iSCSI

# iSCSI

# The Universal
# Storage Connection

# John L. Hufferd

**✦Addison-Wesley**

Boston • San Francisco • New York • Toronto • Montreal
London • Munich • Paris • Madrid • Capetown
Sydney • Tokyo • Singapore • Mexico City

Many of the designations used by manufacturers and sellers to distinguish their products are claimed as trademarks. Where those designations appear in this book, and Addison-Wesley was aware of a trademark claim, the designations have been printed with initial capital letters or in all capitals.

The authors and publisher have taken care in the preparation of this book, but make no expressed or implied warranty of any kind and assume no responsibility for errors or omissions. No liability is assumed for incidental or consequential damages in connection with or arising out of the use of the information or programs contained herein.

The publisher offers discounts on this book when ordered in quantity for bulk purchases and special sales. For more information, please contact:

U.S. Corporate and Government Sales
(800) 382-3419
corpsales@pearsontechgroup.com

For sales outside of the U.S., please contact:

International Sales
(317) 581-3793
international@pearsontechgroup.com

Visit Addison-Wesley on the Web: www.awprofessional.com

*Library of Congress Cataloging-in-Publication Data*

Hufferd, John L.
    ISCSI : the universal storage connection / John L. Hufferd.
        p.   cm.
    Includes bibliographical references and index.
    ISBN 0-201-78419-X (pbk. : alk. paper)
    1. iSCSI (Computer network protocol) 2. Computer networks—Management.
  3. Computer storage devices. I. Title.
    TK5105.5677 .H82 2003
    004.6'068—dc21

                                            2002026086

ISBN  020178419X

Text printed in the United States on recyled paper at Offset Paperback Manufacturers in Laflin, Pennsyl

5th  Printing    February 2007

This book is dedicated to my family, who had to put up
with me during its writing.
My wife Cathy
and my children
Jared, Jeffrey, and Joanne

# Contents

# Credits and Disclaimer

**MUCH OF THE INFORMATION** in this book has been obtained from the IETF drafts relating to iSCSI. That information has been edited and interpreted; however, any discrepancies between this book and the IETF drafts/standards should be resolved in favor of the IETF drafts/standards. This book is written against the IETF RFC3720.

The IETF IPS Internet drafts for iSCSI, and related drafts, from which information has been extracted and referenced, have the following copyright statement:

Note: The above is the copyright statement found within the various IETF documents from which much of the information in this book was obtained. It is *not* the copyright statement for this book.

Credit should go to the many individuals who make up the IETF ips workgroup (iSCSI track) for the many contributions that have been made on the "reflector," which has permitted the iSCSI related drafts to reach their current state.

The IETF drafts are always in a state of refinement. Thus, what was correct when this book was written may be out of date when the book is read. The reader is cautioned to use the information here as important background material and use the only current IETF iSCSI drafts as the correct version.

Special appreciation is hereby expressed to the co-chairs of the IETF ips workgroup: David Black and Elizabeth Rodriguez. I would also like to thank them for their faith in me as reflected in my appointment as technical coordinator for the iSCSI track, within the IETF ips workgroup.

A very big thank you is also sent to Julian Satran not only for the countless hours he has spent being the editor and primary author of the main iSCSI draft, but also for the hours we have spent together working out details and implementation approaches of the iSCSI protocols. Julian led the IBM Haifa Research team that did so much of the early work on iSCSI. He is a man with a large intellect and the willingness to share it with others in a most gracious manner. Thank you, Julian.

Also, my thanks go to the following folks for their major contributions to the main iSCSI draft and several related drafts, as well as to some key people from the early days when the effort was still called "SCSI over TCP/IP."

Mark Bakke, for his work on SCSI and the iSCSI MIB draft, the Naming and Discovery draft, the SLP draft, and the NamePrep and StringPrep drafts and their relationship to iSCSI naming.

Marjorie Krueger, for her work on the SCSI and iSCSI MIB draft, the Naming and Discovery draft, and the iSCSI Requirements draft.

Jim Hafner, for his work on the Naming and Discovery draft and for keeping all our work consistent with the SCSI model.

Prasenjit Sarkar, for his leadership on the iSCSI Boot draft and his leading-edge iSCSI implementation work in the initial SCSI-over-TCP/IP prototyping and measurements, as well as for building the IBM 200i prototype.

Kalahari Voruganti, for his leadership on the iSCSI Naming and Discovery draft and his leading-edge iSCSI implementation work in the initial SCSI-over-TCP/IP prototyping and measurements in the IBM 200i prototype.

Joshua Tseng, for his work on the Naming and Discovery draft and for his leadership on the iSNS draft.

Bernard Aboba, for his leading effort and work on the IP Storage Security draft.

John Sondeno, for his careful reviews and edits of this manuscript.

Steven Hetzler, for his leading effort in getting attention within IBM for pursuit of SCSI over TCP/IP and for leading an IBM Almaden Research team that built some of the initial demonstration projects that proved the concept.

Daniel Smith, for his effort in some of the initial work on the IBM prototype of SCSI over TCP/IP.

Bill Kabelac, for his effort in some of the initial work on the IBM prototype of SCSI over TCP/IP.

Jai Menon, for his work with Clod Barrera to ensure that the SCSI-over-TCP/IP project was continued within IBM and for being instrumental in the agreement with Cisco for co-authoring the original draft.

Clod Barrera, for his work with Jai Menon and for ensuring that the SCSI-over-TCP/IP project was continued within IBM Haifa and Almaden Research, and for being instrumental in the agreement with Cisco for co-authoring the original draft. Additional thanks are appropriate for Clod because of the continued support that he gave me as the IBM iSCSI projects were being defined.

Manoj Naik, for his work in creating one of the very first working SCSI-over-TCP/IP prototypes.

Andy Bechtolsheim, for his vision of bringing Cisco into the iSCSI venture with IBM.

Costa Saputzakis, for his initial work with IBM in developing the Cisco/IBM proposal for the iSCSI protocol.

Tom Clark, for his careful review of this manuscript and his very useful suggestions.

Mallikarjun Chadalapaka, for his dedicated effort in defining the iSCSI protocol for handling errors and for his help in editing this manuscript.

Elizabeth Rodriguez, for her effort as co-chair of the IETF ips work-group and for her efforts in editing this manuscript.

James Pertzborn, for having the foresight to commit IBM to the announcement and development of the IBM 200i target storage controller, over a year before the IETF standard went to last call.

John Kuhn, for his management of the 200i project and for all the techniques he used through the difficult process of bringing out a paradigm-changing product within IBM.

John Dowdy, for his key planning and coordination in getting the IBM 200i target storage controller shipped and updated through all the different versions of the specification.

Efri Zeidner, for building an early primitive target and initiator test bed using a connection-per-LU model that helped to put together the case for TCP.

Kalman Meth, for his help exploring different variants of the early protocol and for his heavy involvement in writing the version that was first submitted to IETF.

Ofer Biran, for his expertise in building a good security story and for his work on the main iSCSI drafts.

Micky Rodeh and Joseph Raviv, for their support of the whole project from the outset, their agreement to fund it, and the energy they spent convincing everyone that iSCSI is good business.

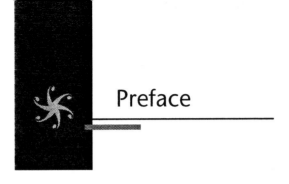

# Preface

**THIS BOOK IS A GUIDE TO UNDERSTANDING** Internet SCSI (iSCSI) and where it fits in the world. It contains discussions of the marketplace where appropriate and of some technology competitors, such as Fibre Channel. However, mostly there will be positioning of the various technologies to emphasize their appropriate strengths. iSCSI is based on such a ubiquitous network technology (TCP/IP) that it seems to play in many different areas that are currently dominated by other technologies. Therefore, one needs to view all iSCSI capabilities and determine its applicability to the area in which the reader is interested.

Since iSCSI is only a transport, that is, a carrier of the SCSI protocol, there is no involved discussion of SCSI itself. Many parts of the book are general enough that a thorough knowledge of SCSI is not needed. There are, however, more detailed parts of the book where SCSI knowledge would be helpful.

I wrote this book to provide both the manager and the technician with a useful understanding of the technology. Product marketing and strategy professionals should also find the information useful and meaningful. The technician should view this book as a primer, in which the iSCSI technology is discussed with enough depth that the IETF iSCSI documents should be readily understandable. Those who want to understand and build a product based on iSCSI should find this book to be a must-read, especially if they plan to dive down into the details of the IETF iSCSI drafts/standards documents.

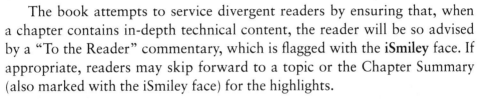

The book attempts to service divergent readers by ensuring that, when a chapter contains in-depth technical content, the reader will be so advised by a "To the Reader" commentary, which is flagged with the **iSmiley** face. If appropriate, readers may skip forward to a topic or the Chapter Summary (also marked with the iSmiley face) for the highlights.

## Organization

The book begins with a general background of the market and an answer to why iSCSI is of interest. A taxonomy of the various markets is given, along with an explanation of how iSCSI fits into them. This is followed by a short history of iSCSI so that the reader can get a sense of what propelled its development.

Next the book heads into the technology itself, with an overview that includes iSCSI layering. This shows the use of the underpinning TCP/IP technology, the concept of a session, and the structure of the message units. Various other key concepts are introduced here to ensure that the reader knows not only the importance of data integrity to storage technology, but also that new hardware is being introduced specifically to address bandwidth and latency issues. A few pages are spent explaining the iSCSI naming conventions, because of their major significance to the use of the technology.

Following the discussion of iSCSI naming conventions, the book takes the reader through the login process and the identification and option negotiation process. These processes are key in the establishment of a communication path between the host system and the storage controller. The process of sequencing the commands and data, as well as controlling the flow of commands and data, is reviewed.

One chapter is dedicated to merging iSCSI concepts with SCSI concepts, by depicting where the various named entities are located. This is perhaps the most tedious chapter, even though not deep in technical content.

The various forms of task and error management are explained in a very technical discussion. The detail and technical depth build from that point to the end of the book. Finally the reader is taken through the various companion technologies that iSCSI uses to complete its suite of capabilities.

The main part of the book concludes with an explanation of what hardware vendors are doing to permit direct memory placement of iSCSI messages without additional main processor involvement.

Of course, there is an overall summary that considers expectations for the future.

Appendix A contains most of the truly technical details of the iSCSI protocol. The message units are presented in alphabetical order for ease of reference. Appendix B contains a compact listing of the various negotiation keywords and values.

Appendix C goes into the relationship of iSCSI to the SCSI architecture. It explains the logical model and its consequences. Appendix D contains the details of the key=value field encodings of numbers, characters, and bits.

Readers may forget from time to time the meanings of various iSCSI and SCSI terms, so a glossary is presented in Appendix E. As a further aid I have included in Appendix F the various acronyms used throughout this book and many of the referenced documents, especially the base IETF iSCSI drafts.

Finally, Appendix G contains the various reference sources, along with their Web page locators (in most cases). Speaking of references, bracketed citations, such as [SAM2], are fully referenced in this appendix.

In iSCSI, serial numbers are always incremented and compared in what is called a 32-bit serial number arithmetic. This is a way to determine, when serial numbers wrap around, if those numbers are greater or less than other serial numbers. Refer to Appendix A for a quick overview and to [RFC1982] for details.

## iSCSI: One of Several Storage Fabrics

iSCSI is the focus of this book, but it is only one of the key storage fabrics that will exist in the next decade or so. The current incumbent is Fibre Channel (FC) and it will continue its advancements even as iSCSI is also advanced. One should expect the FC storage fabric to continue to be used by those installations that currently have FC, and will even have moderate extentions into new installations. The speeds of FC will continue to increase to 8 and 16 Gb/s (and possibly beyond). The speed and functionality of FC should be expected to be enhanced at least through 2015–2020.

Also there is another network technology that is used for large-scale storage interconnect and that is known as InfiniBand (IB). When this IB Network was created it had as its primary focus the coupling of systems together in a low latency high bandwidth fabric. But it has also added storage protocols know as SRP (SCSI RDMA Protocol) and iSER (iSCSI Extensions for RDMA).

Over the next decade or so, in addition to FC one should expect the InfiniBand protocol to exist at the very high end of the performance market (with a variant of iSCSI known as iSER). Ethernet installations carrying iSCSI (and its iSER variant) will probably dominate in all other areas where Fibre Channel is not ingrained as the incumbent. This means that a form of iSCSI will be used in all non FC large storage networks, and possibly in a decade or so, even supplant FC.

# 1 The Background of SCSI

**WHEN IT COMES TO ATTACHING** storage to computers, **ATA** (AT attachment) is the most prevalent method. The characters *AT,* which stand for "advanced technology," come from the name of the first 80286-based IBM PC. ATA drives are found mostly on desktop systems and laptops. Higher-end systems, often called "servers," utilize a connection technique called **SCSI** (Small Computer System Interface) parallel bus architecture. These systems may have several such SCSI buses attached to them. The more SCSI buses that can be effectively connected to a system, the higher the data input/output (**I/O**) capabilities of that system.

## SCSI Bus Interconnect

A SCSI bus permits hard disks, tape drives, tape libraries, printers, scanners, CD-ROMs, DVDs, and the like to be connected to server systems. It can be considered a general interconnection technique that permits devices of many different types to interoperate with computer systems. (See Figure 1–1.)

The protocol used on the SCSI bus is the SCSI Protocol. It defines how the SCSI device can be addressed, commanded to perform some operation, and give or take data to or from the (host) computing system. The operational commands are defined by a data structure called a command description block (**CDB**). For example, a read command would have a CDB that contained an "opcode" defined by the protocol to mean, "read." It would also contain information about where to get the data (e.g., the block location on the disk) and miscellaneous flags to further define the operation.

The protocol that defines how a SCSI bus is operated also defines how to address the various units to which the CDB will be delivered. Generally, presenting the address on the hardware lines of the SCSI bus performs the addressing. This address technique calls out a particular SCSI device, which

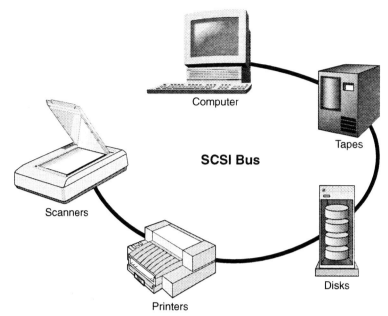

Figure 1-1  Small computer system interface (SCSI).

may then be subdivided into one or more logical units (**LUs**). An LU is an abstract concept that can represent various real objects such as tapes, printers, and scanners.

Each LU is given an address. This is a simple number called the logical unit number (**LUN**). Thus, the SCSI protocol handles the addressing of both the SCSI device and the LU. (*Note:* "LUN," though technically incorrect, will often be used when "LU" is meant.) Servers may connect to many SCSI buses; in turn the SCSI buses can each connect to a number of SCSI devices, and each SCSI device can contain a number of LUs (8, 16, 32, etc.). Therefore, the total number of SCSI entities (LUs) attached to a system can be very large. (See Figure 1–2.)

The next thing to consider is what happens when many computers are in the same location. If there are numerous disks (LUs) for each system, this configuration creates a very large grouping of storage units. Many installations group their servers and storage separately and put appropriate trained personnel in each area. These people are usually skilled in handling issues with either the computer system or the storage.

One of the most prevalent issues for the storage specialist is supplying the proper amount of storage to the appropriate systems. As systems are actually used, the amount of storage originally planned for them can vary—either too

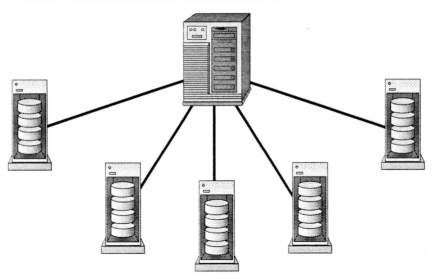

Figure 1–2 Host processors can have many SCSI buses.

much or too little. Taking storage from one system's SCSI bus and moving it to another system's SCSI bus can be a major disruptive problem often requiring booting of the various systems. Users want a pool of storage, which can be assigned in a nondisruptive manner to the servers as need requires.

Another issue with the SCSI bus is that it has distance limitations varying from 1.5 to 25 meters, depending on the bus type (yes, there are multiple types). The bus type has to be matched with the requirements of the host and the SCSI (storage) devices (often called storage controllers), which seriously limits the amount of pooling a SCSI bus can provide.

Further, many SCSI bus storage devices can have no more than one bus connected to them, and unless high-end storage devices are used, one generally has at most two SCSI bus connections per storage device. In that case the storage devices have at most two different host systems that might share the various LUs within the SCSI devices. (See Figure 1–3.)

Often the critical host systems want a primary and a secondary connection to the storage devices so that they have an alternate path in case of connection or bus failure. This results in additional problems for systems that want alternate paths to the storage and, at the same time, share the storage controllers with other hosts (which might be part of a failover-capable cluster).

Often an installation requires a cluster made up of more than two hosts, and it uses a process called file sharing via a shared file system (e.g., Veritas Clustered File System) or a shared database system (e.g., Oracle Cluster

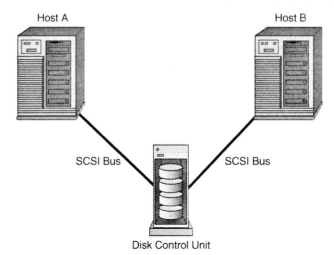

Figure 1–3  Two hosts sharing one storage control unit.

Database). Often this is not possible without the expense of a mainframe/ enterprise-class storage controller, which usually permits many SCSI bus connections but brings the installation into a whole new price range. (See Figure 1–4.)

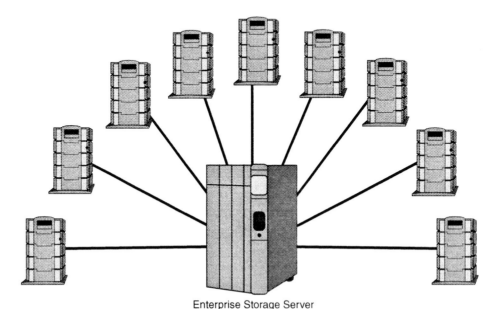

Figure 1–4  Pooled storage via SCSI connections.

## Fibre Channel Interconnect

Understanding the problems with SCSI led a number of vendors to create a new interconnection type known as Fibre Channel. In this technology the SCSI CDBs are created in the host system, as they were in SCSI bus systems; however, the SCSI bus is replaced with a physical "fibre channel" connection and a logical connection to the target storage controller.

The term "logical connection" is used because Fibre Channel (**FC**) components can be interconnected via hubs and switches. These interconnections make up a network and thus have many of the characteristics found in any network. The FC network is referred to as an FC storage area network (**SAN**). However, unlike in an Internet Protocol (**IP**) network, basic management capability was initially missing in Fibre Channel. This has been mostly rectified, but the administrator of an IP network cannot now, and probably never will be able to, use the same network management tools on an FC network that are used on an IP network. This requires duplicate training cost for the FC network administrator and the IP network administrator. These costs are in addition to the costs associated with the actual storage management duties of the storage administrator.

I have had many storage customers request that storage be set up on an IP network, for which they have trained personnel. (See Figure 1–5.) This request comes from the fact that FC networking has not been taught in colleges and universities.* People with FC skills are generally taught by the vendor or by specialty schools, which are paid for by their company. This is a very expensive burden that must be borne by the customer of FC equipment. The more storage shipped that is FC connected, the more ruthless the demand for trained personnel. Without universities providing trained graduates, companies will keep hiring people away from each other.

Some people minimize this point and then go further and state that storage has different needs from other products located on a general IP network. This is true; however, those needs are in addition to the management of the actual network fabric. Fibre Channel needed to invent general FC network fabric management as well as storage management. It is the fabric management that people have been wishing were the same for both storage and the general IP network.

---

*There is at least one important exception: the University of New Hampshire, which has become an important center for interoperability testing for Fibre Channel (and recently for iSCSI).

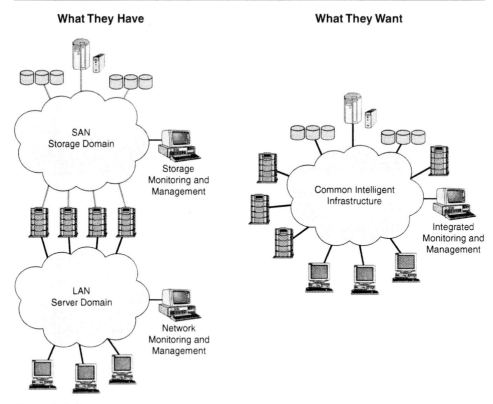

Figure 1–5  Have versus want.

Universities have not been training students because of a combination of factors:

1.  Fibre Channel does not yet replace any other curriculum item.

2.  Storage interconnect is seen as a specialty area.

3.  Few instructors have expertise in storage and storage interconnects.

4.  Many university servers are not FC connected.

5.  The processors used by professors are not likely to be FC connected.

That the main university servers are not Fibre Channel connected is a problem currently being addressed. However, the professors' local systems, which have significant budget issues, will probably be the last to be updated.

There is another solution to the problem of training, and that is the hiring of service companies that plan and install the FC networks. These companies also train customers to take over the day-to-day operations, but remain on call whenever needed to do fault isolation or to expand the network. Service companies such as IBM Global Services (IGS) and Electronic Data Systems (EDS) are also offering ongoing operation services.

The total cost of ownership (**TCO**) with Fibre Channel is very high compared to that with IP networks. This applies not only to the price of FC components, which are significantly more expensive than corresponding IP components, but also to operation and maintenance. The cost of training personnel internally or hiring a service company to operate and maintain the FC network is a significant addition to the TCO.

It is important to understand that storage networks have management needs that are not present in direct-attach SCSI. The fact that Fibre Channel has suffered through the creation of many of these new storage management functions (e.g., host LUN masking, shared tape drives and libraries) means that IP storage networks can exploit these same storage management functions without having to create them from scratch.

## iSCSI Interconnect

The **iSCSI** (Internet SCSI) protocol was created in order to reduce the TCO of shared storage solutions by reducing the initial outlay for networking, training, and fabric management software. To this end a working group within the IETF (Internet Engineering Task Force) Standards Group was established.

iSCSI has the capability to tie together a company's systems and storage, which may be spread across a campus-wide environment, using the company's interconnected local area networks (**LAN**s), also known as intranets. This applies not only to the company's collection of servers but also to their desktop and laptop systems.

Desktops and laptops can operate with iSCSI on a normal 100-megabit-per-second (**Mb/s**) Ethernet link in a manner that is often better than "sawing across"* their own single-disk systems. Additionally, many desktop systems can exploit new "gigabit copper" connections such as the 10/100/1000BaseT Ethernet links. The existing wiring infrastructure that most companies have is Category 5 (**Cat. 5**) Ethernet cable. The new 1000BaseT network interface

---

* "Sawing" is a term used to describe the action of the voice coil on a disk drive that moves the recording heads back and forth across the sectors of the disk. The resultant noise often sounds like sawing.

cards (**NICs**) are able to support gigabit speeds on the existing Cat. 5 cables. It is expected that the customer will, over time, replace or upgrade his desktop system so that it has 1000BaseT NICs. In this environment, if the desktops can operate effectively at even 300 Mb/s, the customer will generally see better response than is possible today with normal desktop ATA drives—without having to operate at full gigabit speeds.

Data suggest that 500MHz Pentium systems can operate the normal host **TCP/IP** (Transmission Control Protocol over Internet Protocol) stacks at 100 Mb/s using less than 10% of CPU resources. These resources will hardly be missed if the I/O arrives in a timely manner. Likewise we can expect the desktop systems shipping in the coming year and beyond to be on the order of 1.5 to 3 GHz. This means that, for 30 megabyte-per-second (**MB/s**) I/O requirements (approximately 300 Mb/s), desktop systems will use about the same, or less, processor time as they previously consumed on 500MHz desktop systems using 100Mb/s links (less than 10%). Most users would be very happy if their desktops could sustain an I/O rate of 30 MB/s. (Currently desktops average less than 10 MB/s.)

The important point here is that iSCSI for desktops and laptops makes sense even if no special hardware is dedicated to its use. This is a significant plus for iSCSI versus Fibre Channel, since Fibre Channel requires special hardware and is therefore unlikely to be deployed on desktop and laptop systems. (See Figure 1–6.)

The real competition between Fibre Channel and iSCSI will occur on server-class systems. These systems are able to move data (read and write) at

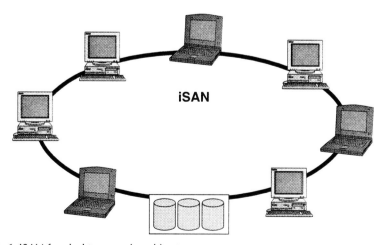

Figure 1–6 iSAN for desktops and and laptops.

up to 2–4Gb/s speeds. These FC connections require special FC chips and host bus adapters (**HBAs**). As a rule, these HBAs are very expensive (compared to NICs), but they permit servers to send their SCSI CDBs to SCSI target devices and LUs at very high speed and at very low processor overhead. Therefore, if iSCSI is to be competitive in the server environment, it too will need specially built chips and HBAs. Moreover, these chips and HBAs will need to have TCP/IP offload engines (**TOEs**) along with the iSCSI function. The iSCSI function can be located in the device driver, the HBA, or the chip, and, in one way or another, it will need to interface directly with the TOE and thereby perform all the TCP/IP processing on the chip or HBA, not on the host system.

Some people believe that the price of FC networks will fall to match that of IP networks. I believe that will not occur for quite a while, since most FC sales are at the very high end of the market, where they are very entrenched. It therefore seems foolish for them to sacrifice their current profit margins, fighting for customers in the middle to low end of the market (against iSCSI), where there are no trained personnel anyway. I believe that FC prices will go down significantly when iSCSI become a threat at the market high end, which won't happen for some time.

Studies conducted by IBM and a number of other vendors have concluded that iSCSI can perform at gigabit line speed, with overheads as low as those of Fibre Channel, as long as it has iSCSI and TCP/IP hardware assist in HBAs or chips. It is expected that the price of gigabit-speed iSCSI HBAs will be significantly lower than that of FC HBAs. It is also felt that two 1Gb iSCSI HBAs will have a significantly lower combined price than current 2–4Gb FC HBAs.

Even though iSCSI HBAs and chips will be able to operate at link speed, it is expected that their latency will be slightly higher than that of Fibre Channel's. This difference is considered to be less than 10 microseconds, which, when compared to the time for I/O processing, is negligible. iSCSI's greater latency is caused by the greater amount of processing to be done within the iSCSI chip to support TCP. Thus, there is some impact from the additional work needed, even if supported by a chip. A key future vendor-value-add will be how well a chip is able to parallel its processes and thus reduce the latency. This is not to say that the latency of iSCSI chips will be unacceptable. In fact, it is believed that it will be small enough not to be noticeable in most normal operations.

Another important capability of iSCSI is that it will be able to send I/O commands across the Internet or a customer's dedicated wide area networks (**WANs**). This will be significant for applications that require tape.

An odd thing about tape is that almost everyone wants to be able to use it (usually for backup) but almost no one wants the tape library nearby. iSCSI provides interconnection to tape libraries at a great distance from the host that is writing data to it. This permits customers to place their tape libraries in secure backup centers, such as "Iron Mountain." A number of people have said that this "at distance" tape backup will be iSCSI's killer app.

At the bottom line, iSCSI is all about giving the customer the type of interconnect to storage that they have been requesting—a network-connected storage configuration made up of components that the customer can buy from many different places, whose purchase price is low, and whose operation is familiar to many people (especially computer science graduates). They also get a network they can configure and operate via standard network management tools, thereby keeping the TCO low. Customers do not have to invest in a totally new wiring installation, and they appreciate the fact that they can use Cat. 5 cable—which is already installed. They like the way that iSCSI can seamlessly operate, not only from server to local storage devices but also across campuses as well as remotely via WANs.

These customers can use iSCSI to interconnect remote sites, which permits mirrored backup and recovery capability, as well as a remote connection to their tape libraries. (See Figure 1–7.) On top of all that, iSCSI will be operating on low-end systems and on high-end systems with performance as good as what FC networks can provide. If that is not enough, it also comes

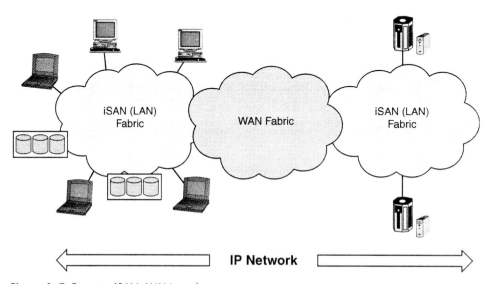

Figure 1–7  Remote iSAN, WAN, and tape.

with built-in Internet Protocol security (**IPsec**), which the customer can enable whenever using unsecured networks.

It is no wonder why customers, consultants, and vendors are singing the praises of iSCSI; it is a very compelling technology.

## File Servers and NAS

For over a decade now, there has been the concept of file serving. It begins with the idea that a host can obtain its file storage remotely from the host system. SUN defined a protocol called Network File System (**NFS**) that was designed to operate on the IP network. IBM and Microsoft together defined a protocol based on something they called Server Message Block (**SMB**). Microsoft called its version LAN Manager; IBM called its version LAN Server.

The original SMB protocol ran only on small local networks. It was unable to operate seamlessly with the Internet and hence was generally limited to small LANs. Microsoft updated SMB to make it capable of operating on IP networks. It is now called the Common Internet File System (**CIFS**).

It should be noted that Novell created a file server protocol to compete with IBM and Microsoft.

A file server protocol places a file system "stub" on each host, which acts as a client of the target file server. Like a normal file system, the file system stub is given control by the OS; however, it simply forwards the host's file system request to the remote file server for handling. The actual storage is at the file server.

File serving began as a means to share files between peer computer systems, but users soon started dedicating systems to file serving only. This was the beginning of what we now call a network attached storage (**NAS**) appliance. Various vendors started specializing in NAS appliances, and today this is a very hot market. These appliances generally support NFS protocols, CIFS protocols, Novell protocols, or some combination. Since NASs operate on IP networks, many people see them as an alternative to iSCSI (or vice versa). In some ways they are, but they are significantly different, which makes one better than the other in various environments. We will cover these areas later in this book.

 ## Chapter Summary

In this chapter we discussed the various types of hard drives, and the type of interconnect they have with the host systems. We also discussed their applicable environment and their limitations. This information is highlighted below.

- There are two main hard drive types available today:

  ➢ ATA (used in desktop and laptop systems)

  ➢ SCSI (used in server-class systems)

- SCSI drives are connected to a host via a SCSI bus and use the SCSI protocol.

- The SCSI command description block (**CDB**) is a key element of the SCSI protocol.

- The real or logical disk drive that the host talks to is a logical unit (**LU**).

- The SCSI protocol gives each addressable LU a number, or **LUN**.

- SCSI bus distance limitations vary from 1.5 to 25 meters depending on the type of cable needed by the host or drive.

- Non enterprise storage controllers usually have only one or two SCSI bus connections.

- Enterprise storage controllers usually have more than two SCSI bus connections.

- Clustering servers without using enterprise-class storage systems is often difficult (especially if each host wants to have more then one connection to a storage controller).

- Fibre Channel (**FC**) connections solve many interconnection problems, but bring their own management problems.

- Fibre Channel requires its own fabric management software and cannot use the standard IP network management tools.

- Fibre Channel needs software to manage the shared storage pool to prevent systems from stepping on each other.

- FC networks are generally considered to have a high **TCO** (total cost of ownership).

- FC HBAs, chips, and switches are generally considered to be expensive (especially when compared to IP network NICs and switches).

- Personnel trained in Fibre Channel are scarce, and companies are pirating employees from each other.

- Universities in general are not teaching Fibre Channel.

- FC can be expected to be viable for at least another decade at the mid to high end of the storage market.

- iSCSI offers the same interconnectivity and the same pooled-storage approach that Fibre Channel does, but over the more familiar IP network infrastructure.

- iSCSI offers the same fabric management capabilities that normal IP networks do.

- iSCSI can use much of the storage management software that was developed for Fibre Channel.

- iSCSI can utilize IP-trained personnel to manage the iSCSI-based SAN.

- iSCSI is believed to offer the promise of lower TCO.

- iSCSI will work not only with server systems but also with desktop and laptop systems via currently installed Cat. 5 cables and 10/100BaseT as well as 10/100/1000BaseT NICs.

- Desktop and laptop systems will probably be very happy even if they utilize only up to 300 Mb/s on the 1000Mb/s-capable Cat. 5 cable.

- The prices of iSCSI HBAs are currently significantly less than those of FC HBAs.

- FC prices won't fall significantly until iSCSI becomes a threat at the high end of the market.

- iSCSI can be expected to enable "at-distance" computing, where storage is located beyond the local environment.

- Tape backup is likely to become the killer app for iSCSI in the future.

- File servers (NASs) can be located on IP networks; therefore, the fabric management that fits NAS fits iSCSI and vice versa.

- NAS and iSCSI storage can be located on the same network; though they have overlapping capabilities, they also each have capabilities that the other does not (which will be discussed later in this book).

# 2

# The Value and Position of iSCSI

## To the Reader

This chapter will take you through the different environments in which network-connected storage may be appropriate. Because market planners and engineers may have different views on the potential market for iSCSI products, we will discuss what the market looks like, in hopes of bridging the divergent views.

A taxonomy of the various environments is listed, and each area's potential relative to iSCSI is explained. This entire chapter is therefore recommended reading for marketers and hardware and software engineers.

Small installations are called **SoHo** (Small office, Home office) environments. In such environments customers will have one or more desktop systems, which they are tired of constantly opening up to install storage devices. They want easy interconnects that permit them to operate with external storage as fast as they can operate with internal storage.

## The Home Office

Often the home office will have multiple computers, some have older applications and some belong to the family. These systems are frequently connected on small locally attached Ethernet 100Mb/s links. These systems typically have more processing power than they have storage access capability. These installations will find value in placing their storage in a central location, dynamically adding it to their personal computer systems with a simple plug-and-play configuration, thereby obtaining additional storage without having to open up their systems.

The home office environment can use standard, low-cost, off-the-shelf networking components. The switches are readily available, and the desktop

and laptop processors usually have more processing power than is needed for
the types of work they do. These home office systems usually come with
Ethernet connections and do not need any special adapter cards. The only
things they need are iSCSI software drivers and the low-cost IP storage devices
that iSCSI will permit.

For the home office, vendors are bringing to market a simple disk controller that can attach from one to four (or more) low-cost ATA desktop-
class drives. These controllers and drives will be purchased at local computer
superstores for very low prices. Moreover, the customer will be able to buy
one or two drives initially with the basic controller and then add drives
whenever they wish.

In addition, these customers can now purchase 10/100/1000 Ethernet
cards that can operate over the inexpensive Cat. 5 Ethernet cable already
installed for their existing 10/100Mb/s network.

Prices for 10/100/1000 Ethernet NICs and switches are dropping rap-
idly. In early 2002, 10/100/1000 Ethernet NICs cost $60. The then current
10/100 Ethernet NICs cost only $30, down from $60 just a year previously.
It seems reasonable to assume that the 10/100/1000 Ethernet NIC will soon
be the default in most desktop systems, which means that the home office will
have gigabit capability and processors fast enough to at least utilize 300 Mb/s.
This will give desktop home office systems as much high performance storage access as they can use.

Usually home offices obtain all their software either from the OS that
came with the unit or from a local computer store. There is almost no software in this environment that knows how to work with shared files, and it is
very rare to see a file server in this environment.

Home offices use peer-to-peer file-sharing functions that come with the
OS to permit one user to operate on a file created by another (serial sharing).
However, the storage is considered to belong to the system to which it is
attached. As a rule, when one home system runs out of space, owners do not
use the space on another system but instead upgrade the storage on each system independently as needed.

iSCSI will permit home office users to set up their own external storage
pool connected via a LAN. The owner will then assign new logical or physical hard disk drives (**HDDs**) to each host system without needing to open or
replace them. (See Figure 2–1.)

We have been talking as if the home office had more than one host system. This is because owners of home offices tend to keep their old systems,

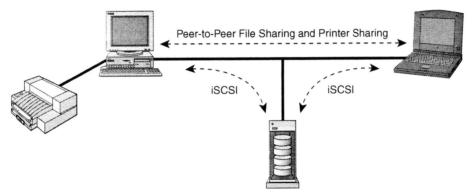

Figure 2–1 The home office and iSCSI.

which have old data and applications that still work. Also, the home/family use dynamic—the multiple computer family—is often envolved. Many times there are two, three, or more computers in the same family—one for each adult and one for the children—but only one person is responsible for maintaining them all. In these environments a shared pool of storage is valuable for ease of both access and administration.

Even though multiple-system households are common, it is also true that home offices may have only a single desktop or laptop system. But even in single-system environments, the owner will want to have storage attached externally to avoid the problems of opening the system and adding new HDDs. Unlike other environments, these systems are often updated to add processing power not only for business but also for game playing. Whatever the reason, they will find iSCSI very useful in avoiding having to transfer all their key files from old systems to new systems, since the storage is all external. (And yes, iSCSI has boot capability.)

It has been pointed out that even in a home office, doctors, lawyers, and others would love to have their data placed on small, inexpensive **RAIDs** (redundant arrays of independent disks) because of their reliability. And iSCSI provides even this "upscale" home office the most appropriate, flexible, and inexpensive interconnect for that need.

### The Home Office and Serial ATA Drives

At least one individual has made the claim that iSCSI's real competition is the new serial ATA (**S-ATA**)—a cabling protocol that travels from the controller chips on the motherboard directly to the HDD. This is not a true considera-

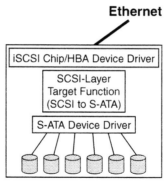

Figure 2–2  Attached serial ATA storage controllers.

tion today, since the S-ATA is currently 1 meter in length and has no sharing capability. Therefore, it is unlikely that it will be used for a cabling interface that hangs out of a home PC for a general storage interconnect. There is a proposal for increasing the length, but this is for rack mount versions and it is not clear if that will ever affect the desktop or home market. Further, the S-ATA specification has not yet defined a technique for permitting the same storage device to be attached to more than one system at household distances. Within the iSCSI target, however, one may find iSCSI coming into a small box and then interconnecting to the ATA disks with S-ATA cables. (See Figure 2–2.)

## The Small Office

Examples of the small office environment are dentists, accountants, construction, real estate, and the like—that is, any office that has a relatively small number of employees working in close proximity and a continuing need to grow its storage. Individual desktop systems in small offices have the same disruptive effect when adding storage as they have in home offices, but they are often connected to a file server. However, these file servers face the same problems that individual office or home systems face when adding additional storage. Their owners do not want to disassemble them to add storage and may instead replace the system altogether.

The real problem starts when the user has to migrate the data from an old file server to a new unit, a difficult and very disruptive process. There are technical solutions, of course. One of them is to just buy an additional file server or a network attached storage (NAS) appliance and leave the old one in place. Thanks to iSCSI there is another, generally less costly approach—pooled storage. Pooled storage may consist of simple iSCSI **JBODs** (just a bunch of disks) or RAID controllers, all connected to the same network via iSCSI. With iSCSI, users can also begin small and add storage as needed, placing it wherever they have room and a network connection. Regardless of how many units they add, all of them are logically pooled and yet any of the individual systems in the office can have its own private storage portion.

With iSCSI all the major storage placement decisions are performed by the various host systems as if the storage were directly connected to them. Because of this fact, iSCSI is fairly simple compared to NAS and this results in low processing requirements in the iSCSI storage controllers. It is therefore expected that iSCSI JBODs and RAID controllers will be significantly less costly, and support more systems, than the same storage in a NAS appliance. Using iSCSI units in this way is *not* always the right answer; however, it does give the customer another option that may meet their needs for flexibility and price. In other words, for the same processor power an iSCSI appliance can support more clients and more storage than is possible with a NAS appliance.

A performance analysis carried out by IBM compared a NAS (NFS) server to an iSCSI target (with the same basic power and equipment). This comparison showed that the iSCSI target used much less processing power than did the NFS server. (Refer to the discussion of measurements in Chapter 3.)

Small offices are similar to home offices, except that they have more links and switches. In most installations, a switch can be used to attach either a new NAS appliance or an iSCSI storage controller. (See Figure 2–3.)

Like home office systems, small office systems are bound together with 100Mb/s links. As a rule, it will be possible for them to upgrade to 1000Mb/s links whenever their 100Mb/s links become congested. They can usually ease into iSCSI storage controllers with 100Mb/s links, but over time these links will be upgraded to 1000Mb/s (1Gb/s). They will operate on the same (Cat. 5) Ethernet cable and provide all the bandwidth needed to support any normal demand for iSCSI access, NAS access, normal interactive traffic, and Web traffic.

In a small office that has NAS, iSCSI storage can be added to the existing network with no more network congestion than would exist if its current file server were updated or if a new NAS server unit were added.

A question that needs to be asked is when it is appropriate to add a NAS unit and when it is appropriate to attach an iSCSI storage controller. The answer depends on the customer application. Some small offices, such as

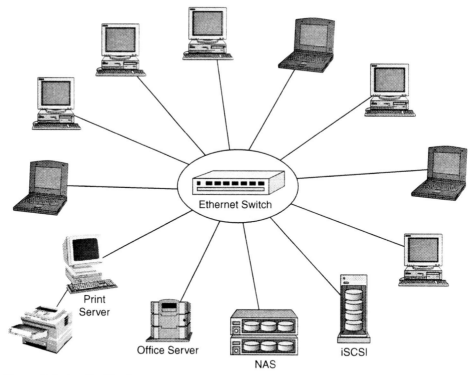

Figure 2–3  Small-office interconnect.

dentists and accountants, use specialty software, acquired from a salesperson who supplies them with other tools of their trade. It might be an appointment management system or a billing system, or sometimes a trade/business-specific system. Some are database applications; others are just file based.

The first thing to determine is whether the software is a database application or a file system application. If a database application, the normal choice for additional external storage is iSCSI. This is true whether or not the database uses a local file system or a "raw" partition (without file system formatting). In either case the most efficient process is to let the database or file system allocate its own data blocks and then use iSCSI to access them. Oracle and IBM DB2, for example, can operate efficiently with a raw partition, but they also have been set up to interface efficiently with many local file systems. The use of iSCSI exploits that fact. As indicated above, the iSCSI storage controller can handle more loads, at higher performance, than a NAS system with similar hardware can.

The clear trend in the industry is to tie applications to databases. When this is done, for the most part the question of sharing files becomes academic since almost all major databases* use "Shared Nothing." In this model the storage is not shared with other systems. This is true even in larger "clustered" installations, where the database query is "parsed" and divided up among the different database systems in the cluster that "own" the data. In this way the more database servers an installation has, the less it needs to share files and the more useful iSCSI becomes.

If the application uses a file system instead of a database, we need to ask if the application is capable of sharing data with other users in either a serial or parallel manner. If so, then we need to ask if the user actually does any file sharing. The answers to these questions will generally indicate that 90% or more of the data at the site is not shared. In fact, the answer with the highest probability in a small office is that *no* file sharing occurs.

Normally the only data sharing in a business environment is via a database. The main exception to this is in an engineering environment. For example, physical design engineers—such as those working at a company like Boeing—may share design files that need to be integrated from time to time so that full simulations can be done. The wing designer might need to share his design file with the engine mount designer, and both might need to share files with the engine designer.

We can find a similar situation with chip engineers, who need to share macro files and their own design files with other designers and the simulation system. Software engineers are still another example. They share their development libraries, their resultant components, and even their documentation library.

The engineering environment is the primary environment where files are shared. Much of the rest of the world shares by sending things around in e-mails. In general, they usually do not have a file sharing need.

When incidental serial file sharing occurs, the small business office, like the home office, is more apt to use peer-to-peer sharing and not put in a NAS server. However, this probability varies with the size of the office; the larger it is, the higher the possibility that it will devote a system to file serving or

---

*Oracle offers a special version of its database that uses shared disks (LUs) in clustered systems. This is called Oracle Real Application Clusters, but it is usually found on high-end enterprise database servers and is not normally used with NAS servers.

install a NAS appliance. Even when the file sharing is not very important, the office often finds use for the file server/NAS as a backup device.

Once file-sharing requirements are understood, we can determine if a NAS unit or an iSCSI storage controller best meets the need. If we have a large file-sharing requirement, NAS is usually the best fit. If not, the best fit is usually iSCSI. Then, in the rare case when file sharing is needed, the peer-to-peer type is appropriate.

If the installation has a lot of sharing and nonsharing requirements, we determine the minimum number of NAS systems needed for file sharing and the number of iSCSI systems needed for nonfile sharing, buying the minimum of both. If all workload can fit into a single inexpensive NAS unit, often this is the best approach. In general, it is best for an installation to fit the entire file-sharing workload into the fewest number of NAS units that can support it. Then it can either try to fit some amount of the nonfile sharing storage access into the unfilled NAS capacity or leave it for subsequent NAS growth. The rest of the storage access load, which will probably be a large majority of the total storage requirement, should exploit the efficiencies of iSCSI storage controllers. This approach is usually much more cost effective than pushing all workload into NAS units.

One other solution is the single unit that supports both NAS and iSCSI functions, which I call a "dual dialect" storage server. With this type of system the installation does not need much precision in its NAS/iSCSI planning. As an example, let's suppose the installation only needs 10% of its clients, or applications, to have file sharing. In this case, one dual dialect storage server can devote 70% of its processing capability to 10% of its clients and use the remaining 30% for the 90% of its clients that have no file-sharing requirements. (See Figure 2–4.)

Of all environments, a small office environment is the least capable of anticipating and designing the storage layout that can optimally support its workload. I therefore expect dual dialect systems to be very successful in small office environments that include both engineers and nonengineers. Environments without heavy engineering design work will generally find iSCSI storage controllers to be the most appropriate equipment for providing IP-based storage.

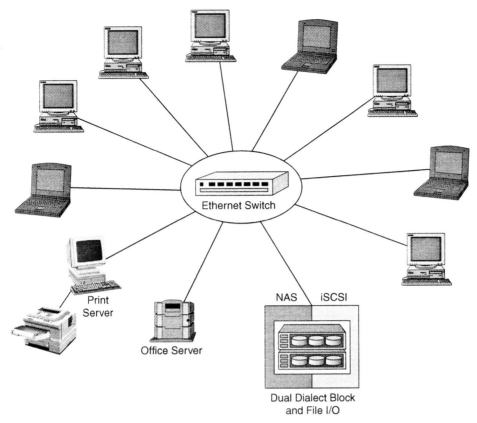

Figure 2–4  Storage combo—NAS and iSCSI.

## The Midrange

Moving up to the midrange company environment, we find multiple server systems. These are unlike desktop or laptop systems, which usually have more processing power than they can use. Servers are heavily loaded performance-critical systems that consume all the CPU cycles they have and often want more. They need access to storage with the smallest amount of lost CPU cycles possible. In an FC, or a direct-attach environment, these systems expend approximately 5% processing overhead to read and write data from and to a storage device. If iSCSI is to be competitive in the server environment, it needs a similar overhead profile. This requires that the processor overhead associated with TCP/IP processing be offloaded onto a chip or host bus adapter (HBA).

Offloading requires a TCP/IP offload engine (TOE), which can be completely incorporated in an HBA. All key TOE functions can be integrated on a single chip or placed on the HBA via the **"pile-on"** approach. The pile-on approach places a normal processor and many discrete components on the HBA (along with appropriate memory and other support chips) and includes normal TCP/IP software stacks. The integrated chip and the pile-on technique both permit the host processor to obtain iSCSI storage access without suffering the overhead associated with host-based TCP/IP processing.

We will be seeing a number of HBAs of all types from a collection of vendors. These will include not only a TOE but also in many cases full iSCSI offload. We will also see a pile-on HBA that can support 70% to 100% of the line speed while operating at close to 100% CPU utilization on the HBA. The customer of the server processor will care not how hard the HBA is working, but only that it can keep up with line speed and offload the iSCSI overhead (including TCP/IP) from the host processor.

The pile-on HBA approach will have higher latency than an HBA that has TCP/IP and iSCSI processing integrated onto a single chip. Even if the pile-on HBA can operate at line speed (1 Gb/s), the latency caused by this type of adapter is unlikely to permit its ongoing success in the market. That is because HBAs with full iSCSI and TOE chips will permit not only operation at line speed but also very low latency. We should consider the pile-on approach to be a time-to-market product that vendors will replace over time with faster and cheaper HBAs using iSCSI and TOE integrated chips.

The goal of iSCSI HBAs is to keep latency as close to that of Fibre Channel as possible (and it should be close when using integrated chips) while keeping costs significantly under those of Fibre Channel.

Some people have argued the price issue, saying that Fibre Channel can easily lower its prices to match iSCSI's because an FC chip will have less silicon than an iSCSI TOE chip. This is of course an important consideration, but sales volume is the key, and iSCSI has the potential for high volume with a technology that operates in an Ethernet environment. This includes operating at gigabit speeds with normal Cat. 5 Ethernet cable attachments so that the customer doesn't have to install and manage a new cable type.

As stated previously, I do not believe that FC vendors will give up their high margins in the high-end market in order to fight iSCSI in the low-end and midrange markets. This will only occur when iSCSI is considered a threat in the high end, but by then iSCSI will have large volumes in the rest of the market and will be able to push the price envelope against Fibre Channel. Also remember that TCP/IP (and Ethernet) connections will always be needed on these systems anyway. Therefore, since FC is always a "total cost adder," whereas iSCSI will have much of its cost supported by other host requirements for IP interconnect, price advantage will clearly go to iSCSI.

There has been talk that FC vendors will attempt to move their 1Gb offerings into the midrange while keeping their 2Gb offerings at the high end. However, the total cost of ownership (TCO) to the midrange customer will still be higher than iSCSI because of the shortage of FC-trained personnel, the use of new special cables, and, as mentioned above, the fact that Fibre Channel is always a total cost adder.

The goal is for the midrange environment to be able to obtain iSCSI-block I/O pooled storage, with performance as good as that of Fibre Channel but at lower cost. However, the midrange customer will still face the dilemma of iSCSI versus NAS. The same consideration and planning should be done in this environment as in the small office environment. The only difference is in the capabilities and price of the competing offerings.

In addition to the normal NAS and iSCSI offerings in this environment, there will be dual dialect offerings also. The difference is that the iSCSI-offload HBAs and chips can be employed to reduce the iSCSI host overhead to a point where they are competitive with Fibre Channel and direct-attached storage. This is not currently possible with NAS.

The other consideration in midrange company environments is that they have desktops and laptops that feed the server systems, which will also, from time to time, need additional storage. Their users will want to get the additional storage and have it managed along with the server storage. This is similar to the needs of SoHo environments: Instead of spending time upgrading internal disk storage, they want to get their additional storage via the network they are already plugged into.

With the new copper 1000Mb/s Ethernet adapters, users can have both a high-speed interactive network and a high-speed storage network, all without changing the Cat. 5 Ethernet cable already installed throughout their company. iSCSI storage controllers can supply the needs of both servers and client desktops. And when connected at 1Gb/s the storage can be supplied at 3+ times normal desktop speeds.

Still, the argument is often made that a NAS solution can address the needs of desktops and laptops. This is true, but at a higher cost. As pointed out earlier, in the small office environment many applications are being written to use databases. They generally use a "shared nothing" approach and therefore provide an information-sharing environment in which NAS is

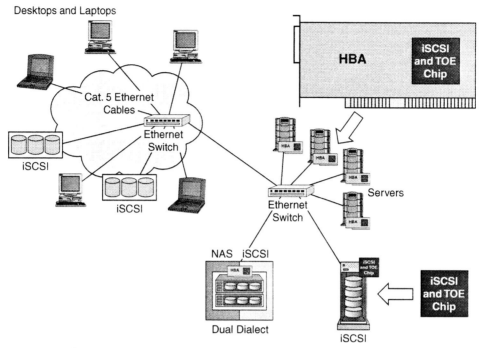

Figure 2–5  The midrange environment.

not required. Again, if files need to be shared, NAS is appropriate; otherwise, a block I/O interface best meets the requirements. iSCSI is the most cost-effective approach for non-shared pooled storage.

Many of these midrange companies will be building iSANs. These are logically the same as FC SANs but are made up of the less expensive iSCSI equipment—less expensive because the entire Ethernet and IP equipment market is relatively low priced (at least low priced when compared to Fibre Channel). Even iSCSI HBAs are cheaper than current FC components. Intel, for example, has declared that its HBA will be available at a street price of under $500. It is further expected that iSCSI HBAs and chips will have even lower prices as sales volumes go up.

One significant difference between the midrange and small office computing environments is that the I/O requirements of the various servers can be as demanding as that found in many high-end servers. Therefore, in the midrange one tends to see more use of iSCSI HBAs and chips in various servers and storage controllers, and a smaller reliance on software versions of iSCSI. (See Figure 2–5.)

# The High End

High-end environments will have the same processor offload and performance requirements that midrange environments have. However, they will probably be more sensitive to latency, so it is expected that the pile-on type of HBA will not be very popular. Because of the never-ending throughput demand from high-end servers, it is in this environment that HBAs with multiple 1Gb Ethernet connections and 10Gb implementations will eventually find their most fertile ground.

Another important distinction is that the high-end environment will probably have some amount of FC equipment already installed. This means that the cohabitation of iSCSI and Fibre Channel will be required.

Because of the usefulness and flexibility of iSCSI-connected storage, and because high-end servers are probably already connected with Fibre Channel, it is expected that high-end environments will first deploy iSCSI in their campus, satellite, and "at-distance" installations. (See Figure 2–6.) The following sections will break out each of these subconfigurations and then address the central facility.

## The Campus

The campus is the area adjacent to the central computing site—within a few kilometers—where private LANs interconnect the buildings containing local department servers as well as the desktops and laptops that are also spread throughout. The different department areas are analogous to the midrange and small office environments. Their general difference is that, with the use of iSCSI, they can exploit the general campus IP backbone to access the data, which may be located at the central computing location.

Often these department areas have policy or political differences with the organization that runs the central computing complex, and so they want their own independent server collections. Generally they want the flexibility that a storage area network (SAN) can provide (such as device pooling and failover capability), but they do not want to get into the business of managing an FC network.

In spite of their independence, these departments want access to the tape libraries at the central location. They want access to these robust backup devices, which they consider essential but which they do not want to service, manage, or maintain. (See Figure 2–7.) The departments also want to access disk storage at the central location as long as they do not have to abide by

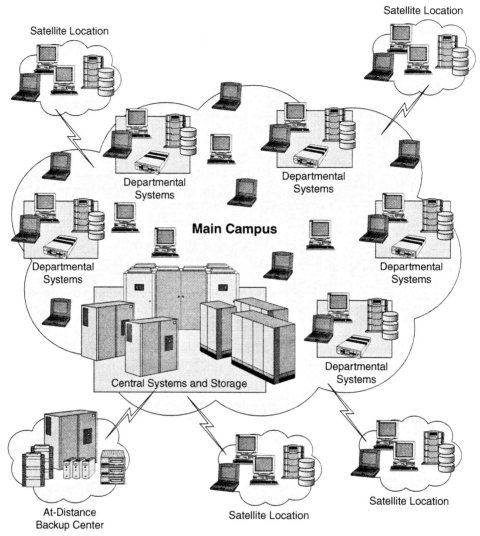

Figure 2–6  The high-end environment.

what they perceive as excessive centralized regulation and control requirements.

Today, even if the FC cables could be pulled to the various campus locations, since Fibre Channel has no security in its protocols, the access control
demands of the central computing location may be more than the departments want to put up with. iSCSI, on the other hand, has security built into
the basic protocol (both at the TCP/IP layer and at the iSCSI layer), which
permits fewer invasive manual processes from anyone, including the disk

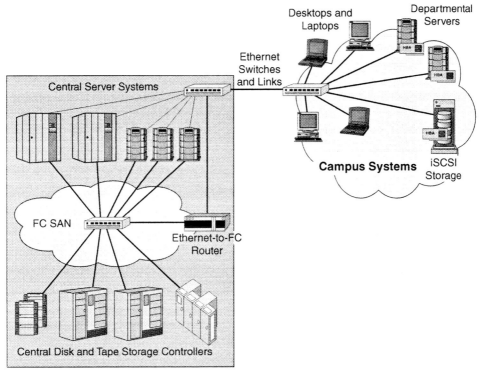

Figure 2–7 Campus and central system/storage.

storage administrator at the central location. iSCSI also permits the department servers to be booted as often as necessary, while still getting at central storage, something that probably would not be done if located within the main computing center.

Because of their needs and desires, campus departments are very likely to view iSCSI as key to their strategic computing direction. However, the campus environment is made up of more than just the department servers. It also has individual desktops and laptops distributed throughout that look like home office systems. A major difference, however, is that their users are not encouraged to modify them. Instead, every time they need additional storage, they have to justify it to either the department or the central computing location. Then the central or department "guru" who handles the system, must schedule time to come out and do an upgrade. Since these guru types handle many different users, they take approaches that can be unpleasant for the end user, often causing the loss of data or carefully constructed "desktop screens." Gurus are in a no-win scenario. They do not like taking end users' systems apart, especially since users can be abusive about procedures, scheduling, and so forth.

Some installations have been known to just upgrade the entire system whenever new storage or processor power is needed. In the past this was often a reasonable approach since the need for processing power was keeping pace with the creation of storage. Now, as a rule, this is not the case. The 1-to-2 gigahertz (**Gh**) processors seem to have reached a plateau where the productivity of the office worker does not benefit from the additional speed of the laptop or desktop. However, one can still generate a lot of storage requirements with these processors, and it is beginning to occur to many companies that replacing systems just to upgrade the storage is a waste of time and money. Further, it greatly disturbs employees when they lose their data, their settings, or their visual desktop. Even when things go right in the backup and restore stages of bringing data from one system to another, the process is lengthy and tedious. Companies that believe time and productivity are money dislike these disruptions.

Both the end user and the guru will love iSCSI. To get additional iSCSI storage the end user just has to be authorized to use a new logical volume, and the issue is done. Often this can be accomplished over the phone.

Over time, desktops will be "rolled over" for newer versions, which will come equipped with the 10/100/1000BaseT (**gigabit copper**) IP adapter cards. 1000BaseT-capable adapter cards permit desktop performance of up to 1 Gb/s, which will greatly improve the performance of iSCSI storage. Note that most installations use Cat. 5 copper cables for 10/100Mb/s Ethernet connections, and these same Cat. 5 cables are adequate for gigabit speeds. Therefore, installations do not have to rewire in order to get gigabit iSCSI storage access for their ubiquitous desktop systems.

Since iSCSI also supports remote boot, one can expect many desktop systems only to support storage connected via iSCSI in the future. The desktops can then be upgraded as needed independently of the data.

### The Satellite

A remotely located office, known as a satellite, will have an environment similar to that of a campus. It often functions like a department or small office. Satellites have their own desktop systems and sometimes their own servers. They generally suffer from the lack of adequate "remote support," which often means slow response to their needs.

As in the small office, satellite users do not usually touch the system but instead get a guru to come to the remote location to fix things. With the use of iSCSI many satellite installations can have their storage-related needs handled via the phone. As they need more storage, they can call in the storage administrator, who enables more logical volumes for their use. This is possible since with iSCSI they are connected to the central location via a virtual private network (**VPN**).

A VPN is provided by a combination of carrier and user equipment. A carrier or ISP delivers some type of "IP tone" to the remote location, and the remote office uses encrypting firewalls and the like to secure access to a central computing facility, even across the Internet or other public infrastructures.

When the various satellite offices are located in a metropolitan area, a VPN becomes very attractive, since there will not be a large problem with "speed of light" latency issues. These network types are called metropolitan area networks (**MANs**). However, the greater the distance, the more local (iSCSI) storage will be deployed at the satellite location and the less central storage will be used for normal operations. These more remote locations will like the feature of local pooled storage that they get with iSCSI, without having to learn Fibre Channel.

When metropolitan area satellite offices need more iSCSI-based storage, they just ask the storage administrator at the central installation to logically attach more virtual volumes to the user's iSCSI access list. All this is possible without significant effort at the satellite location, assuming, of course, that adequate bandwidth exists between the central location and the satellite office.

In the past, satellite office connections required private or leased phone lines, but it is now becoming prevalent in many areas for carriers to offer "IP tone" at a much lower cost than leased lines. Thus, the customer is now more likely than before to have high-speed connections between the satellite office and the central office.

Satellite locations may also have local servers and storage requirements, and will want the flexibility offered by a SAN. They will find iSCSI a more cost-effective solution than Fibre Channel, especially since the network management can still be handled at the central location.

The satellite installation, like the campus environment, will also want to be able to use centralized tape units for backup without having them located at the satellite location. This also is an ideal exploitation of the capabilities of iSCSI. (See Figure 2–8.)

## The At-Distance Site

"At-distance" reflects the needs of many centralized computing locations that use storage equipment placed at remote locations.

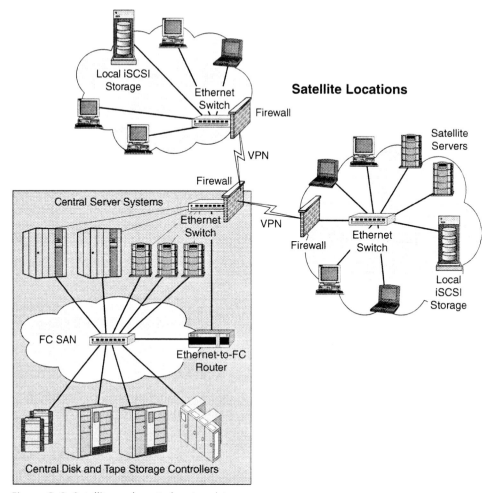

Figure 2–8  Satellite and central system/storage.

The remote equipment can range from small RAID arrays to large disk RAID arrays, tapes, and tape libraries. Even the central location prefers to have the tape library "at distance" from the central site. Often this is a tape vaulting area (such as "Iron Mountain"). iSCSI permits "natural" access to such remote units, without undue gateways, routing, or conversions from one technology to another. (See Figure 2–9.)

Part of this "natural" access is the ability of either the servers, the storage controller, or some third-party equipment to create dynamic mirrors at remote locations, which can be "spun off" at any time and then backed up to tape. This permits remote backup without impacting online applications. The

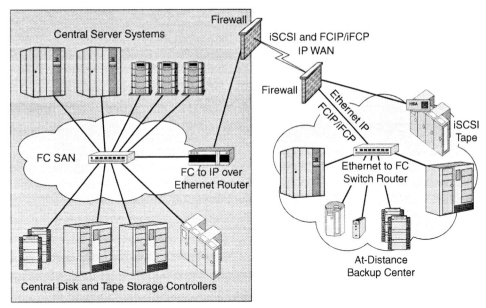

Figure 2–9 The at-distance environment.

remote mirror can be located at the tape-vaulting site, or iSCSI can be used to send it to another remote location. This type of process, though possible at a local site, seems to be very valuable when located at a secure remote site.

Today this remote storage access is done with proprietary protocols, devices, and often expensive leased lines. In the future it will be done with standard IP protocols, primarily iSCSI, often utilizing carrier-provided IP tone interconnects.

### The Central Site

The central site will receive iSCSI storage requests from campus department servers, from desktops and laptops, and from satellite locations. Likewise it will issue storage requests to remote locations for backup and disaster recovery. (See Figure 2–10.)

The central environment is considered to be the high-end processing and storage environment. It has the highest speed requirements not only on the processor itself but also on the I/O network it uses. Further, it has an overarching need for high reliability, availability, and serviceability (**RAS**).

In the central site iSCSI must be able to perform as well as Fibre Channel and match the same RAS requirements. These difficult but attainable requirements dictate that hosts use top-of-the-line iSCSI HBAs and that these

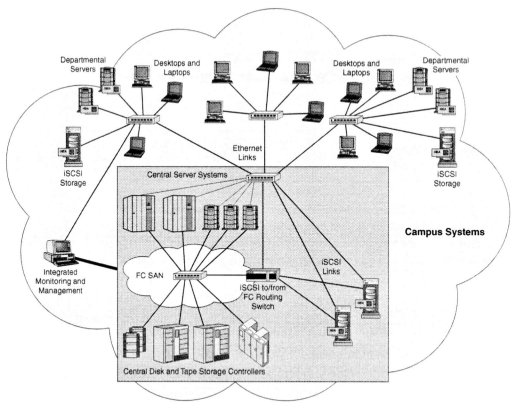

Figure 2–10  The campus environment.

HBAs be configured to operate in tandem such that failover is possible. Also, they need to be usable in a parallel manner such that any degree of throughput can be accomplished. The iSCSI protocol has factored in these requirements and supports a parallel technique known as Multiple Connections per Session (**MC/S**). This permits multiple host iSCSI HBAs to work as a team, not only for availability but also for maximum bandwidth. The same set of capabilities within the iSCSI protocol also permits iSCSI target devices to perform similar bandwidth and availability functions.

The high-end environment will have both the FC and iSCSI storage controllers. And since Fibre Channel is already there and can't be ignored, the installation must be able to interconnect the two storage networking technologies and expect them to "work and play" well together. The installation will have the problem of how to begin and how to integrate the two networks. Customers will want to invest in iSCSI storage controllers and yet continue to capitalize on the FC SAN investments they already have.

Various vendors offer "bridge boxes" that convert iSCSI host connections to FC storage connections. Some boxes convert FC host connections to iSCSI storage connections. Both of these functions are accomplished via routers, gateways, and switches (**switch routers**).

The thing that will actually make all this interconnection capability work is the management software. Probably there will be storage network management software that can operate with all FC networks and similar software that can control the iSCSI network. Clearly, though, there is a need for storage management software that can manage a network made up of both FC and iSCSI.

Even though multi-network software is sophisticated, some vendors are bringing it to market now. Luckily, the iSCSI protocol has defined a set of discovery processes that can be shipped with each iSCSI device which will permit a full iSCSI discovery process. This process, when used in conjunction with the FC discovery processes, will permit the interplay of iSCSI and FC SANs.

Since iSCSI and Fibre Channel share the SCSI command set, most existing LUN discovery and management software will continue to operate as it does in SCSI and Fibre Channel today. Therefore, there should not be significant changes to the SAN LUN management software.

The key problem is that the combined "SCSI device" discovery processes need to be carried out when there are both FC and iSCSI connections. It needs to be done both to and from the hosts and to and from the storage controllers. When an FC network manager performs its discovery process and detects an FC device, which just happens to be available to an iSCSI host (via a gateway device of some kind), it is important that the iSCSI network manager also know about the device. Therefore, an FC/iSCSI network manager needs to combine the results of the FC discovery process with its iSCSI discovery process so that all appropriate devices can be offered to the host systems as valid targets.

In addition to knowledge about each other's hosts and storage controllers, there has to be a melding of names and addresses such that iSCSI hosts can actually contact the FC target storage controllers and vice versa. Luckily, a companion protocol/process called **iSNS** (Internet Storage Name Service) deals with this problem by mapping the names and address between the FC and iSCSI views. In this way, with the appropriate surrounding management software, both networks can be seen as a seamless interconnected SAN.

To sum up, the high-end environment contains all aspects of the low-end (SoHo) and midrange environments, plus additional requirements for high availability and large bandwidth, along with campus and WAN (intranet) connections. It also requires seamless interconnect between FC and iSCSI networks.

## FC and iSCSI

Many have asked, "Will the integration of iSCSI and Fibre Channel continue indefinitely?" Since that question has an open-ended timeframe, the answer has to be no. A more important question, however, is, "What is the timeframe for when the customer will more likely buy iSCSI products than Fibre Channel products?" Said another way, "When will the sales of iSCSI equipment surpass the sales of Fibre Channel equipment?" My guess is 2006–2007. Other analysts have said 2005 and even 2004, but this seems to me to be wishful thinking.

I believe that the volumes will tip in favor of iSCSI (regardless of the timeframe) because iSCSI can perform all the functions that Fibre Channel can. In addition, iSCSI will operate on the wide area network (WAN), the Internet, and campus LANs up to the individual desktop and laptop level. Thus, when an installation is considering what to purchase next, it is probably going to choose the most flexible technology, especially since that seems to be the technology with the lowest projected price. This applies to both the initial costs to purchase and, as addressed earlier, the ongoing cost of management, training, and the like.

I did not say that Fibre Channel was going to go away in 2006–2007, just that iSCSI would begin to outsell it. That is because iSCSI will make significant gains by playing to a larger market, not just by displacing current Fibre Channel. I think Fibre Channel will continue to evolve for a while and continue to support its customer base. In other words, if I could project myself to 2010, I would still see sales of FC equipment. This means that not only will there be **iSANs** (SANs made up of only iSCSI network entities), but there will also be long-term business in the area of integrating iSCSI and FC SANs via various gateways and switching routers.

 ## Chapter Summary

This chapter focused on the various environments where iSCSI would be of value. In it we discussed **SoHo** (Small office, Home office) environments and where iSCSI fits in them.

Home offices:

- Purchase software as part of the OS.

- Purchase software from a local computer store.

- Seldom share files.

- Share files via e-mail or peer to peer.

- Find iSCSI solutions useful for easily adding storage without opening systems.

Small offices:

- Sometimes install specialty software, which often uses a database.

- Sometimes have NAS servers.

- Can use iSCSI to ease the impact of storage growth.

- Find software iSCSI initiators and software-based iSCSI targets acceptable.

- Are attracted to dual dialect servers.

Midrange environments:

- Use dedicated server systems to process their business needs.

- Prefer HBAs instead of software iSCSI device drivers in their server systems.

- Require their target storage controllers to have hardware iSCSI HBAs or chips to ensure maximum capacity and performance.

- Have desktop and laptop systems that use software iSCSI device drivers.

- Use dual dialect boxes.

The size of the midrange market will be so large that the price of iSCSI adapters and chips will bring significant cost reductions to the iSAN market. iSCSI will tend to dominate the markets

- At the midrange.

- In the low end.

- Over time in the high-end environment.

The high-end company has

- A central computing location.

- Well-trained personnel.

- Backup tape drives.

- Tape libraries.

- Many storage controllers.

- A campus made up of:

  ➤ Many small fiefdoms of key managers who need to *own* their own systems.

  ➤ Subenvironments that in many respects map to SoHo and midrange environments, including desktops and laptops.

- Satellite locations.

- At-distance installations.

Satellite offices find that

- VPNs and iSCSI are valuable technology partners.

- They can access central storage as if it were located at the satellite location.

- They will be able to operate in a manner similar to the operations of small offices and midrange companies.

- They can have their own local iSCSI SANs with local storage.

- They can have all their disk storage requirements coordinated with a central location.

- They can use the central tape library for backup.

The bigger the satellite office, the more it will function independently, but even a small satellite office will have its logical SAN extend across VPNs to the central location. This will be especially true in metropolitan area networks (**MAN**s). MANs will permit central iSCSI storage to be used as if it were local to the satellite location.

The high-end environment will be composed of "at-distance" environments:

- These environments want access to devices such that tape can be located in some remote area (called tape vaulting).

- Backup to tape at a remote location will be one of iSCSI's "killer apps."

The central location holds all the big servers and big storage controllers.

- This is the primary location for FC devices.

- The key requirement is to ensure that iSCSI and Fibre Channel "work and play" well together.

- A centralized technique is needed to

  ➤ Perform discovery.

  ➤ Manage the total storage environment.

  ➤ Permit both Fibre Channel and iSCSI to work as a single transport network.

- Fibre Channel is not going away, or at least not quickly.

- iSCSI does not have to take on all FC deployments to be successful.

- iSCSI will be considered a very successful transport if it can meet all the needs of SoHo, midrange, and campus environments.

- Routers, gateways, and switches will permit access by campus systems to the FC storage in the central computing center.

- Any amount of native iSCSI installation in the main computing center should be considered to be net added value to the iSCSI business plan.

# 3 The History of iSCSI

## To the Reader

This chapter will describe the events that brought iSCSI to the storage industry. Key individuals involved in these events are acknowledged in the Credits and Disclaimer section at the beginning of this book.

The chapter will focus on the early days of iSCSI development. Included is an important set of measurements that helped IBM set its iSCSI direction with respect to NFS, Fibre Channel, and the need for a TCP/IP offload engine. Readers not interested in history should at least read the Measurements section and then pick up with the Chapter Summary.

## SCSI over TCP/IP

In 1996 IBM Research was investigating networked storage using Ethernet. That ultimately led to meetings in which IBM Haifa Research, IBM Watson Research, and IBM Almaden Research came together to discuss joint investigations.

The researchers debated the appropriate way to interface storage to common networks. The debate was focused on SCSI over TCP versus SCSI over IP and SCSI over raw Ethernet. It was agreed that the investigations would pursue SCSI over TCP/IP because of TCP/IP's network flexibility and ubiquitous availability. As a result the work was divided up and decisions were made about what tests and proofs of concept to run. The researchers built prototypes on an NT base and on a Linux base.

By October 1998 the researchers had the first working prototype of SCSI over TCP/IP. Numbers of performance measurements were taken comparing the overheads of Fibre Channel and of SCSI over TCP/IP and of SCSI over raw gigabit Ethernet. The bottom line was that the TCP overhead was not as great as feared, and it was felt that processor power, as it kept increasing, would make the differences negligible.

The researchers determined that if all they wanted to do was to operate on local networks, then SCSI over raw gigabit Ethernet or SCSI over IP should be considered. However, the goal they had in mind was to permit the SCSI protocol to flow on any network, including the Internet, and that required TCP/IP. Therefore, based on the measured results, the extrapolation into the future, and network goals, SCSI over TCP/IP became the direction of further research.

This was not a sufficient condition to set new directions within IBM development, however. There were more questions to answer, key among them whether SCSI over TCP/IP could be made to perform well in "enterprise" environments or would remain only a niche technology. Several things needed to be measured and understood, to arrive at an answer:

- How did this technology stand up to Fibre Channel?

- Was there a future for the technology in areas where Fibre Channel would not go?

- Was there a definable path to get to the technology promises?

To get a handle on these questions, measurements were taken where data was sent from client to target systems. In some cases the connection was Fibre Channel and in some it was TCP/IP. The measurements showed very clearly that TCP/IP had a long way to go before it could be competitive with Fibre Channel in the enterprise machine room. It also became very clear that, unless TCP/IP could be offloaded onto a chip or an HBA, as was done with the networking overhead of Fibre Channel, there would never be a sufficient reduction of CPU overhead to convince customers to use TCP/IP instead of Fibre Channel in fully loaded servers, especially with high-end systems. In addition, some key measurements also needed to be run to answer the following questions:

- Will SCSI over TCP/IP perform better or worse at the target than a Network File System (NFS) server?

- Where in the protocol stack is the processor time most impacted?

- Is there a way to have a reasonable software-based SCSI over TCP/IP target before there is a TCP/IP offload engine (TOE)?

These were critical questions, especially since most pundits at that time held the position that a reasonable TOE could not be created.

*Note:* During the second half of 1999, I met with a number of TCP/IP and NIC vendors to discuss the possibility of a TOE. They said that a TOE on a chip was not possible or reasonable.

## Measurements

The question of NFS versus SCSI over TCP/IP was considered to be a key consideration regarding the future of iSCSI. If NFS could operate as well as SCSI over TCP/IP, why would one ever want to use SCSI over TCP/IP? A number of measurements were taken in 1998–1999 to get a basis for answering this question.

By early 2000 the measurements had led to the creation of an IBM internal white paper. A key set of measurements showed how a file of a given size could be transferred from a client to a target/server using TCP/IP NFS and using SCSI over normal TCP/IP, and how the CPU utilization compared in these two approaches. To ensure that they were measuring apples to apples, the researchers put everything on a RAM disk at that target to eliminate some of the variability.

Later some additional measurements were taken of the SCSI-over-TCP/IP approach. One of them modified the TCP/IP stack so that SCSI could use a special, single buffer-to-buffer copy interface. It had only one data movement in main memory instead of the usual two buffer-to-buffer copies in the unmodified TCP/IP. These measurements went even further when another special TCP/IP version was created that used a scatter/gather approach and had *no* buffer copies.

The results can be seen in Figure 3–1, which shows a significant difference between the CPU utilization in the NFS server and the SCSI-over-TCP/IP server. The client side of the operation is not shown, but the client-side overhead was about a wash between SCSI and NFS.

The measurements also determined that reducing the buffer-to-buffer moves would achieve some important performance improvements. That is, just moving the SCSI over TCP/IP to an implementation with only one buffer move saved over half the processor cycles. Likewise, eliminating all buffer-to-buffer moves could save more than half of the remaining processor cycles.

Figure 3–1 shows that SCSI over unmodified TCP/IP consumed only 26% to 31.4% of the CPU cycles consumed by an NFS server with unmodified TCP/IP. The single-buffer-copy version of SCSI over TCP/IP reduced

Percent CPU Overhead

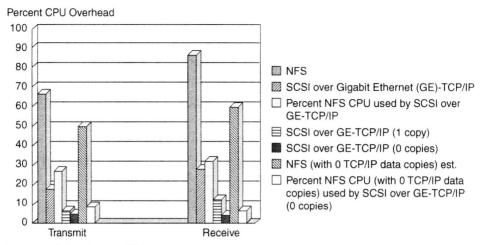

Figure 3–1  NAS versus iSCSI.*

those numbers to 9% when sending and 14% when receiving. A zero-copy version consumed only 6% of the CPU cycles that were consumed by the NFS server when sending and 4% when receiving.

One can extract two important pieces of information from the measurements.

■ Since NFS and SCSI over *normal* TCP/IP:

➢ Use the same TCP/IP interfaces.

➢ Have the same Ethernet frame size.

➢ Transfer the same amount of data.

Then

➢ *NFS (over TCP/IP) processing consumes three to four times more CPU processing than does SCSI over TCP/IP.*

■ Assuming that

➢ The total NFS TCP/IP overhead for data transfers is about the same as that of SCSI over TCP/IP.

---

*The base performance numbers used in this graph were provided courtesy of the IBM Corporation [Performance].

> ➤ The TCP/IP overhead left in SCSI over TCP/IP (after elimination of copies) is negligible. (It is not, but this assumption provides a worst-case comparison.)

Then

> ➤ *The processing left in SCSI over TCP/IP is 6% to 8% of the processing needed for NFS, even if NFS uses a zero-data-copy TCP/IP.*

This meant that one could handle around 12 to 16 times the I/O workload with SCSI over TCP/IP than was possible with NFS, even if both offloaded the TCP/IP data copy overhead.

These measurements were a big help in understanding the value of SCSI-block I/O over TCP/IP versus file I/O via NFS over TCP/IP. They also clearly showed what hardware TCP/IP offload, as well as specially modified TCP/IP stacks, could accomplish.

## Cisco and IBM's Joint Effort

In the fall of 1999 IBM and Cisco met to discuss the possibility of combining their SCSI-over-TCP/IP efforts. After Cisco saw IBM's demonstration of SCSI over TCP/IP, the two companies agreed to develop a proposal that would be taken to the IETF for standardization.

The combined team from Cisco and IBM developed a joint iSCSI draft during the fourth quarter of 1999. They had an initial external draft ready by February 2000, when a meeting was held in San Jose attended by HP, Adaptec, EMC, Quantum, Sun, Agilent, and 3Com, among others, to solicit support for presentation of the draft to the IETF. At this meeting several proposals were talked about that used SCSI over Ethernet. At least one suggested not using TCP/IP; however, the general consensus of the group was for SCSI-over-TCP/IP support. With backing from this group, the draft was taken to the IETF meeting held in Adelaide, Australia (March 2000).

## iSCSI and IETF

At Adelaide there was a **BOF** (birds of a feather) meeting at which the draft was presented, and it was agreed that a group would meet in April 2000 in Haifa, Israel, to do additional work on it. The goal was to enlarge the working team, secure consensus, and prepare to take the proposal to the next IETF meeting so that a new workgroup for *iSCSI* could be started. (By this time we had coined the name iSCSI to represent the SCSI-over-TCP/IP proposal being developed.)

The next meeting of the IETF was in Pittsburgh in August 2000. At that meeting the draft was presented and a new workgroup was started. This group was called IP Storage (**ips**) workgroup, and it included not only iSCSI but also a proposal for bridging FC SANs across IP networks (**FCIP**). Subsequently a similar draft from Nishan Systems Corporation, called **iFCP**, was added to the workgroup. David Black and Elizabeth Rodriguez were chosen to be the co-chairs of the IETF ips workgroup, and Julian Satran was made the primary author and editor of the iSCSI working draft. Subsequently I was chosen by David Black to be the technical coordinator of the iSCSI track.

The process moved the draft though several iterations until it was agreed that all outstanding issues had been resolved.

It should be noted that parallel efforts were under way within Adaptec and Nishan Systems. Adaptec was focusing on SCSI over Ethernet, and Nishan was focused on Fibre Channel over UDP. These efforts were not accepted by the IETF ips workgroup, but the Adaptec and Nishan efforts, as they joined the iSCSI effort, have given additional depth to the project.

Subsequent to forming the IETF ips workgroup, we established an IP Storage Consortium within the charter of the Storage Networking Industry Association (**SNIA**), which was called the SNIA IP Storage Forum. An SNIA technical working group was also established to assist in areas that did not directly effect the IETF iSCSI protocol standardization effort. An example of this is the definition of a common application programming interface (**API**) for use by various vendors' iSCSI HBAs.

## The End of the Story

IBM announced in February 2001 (and started shipping in April–June 2001) an iSCSI native RAID storage controller called the 200i. Also,

- At about the same time Cisco started shipping its 5420 bridge/router (iSCSI to Fibre Channel).

- Nishan is shipping a multiport iSCSI and FC switch/router.

- Adaptec is shipping iSCSI HBAs and chips with iSCSI and a TOE.

- Intel is shipping its HBA.

- Alacritech is shipping an iSCSI-compatible HBA.

- Most of the current FC chip vendors are shipping, or planning to ship soon, iSCSI chips and HBAs.

- IBM has stated their intention to make iSCSI part of their main line fabric and not just a connection to its 200i product.

In addition, Nishan, Alacritech, and Hitachi Data Systems have demonstrated that iSCSI initiators can drive an FC storage controller from the West Coast to the East Coast at full gigabit speeds.

Membership in the IETF ips workgroup has grown to over 650 people representing over 250 different companies. The SNIA IP Storage Forum (which requires an additional membership fee above the fee to join SNIA) has 55 active companies contributing to joint marketing efforts for IP storage.

## Chapter Summary

The chronology of iSCSI is as follows:

- In 1996 IBM was performing research into SCSI over Ethernet.

- In 1997–1999 several companies were doing parallel work on SCSI over Ethernet and other IP networks.

- By 1998 IBM had developed prototypes and important demonstration units of its SCSI-over-TCP/IP protocol.

- IBM performed some key measurements that showed that SCSI over normal TCP/IP uses only about a third to a quarter of the CPU processing power used by NFS with normal TCP/IP.

- The performance analysis showed that, if all the overhead for TCP/IP data movement was removed from both iSCSI and NFS, the remaining iSCSI CPU utilization would be only 6% to 8% of the remaining NFS CPU utilization.

- IBM's measurements were able to show that, if a SCSI-over-IP protocol could remove TCP/IP's extra data moves, a software version might be reasonable.

- IBM's measurements clearly showed the value and importance of a TCP/IP TOE.

- Cisco and IBM worked together to bring out a new SCSI-over-TCP/IP protocol.

- IBM and Cisco developed an initial draft proposal for presentation to the IETF.

- IBM and Cisco obtained support from a number of additional companies in February 2000 to bring the draft to the IETF.

- IBM and Cisco brought the draft to an IETF BOF meeting in Australia.

- A team of companies came together in Haifa to refine the draft for the IETF (draft level 0).

- IBM, Cisco, and the new team of supporting companies brought the draft to the IETF, where it was part of the new IETF working group called IP Storage (ips).

- Adaptec and Nishan had parallel efforts but over time joined the iSCSI bandwagon.

- Many vendors are now shipping iSCSI products, and full gigabit line speed has been demonstrated between an iSCSI initiator on the East Coast and a target FC controller on the West Coast.

# 4 An Overview of iSCSI

## To the Reader

The following text is at a fairly high level. However, readers can skip to the various summaries within the chapter and then pick up with the overall chapter summary.

iSCSI is a transport protocol that carries SCSI (Small Computer System Interface) commands from host computer systems (referred to as initiator systems) to target devices. To understand how this is done, we need first to understand the system structure behind SCSI command creation and delivery. (See Figure 4–1 for an iSCSI version of this structure.)

The host system is made up of applications that communicate with the SCSI-connected devices via one of the following, to a SCSI-class driver:

- A file system.

- An application programming interface (API).

There is a SCSI class driver for each type of SCSI device (tape, disk, etc.). The SCSI processing flow is as follows:

1. The SCSI class driver converts a device request from applications or file systems into SCSI commands. SCSI commands are carried in command description blocks (CDBs).

2. The SCSI class driver invokes the appropriate hardware device driver.

3. The hardware device driver interacts with the HBA via a vendor-specific interface.

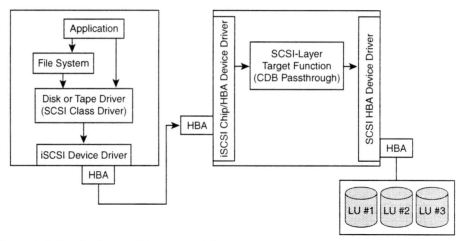

Figure 4–1  Application-to-LU command flow.

4.  The HBA sends the SCSI commands (CDBs) and data to the remote
    SCSI device's HBA and device driver.

5.  Within the SCSI device, a SCSI process

    ■ Interprets the commands.

    ■ Receives the data.

    ■ Sends instructions to the appropriate subordinate LU.

The actual SCSI communication is thus from the SCSI class driver to the
SCSI process in the target device. The SCSI class driver gets its instructions
from the application, and the SCSI target process gives the instructions to the
LU. Communication is from application to LU via SCSI protocols. The section on iSCSI protocol layers further on discusses this process.

    In Chapter 1 we talked about the SCSI parallel bus protocol that delivers
the SCSI commands to the SCSI device. To observe the semantics of SCSI we
must deliver SCSI commands in order to the LU and deliver data to or from
the LU as that LU requires. We also need to understand that, even with the
SCSI parallel bus protocol, commands for different LUs can be multiplexed
with each other, as can the data.

## TCP/IP

The requirement for in-order delivery of commands and data seems straightforward; however, as we get into networks of various kinds the possibility

of congestion, alternate routes, lost data or command packets, and the like, becomes a significant design problem. iSCSI designers decided to build their protocol on top of a reliable delivery transport known as TCP/IP (Transmission Control Protocol over Internet Protocol). This transport guarantees the error-free delivery of every byte of data, delivered in the same order in which it was sent. This solved many problems, and, since almost every system in the world includes TCP/IP, any problematic prerequisites that iSCSI otherwise might require were eliminated. In addition, and perhaps foremost in the minds of iSCSI architects, the TCP/IP protocol can operate in a congested network such as the Internet. Other protocols, like **UDP/IP** (User Datagram Protocol over Internet Protocol), were considered, but they either lacked the ubiquitous availability of TCP or did not have TCP/IP's congestion management.

As will be seen later, error-free in-order delivery has great value, but storage needs an even higher degree of error detection than is normally available to TCP/IP. Therefore, iSCSI designers added optional additional enhancements that can be used in some environments to ensure better end-to-end data protection. These additional features will be described later.

iSCSI's basic unit of transfer is called a protocol data unit (**PDU**). A PDU is designed to carry, along with other information, the SCSI CDBs and the appropriate data components from the initiator to the target, and to receive the required data or reply in response. However, a CDB only describes the function that the initiator wants the target to perform. It does not carry any information about the address of the SCSI target or the LU to which it is directed, because SCSI follows a procedure call model, in which the CDB is only one argument. The other arguments, such as the LUN, are encapsulated by iSCSI in the same PDU with the corresponding CDB, and the IP address of the target is encapsulated in the TCP and IP portions of the protocol packet.

Let's say the above in a different way. Assume that the initiator discovers the location of an iSCSI device, which it is authorized to access. This device will have an IP address. The iSCSI device driver, or protocol handler within the HBA, will build a PDU with the appropriate CDB and LUN. It will then hand that packet over to a TCP/IP socket. TCP will encapsulate the PDU further with TCP headers, then turn the resulting packet over to IP. IP will determine the detail routing address, place it in a packet header, and send it to the Ethernet component, which will add the physical-link-level headers and trailers and send the final packet on its way. (See the encapsulations shown in Figure 4–2.)

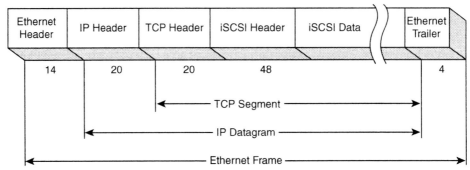

Figure 4–2  iSCSI/TCP/IP/Ethernet transport encapsulation.

That, in a nutshell, describes the main processing path for the iSCSI transport protocol. The next section will describe how the various layers of the iSCSI-related protocol stack exploit the TCP/IP message structure.

### TCP/IP Summary

■ TCP/IP was chosen as the base transport because of its universal availability and its ability to cross almost any network media.

■ TCP/IP can operate on congested networks as well as on dedicated networks.

■ TCP/IP delivers data (almost) error free and in order.

■ Protocol data units (**PDUs**) are the basic form of message unit exchange between hosts and storage controllers.

■ A PDU carries the SCSI command in a command description block (**CDB**) and the logical unit number (**LUN**) of the end device.

■ Each PDU is encased in a TCP segment with IP headers and an Ethernet frame.

## iSCSI-Related Protocol Layers

As mentioned earlier, iSCSI is built on TCP/IP, which it uses to transport its iSCSI PDUs. Also, SCSI looks at iSCSI as a transport to send SCSI commands (CDBs) from the SCSI initiator to the SCSI target.

Note that TCP looks at IP as its transport for sending packets of information to its remote counterpart. Further, IP looks to a set of link-level wire protocols to transport its packets across the network. These protocols can follow the Ethernet standard or one of the **OC** (optical connection) standards. We will focus on the Ethernet links here.

As you can see, a definitive layering is associated with the transport of SCSI commands and data across the network.

Figure 4–3 illustrates the layering structure. Notice that the objects at the top of the layering are the application and the LU to which the application is trying to execute an I/O operation. To do that, it sends an I/O request to the OS kernel which is directed in turn to the appropriate SCSI class driver. Sometimes this is done indirectly through a file system. The SCSI class driver

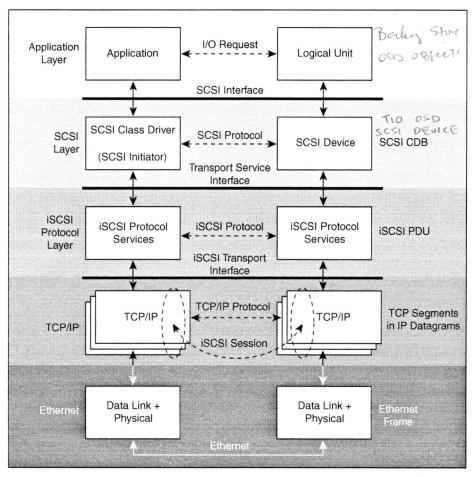

Figure 4–3  The iSCSI layers.

forms the I/O request into an appropriate SCSI command, which is placed in
a data packet called a CDB and sent to the SCSI device via the appropriate
local device driver, indicating the required LU.

From an architecture standpoint the iSCSI device driver is the beginning
of the iSCSI transport layer. The iSCSI layer places the CDB in a PDU along
with the LUN, and sends it to its remote iSCSI partner over a "session,"
which is made up of one or more TCP/IP connections. Systems without a special iSCSI offloaded HBA create all the iSCSI PDU packets within the logical
device driver and then invoke TCP/IP. If the system has an iSCSI HBA, the
iSCSI layer extends into the HBA. In this case, the iSCSI function on the HBA
creates the PDUs. This offloaded function in turn interfaces to the TCP/IP
TOE, which is also on the HBA. In either case (with or without the iSCSI
HBA), the iSCSI layer interfaces to the TCP/IP layer and uses one or more
TCP/IP connections to form a session to carry the PDUs.

The sending TCP/IP layer passes packets to the remote TCP/IP layer by
delivering them to the data link layer below it (for example, the Ethernet
data link layer). As was shown in Figure 4–2, the data link layer places a
header and a trailer on the physical link along with the TCP/IP packet. It
then passes the total Ethernet frame to the remote data link layer, which
passes it to the TCP/IP layers above it.

Note that the PDU might span more than one TCP segment and that each
of the TCP segments will be encapsulated within an IP datagram which is further encapsulated by the data link layer into an Ethernet frame. It is the job of
TCP/IP to reassemble the TCP segments in the right order on the target side
and deliver them to the iSCSI layer in the same bytewise order in which they
were sent. iSCSI will then extract the CDB from the PDU and deliver it to the
SCSI target device code, indicating the appropriate LUN. Then the SCSI target
code will deliver the CDB to the actual LU. When the SCSI layer needs data for
the command (e.g., a write command) it requests it from the iSCSI layer and
passes it through to the LU. The target iSCSI layer extracts the requested data
from PDUs sent from the initiator, which can be one of the following:

- The PDU that held the command (called "immediate" data)

- PDUs that were unsolicited but sent by the initiator and contain only
  data (called "unsolicited" data)

- Data PDUs that the iSCSI target explicitly requested on behalf of a
  direct SCSI layer solicitation

## Protocol Summary

iSCSI uses TCP/IP as the "network transport" to carry the basic elements of the SCSI Protocol. It carries all the SCSI functions that would otherwise take place on a physical SCSI bus. TCP/IP provides iSCSI with inherent reliability along with byte-by-byte in-order delivery. iSCSI added the additional capacity and reliability of multiple physical/logical links (TCP/IP connections) while ensuring that the commands and data, which are spread across the multiple connections, arrive in order at the target SCSI device.

1. In order to send data to a storage device (LU), the application will invoke a "write" API on the initiator.

2. The API will deliver the "write" request to the SCSI layer (the SCSI class driver).

3. The SCSI class driver will build a CDB for the "write" request and pass it to a device driver in the iSCSI protocol layer.

4. The iSCSI protocol layer will place the CDB (and other parameters) in an iSCSI PDU and invoke TCP/IP.

5. TCP will divide the iSCSI PDU into segments and place a TCP header on them; the IP processing will additionally place an IP header before the TCP header.

6. TCP/IP will deliver the segment to the Ethernet data link layer, which will frame the segment with Ethernet headers and trailers.

7. The iSCSI PDU, wrapped in a collection of headers, will traverse the network until it reaches the intended target.

8. At the target, the data link layer will check and strip off the Ethernet framing and pass the remaining segment to TCP/IP.

   ■ TCP and IP will each check and strip off their headers, leaving only the iSCSI PDU, which they will pass to the iSCSI layer.

   ■ The iSCSI layer will extract the "write" CDB from the iSCSI PDU and send it along with related parameters and data to the SCSI device.

   ■ The SCSI device will send the SCSI "write" request and the data to the LU.

## Sessions

The logical link that carries the commands and data to and from TCP/IP endpoints is called an **iSCSI session**. A session is made up of (at least) one TCP/IP connection from an initiator (host) to a target (storage device).

In general this concept is simple and straightforward. There are several things, however, that conspire to make the protocol more sophisticated and involved. The first is the need to send out more I/O commands and data than can be accommodated with a single TCP/IP connection. In Fibre Channel this is handled by the host system adding more sessions between the initiator and the target. This can also be done for iSCSI.

The only problem with this approach is the lack of a SCSI-defined method for sending commands and data across multiple links. As a solution each target vendor has created what the industry calls an **initiator wedge driver** to balance the workload over the multiple FC links. This means that storage vendors need to include their own code in the host system. The more types of storage controllers the customer has, the more vendor-specific wedge drivers are needed around the SCSI class drivers. This can cause a lot of operating system software conflicts. In order to prevent this confusion in the iSCSI space, and to allow any small system in the network to get to the appropriate storage controller without having to add vendor-specific wedge drivers, iSCSI added some additional functions (complexity) in its protocol.

One such function is the concept of multiple connections per session (**MC/S**). (See Figure 4–4.) This is the ability for several TCP/IP connections to make up a session and be used as if they were parts of a single conduit between the initiator and the target. It allows commands and data to be transported across the different links (connections) and to arrive at the ultimate SCSI layer target in the same order as if they had been transported over a single connection. To enable this, the iSCSI PDU must contain, in addition to the CDB and LUN, ordering information. This is somewhat ironic, since TCP/IP was chosen for its ability to deliver data in order, but now we have to add information, counters, and additional flow control to ensure the appropriate order across multiple connections.

The problem of enabling MC/S is that the iSCSI protocol becomes more complicated. Complexity is somewhat eased, however, since each TCP/IP connection that is part of the session delivers its part of the data flow in order and usually error free. Thus, only PDU order between the connections needs to be ensured by iSCSI.

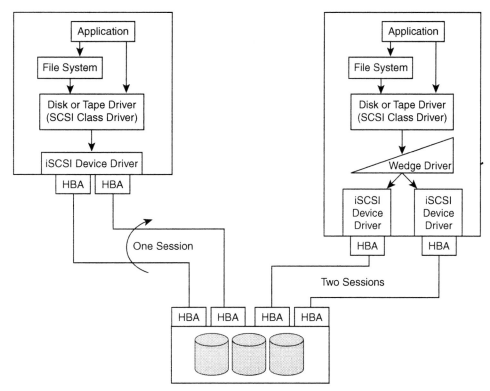

Figure 4–4 Multiple connections between hosts and storage controllers.

**Session Summary**

- An iSCSI session can be made up of one or more physical or logical links.

- These links carry TCP/IP protocols and the iSCSI PDUs, which in turn carry the commands and data.

- Even though TCP/IP ensures in-order delivery within a connection, iSCSI permits the commands to be spread across the different links and the data to be spread with the commands (called multiple connections per session, or **MC/S**).

- The iSCSI protocol defines how the commands and data can be spread over all of the session links yet to be delivered in order to the target SCSI device.

## Protocol Data Unit (PDU) Structure

Figure 4–5 shows the overall format of a PDU. Notice that it is made up of several segments. It has a 48-byte basic header segment (**BHS**), which contains the CDB, LUN, and so forth. This BHS will be studied in more detail a little further on. Descriptions of the additional header segments (**AHS**) will be shown in detail in Appendix A.

To understand the construction of the general PDU, it is important to understand that most PDUs have only the BHS since everything else is optional. The AHS is defined so that the PDU can carry instructions for bidirectional commands (SCSI third-party commands). These commands (extended copy and compare) have a "master CDB" that is contained in the BHS and may have multiple extensions (each with source and target LU addresses along with descriptions of that part of the extended operation). These extensions describe the totality of the operation to a function called the copy manager. The copy manager is a SCSI entity that performs copy functions remote from the host when appropriately commanded (via third-party commands) from the host. Since third-party commands are rare compared to normal SCSI commands, the usual PDU only contains a BHS.

| Byte | 0 | 1 | 2 | 3 |
|---|---|---|---|---|
| Bit | 0 1 2 3 4 5 6 7 | 0 1 2 3 4 5 6 7 | 0 1 2 3 4 5 6 7 | 0 1 2 3 4 5 6 7 |
| 00 -------- -------- 47 | Basic Header Segment (BHS) | | | |
| 48 -------- -------- nn | Additional Header Segment (AHS) (Optional) | | | |
| nn+1 ----- ------- mm | More AHSs (Optional) | | | |
| mm+1 --- --- mm+4 | Header Digest (Optional) | | | |
| mm+5 --- -------- pp | Data Segment (Optional) | | | |
| pp+1 ----- ----- pp+4 | Data Digest (Optional) | | | |

Figure 4–5  General structure of the PDU.

As one can see in Figure 4–5, there are three other extension types. One of those is the data segment, which contains the data being sent to the target device. The other two extensions are digests. "Digest" is a fancy term for an error check word. It works similarly to the TCP/IP checksums, but with 32 bits (instead of 16) and a more robust algorithm, called **CRC-32c** (cyclical redundancy check, 32-bit wide, as proposed by G. Castagnioli et al. [Castagnioli]). The reason for this CRC will be discussed later.

Figure 4–6 shows the basic header in some detail. We can see that it has some flags (discussed later), an iSCSI opcode (which specifies the type of iSCSI operation being performed), and the lengths of the additional header segment and of the data segment, if any. It may also contain, depending on the opcode, the LUN, and the SCSI CDB. For request PDUs, if the I bit is set to 1, the request is "immediate."

| Byte | 0 | 1 | 2 | 3 |
|---|---|---|---|---|
| Bit | 0 1 2 3 4 5 6 7 | 0 1 2 3 4 5 6 7 | 0 1 2 3 4 5 6 7 | 0 1 2 3 4 5 6 7 |
| 0 to 3 | .\|I\| Opcode | Opcode-Specific Fields | | |
| 4 to 7 | Total AHS Length | Data Segment Length | | |
| 8 to 15 | Logical Unit Number (LUN) or Opcode-Specific Fields | | | |
| 16 to 19 | Initiator Task Tag (ITT) or Opcode-Specific Fields | | | |
| 20 to 31 | Opcode-Specific Fields | | | |
| 32 to 47 | Command Descriptor Block (CDB) or Opcode-Specific Fields | | | |

Figure 4–6 Basic header segment (BHS) layout.

We have examined the relatively straightforward main path, the use of TCP/IP connections, and the format of the PDU that carries the SCSI commands. Now we will make things a bit more complicated. As mentioned in Chapters 1 and 2, the market requires the building of iSCSI HBAs. And many of the vendors that are building them—in order to increase performance and reduce cost—have decided to embed their iSCSI processing with their TOE. This permits the HBA or chip to move the TCP/IP packets directly to the host system without additional moves within the main host processor memory. However, to do this the iSCSI processor needs to see the TCP/IP segments as they arrive so that the iSCSI PDU header can supply the information that permits the placement of the data directly in the host system memory, at the appropriate locations, with no additional data movement. This will be covered in more detail in Chapter 8.

### PDU Structure Summary

The protocol data unit (**PDU**), which is the basic message packet that travels between the host and the storage device, is made up of

- A basic header segment (**BHS**).

- A number of optional additional header segments (**AHS**s).

- An optional header digest, which is a cyclic redundancy check (**CRC**) value.

- An optional data segment.

- An optional data digest (a CRC value).

The BHS has the opcode for the PDU and various flags; some PDUs have the CDBs, the LUN, and a series of counters.

## iSCSI and TOE Integration on a Chip or HBA

If the PDU header arrives on the HBA before the rest of the PDU, then all parts of the PDU can be directly placed in their ultimate system memory location. However, if the header arrives later than the other packets, the TOE will need to buffer the packets until the header's arrival (we call that the "reassembly buffer"). When the header arrives, the iSCSI processor will store the packets directly in the correct target system memory location.

In normal situations the reassembly buffer is not very large. This permits a very-low-cost HBA, since the RAM memory on it is minimal. It is only when error processing causes retransmission that there needs to be a considerable amount of RAM to hold all the fragments that come in before the in-error (and retransmitted) PDU header.

HBA vendors, as a result of combining the iSCSI processing and the TOE on the HBA or chip, are offering a product that can assist greatly in the performance of the normal operation path. However, the amount of on-HBA RAM needed for the reassembly buffer, in the presence of an error, can be quite high. This is especially true if the distances between endpoints are great (say from Los Angeles to New York). Therefore, iSCSI has added an optional additional protocol, called Fixed Interval Marking (**FIM**). FIM will permit the integrated iSCSI/TOE HBAs to locate the next iSCSI PDU header in the stream without waiting for any missing iSCSI headers to arrive. This will enable the vendor to build a highly functional HBA but still limit the amount of additional RAM required on it. Thus, HBA vendors not only can offload the TCP/IP overhead but also can keep their HBA RAM memory requirement low and thereby keep their cost low.

 See Chapter 13 for additional information on the RAM Minimization.

### TOE Integration Summary

- **TOE** stands for TCP/IP offload engine.

- Various vendors are building TOEs so that they can offload the CPU processing of TCP/IP.

- The TOE allows rapid processing and low host CPU cycles.

- Vendors are combining iSCSI processing with TOEs to create an iSCSI HBA that will be functionally similar to the FC HBA.

- iSCSI and TOE HBAs can work together to provide direct data placement into the final host memory location.

- A protocol called FIM will help the iSCSI and TOE HBA vendors to perform direct memory placement without stalling the data flow when a BHS arrives out of order at the TCP/IP buffers.

## Checksums and CRC (Digests)

Even though we chose TCP/IP for its ability to deliver data in error-free byte order, the fact is that the TCP/IP 16-bit one's complement checksum is not always strong enough to ensure that all transmitted data is in fact received correctly. This should not be viewed as a frequent problem, but it is frequent enough that major enterprise environments cannot ignore the possibility of undetected errors.

Before we panic, let's see what the TCP/IP network has going for it. The Ethernet links themselves are protected by a 32-bit cyclic redundancy check (**CRC-32**) calculation that travels with the packet across the Ethernet links.

The weakness of this is that it offers no protection for the packets as they pass through routers, gateways, and switches, many of which leave their circuits susceptible to data corruption. Therefore, it is possible for the data to be delivered error free to a switch or router, yet have the switch or router cause some errors before the outgoing packet is sent. Since the packet gets a new Ethernet CRC as it is sent on to the target, the resultant corrupted data packet is delivered to the target without an Ethernet error. And since the TCP/IP 16-bit checksum is a weak detector of errors, the corrupted data can be delivered to the application. When I say a "weak detector of errors," I mean weak compared to a CRC-32 error checker. Looking at the combination of Ethernet CRC-32 error checking on the links and TCP/IP checksum end to end, we can conclude that the data is reasonably protected.

The usual approach to handling the issue of undetected error loss is to use better routers and switches, perhaps ones that have internal checks on the integrity of their memory and data paths. In this way the probability of an undetected error is greatly reduced. However, when it comes to data, many storage vendors are *very* protective and they want to add even further corruption protection.

The architects of iSCSI have determined that they cannot ensure the integrity of the data in installations that have less than perfect routers and switches. Therefore, they have decided to include as an execution option their own 32-bit CRC. Also, in order to permit iSCSI-specific routers and gateways, the iSCSI CRC (when used) will be applied to the PDU header and data separately. In this way, the iSCSI router will be able to change the PDU header and reroute the PDU with its data, yet not have to reconstruct the data CRC. Thereby it leaves the 32-bit CRC able to accompany the data end to end.

The fact that iSCSI can detect an error that TCP/IP has not detected, and therefore that iSCSI must handle itself, is both good news, from an installation standpoint, and bad news, from a protocol standpoint.

When TCP/IP finds the error, it silently retransmits it; the iSCSI layer does not see any of it and does not need to do anything special for error recovery. On the other hand, if TCP/IP does not discover the error but iSCSI does, iSCSI must do the retry without assistance from TCP/IP. This will be discussed further in Chapter 11.

Note that the CRC-32 feature is optional in iSCSI, and customers can choose not to use it. Perhaps they have top-of-the-line equipment that does not need the extra protection, or they may be operating with the integrity (cryptographic digest) or privacy mode (encryption) of IPsec (See Chapter 12). It is also expected that for most laptops and desktops that have a software iSCSI implementation, the risk will be low enough and the overhead so noticeable that they also will operate without the CRC feature.

### Checksum and CRC Digest Summary

- Ethernet links are each protected by a 32-bit cyclic redundancy check (**CRC-32**).

- TCP contains a 16-bit checksum within its header.

- iSCSI adds an optional additional 32-bit CRC (**CRC-32**).

  - ➤ The CRC-32 value is called a digest.

  - ➤ iSCSI has a "required to implement but optional to use" header digest that protects the iSCSI PDU headers.

  - ➤ iSCSI has a "required to implement but optional to use" data digest that protects the data part of the PDU.

- With IPsec, generally the additional iSCSI digests are unnecessary.

## Naming and Addressing

In order to explain some of the following, we must cover the naming issue. Naming in iSCSI eases the administrative burden somewhat. As a goal, the initiator node and the target node should each have a single name, which is used as part of all sessions established between them. Also, there is a requirement that iSCSI initiator and target nodes have one of two types of names:

- **iqn** (iSCSI qualified names)

- **eui** (enterprise unique identifier)

Both types are meant to be long lived as well as unique in the world and independent of physical location. Both have a central naming authority that can ensure their uniqueness. Examples of each are *iqn.1998-03.com.xyc.ajax.wonder:jump* and *eui.acde48234667abcd*.

## Details of Naming and Addressing

The eui name is a string constructed from the identity formed using the IEEE EUI (extended unique identifier) format (EUI-64). (EUI-64 identities are also used in the formation of FC worldwide names.) Each EUI-64 identity is unique in the world. Its format in an iSCSI name is *eui.* plus its 16 hex digits (64 bits).

The most significant 24 bits of the EUI-64 identity are the *company id* value, which the IEEE Registration Authority assigns to a manufacturer (it is also known as the **OUI**, or the organization unique identifier). The manufacturer chooses the least significant 40-bit extension identifier; however, the results must be a string of 16 hex digits, which is unique within the world.

For example, assume that a manufacturer's IEEE-assigned *company id* value is hex *acde48* and the manufacturer-selected extension identifier for a given component is hex *234567abcd*. The EUI-64 value generated from these two numbers is hex *acde48234567abcd*. Thus, the iSCSI eui is *eui.acde48234567abcd*.

The iqn names are formed by a different set of policies. The characters following the *iqn.* are the reverse **DNS** name (the name resolvable by the Domain Name Service) assigned by an Internet naming authority and an additional naming authority within a company, which can assign additional unique qualifiers. For example, suppose the company has the base name *ajax.xyc.com*. The company naming authority would pick an additional string of characters that make the initiator node name unique in the world. Thus, if a fully qualified domain name (**FQDN**) format is *jump.wonder.ajax. xyc.com*, the *iqn.* form of the iSCSI initiator node name will be that string reversed: *com.xyc.ajax.wonder.jump*.

However, the name of an iSCSI node might last longer than the company that created it, or the division of the company could be sold. Subsequent administrators in the new company may not have a clue about what names were previously allocated and thus could create a naming conflict with subsequent allocations. To avoid this, a date field is required before the Reversed FQDN name, the format of which is *yyyy-mm* where *yyyy* is the year and *mm* is the month. For example, *iqn.1998-03.com.xyc.ajax.wonder.jump*.

The date should be when the root name was assigned to the company— that is, when the company received the *xyc.com* DNS root name segments from a Domain Names Registry company (such as VeriSign). In the case of a purchase or merger, the date should be when that merger or purchase took place. To be safe, choose a previous month in which the DNS was valid as of the first of that month. The point is to ensure that a later sale of the company or the name will not cause a conflict, since at the date of assignment the iqn name was unique in the world.

Because some companies have suborganizations that do not know what other parts of the organization are doing, iSCSI has added the option of demarcating the name so that conflicts can be reduced. In other words, it is possible for one organization to own the root and then hand out subdomain names like *ajax* to one group and *wonder.ajax* to another. Then each suborganization can self-assign its iSCSI node names. The *ajax* group might, however, assign the string *wonder.jump*, and the *wonder.ajax* group might assign the string *jump*. The resulting two locations might both have an iqn name that looks like the example above. (Remember that the iqn name format is the reverse of the domain name format.)

To avoid this duplication, iSCSI gives an installation the capability to apply a colon (:) as a demarcation between the DNS assigned string and the iSCSI unique string. The following are some examples (also see Figure 4–7): *iqn.1998-03.com.xyc.ajax:wonder.jump* for the *ajax.xyc.com* group; *iqn. 1998-03.com.xyc.ajax.wonder:jump* for the *wonder.ajax.xyz.com* group; and *iqn.1998-03.com.xyc.ajax.wonder.jump* for organizations when the iSCSI name string matches the reverse DNS string.

The reverse name format ensures that the name is not confused with a real FQDN name. This is necessary since the address of a target or an initiator is actually both the TCP/IP address port and the iSCSI name. Now, since the IP address port can be resolved from a real FQDN name, the FQDN can be used in place of the absolute address port. Because the iqn is the reverse of the FQDN, there will never be any confusion when they are used together. Also, the fully qualified address will not have the same name repeated. It is intended to look different and so is not resolvable to an IP address yet is unique in the world.

While we are on the subject, let's define the fully qualified address of an iSCSI node. This address can be specified as a **URL** (uniform resource locator) as follows: *<domain-name>[:<port>\*]/<iSCSI-name>*. Note that items enclosed in angle brackets (< >) are variables to be specified. Anything in square brackets ([ ]) is optional. The slash (/) is syntactically required.

The domain name is either an IPv4 or an IPv6 address. The iSCSI name is an iqn or eui name. If an IPv4 name is supplied, it is made up of four sets of decimal numbers from 0 to 255, separated by periods—for example,

---

*The port can be omitted only when the well-known iSCSI TCP port number (currently 3260) is used.

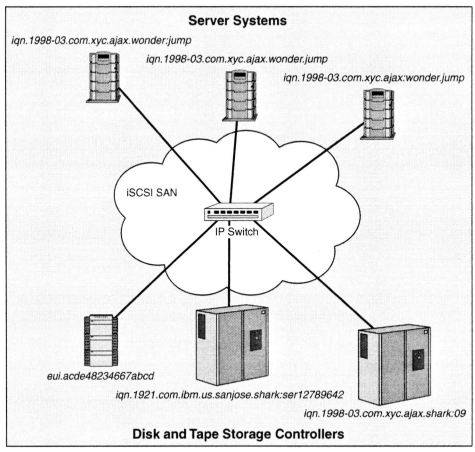

**Server Systems**

*iqn.1998-03.com.xyc.ajax.wonder:jump*

*iqn.1998-03.com.xyc.ajax.wonder.jump*

*iqn.1998-03.com.xyc.ajax:wonder.jump*

iSCSI SAN

IP Switch

*eui.acde48234667abcd*

*iqn.1921.com.ibm.us.sanjose.shark:ser12789642*

*iqn.1998-03.com.xyc.ajax.shark:09*

**Disk and Tape Storage Controllers**

Figure 4–7  iSCSI node names.

*129.25.255.1.* If an IPv6 name is supplied, it is enclosed in brackets with eight groups of 2-byte hex numbers, separated by colons—for example: *[abfe:124a:fefe:237a:aeff:ccdd:aacc:bcad].* Examples of fully qualified URLs are *129.25.255.1:3260\*/iqn.1998-03.com.xyc.ajax:wonder.jump* and *[abfe: 124a:fefe:237a:aeff:ccdd:aacc:bcad]:3270/iqn.1998-03.com.xyc.ajax.wonder: jump.*

It is also possible to have a fully qualified domain name (a host name) instead of the resolved address. Below is an example of using the FQDN within the iSCSI address. As with normal mail, one needs more than the address of the entry point; it is often the case that names are needed so that the mail is delivered to the right person at the address. That is why a

---

\*This port number could have been omitted (it is the default).

fully qualified iSCSI address has both the FQDN (optionally resolved into an IPV4 or IPV6 address) and the iSCSI name. For example, *customer-1.wonder. mother.us.com:330/iqn.2000-1.com.us.mother.wonder:dbhost-1.*

The important thing is that at any given IP address there could be more than one iSCSI name. This is usually the case at iSCSI gateways, but it is legal in other iSCSI entities such as target devices. Of course, it is more customary to see multiple IP addresses with the same iSCSI name.

## Naming and Addressing Summary

- The iqn name form can be made unique in the world. Because of this unique identification, a session can be established between any two iSCSI network entities anywhere in the world.

- There are two types of node name:

  - **iqn** (iSCSI qualified name)

  - **eui** (enterprise unique identifier)

- The iqn form of a node name is human readable:

  - *iqn.1998-03.com.xyc.ajax.wonder.jump*

  - *iqn.1998-03.com.xyc.ajax:wonder.jump* (note the : variant)

- The eui form of a node name is written in hex notation:

  - *eui.acde48234667abcd*

  - *eui.f73ab973e5ac89d1*

- An eui node name should be DNS based but reversed to avoid confusion with the DNS name itself.

- We also discussed how to record the IP address and TCP port (depending on whether it is an IPv4 or an IPv6 address).

- The default iSCSI TCP port number is currently 3260.

Now that we have explained the concept of a URL and how we might combine the iSCSI name with the iSCSI IP address and TCP port, we should keep in mind that the URL syntax, as such, is *not* directly used in the iSCSI protocol. iSCSI has no direct reason to combine the name string with the IP address and TCP port string. However, the two strings are used in separate key–value pairs in the login request, login response, and text PDUs. In spite of all that, the URL form is a convenient way of explicitly specifying a fully qualified iSCSI name and TCP port address for written communication and is expected to be used for administrator input to management software.

## Chapter Summary

In this chapter we explained the use of TCP/IP:

■ TCP/IP was chosen because it is ubiquitous and robust, and because it delivers data from point to point in order and free of as many errors as it can detect.

■ There are appropriate levels of encapsulation—the Ethernet frame, the IP header, and the TCP segment that carries the iSCSI protocol data unit (**PDU**).

We also discussed the concept of an iSCSI session, including multiple connections per session (**MC/S**):

■ A session is the basic communication "pipe" from an iSCSI initiator to the iSCSI target.

■ The session can be made up of several TCP/IP connections.

■ Connections can be logically separate on the same physical link or can be separate connections on different physical links.

Vendors are integrating iSCSI and TOE functions on the same HBA or chip.

■ With that integration, the iSCSI code can place iSCSI PDUs directly at final locations in main memory, thereby avoiding host CPU cycles moving the data from buffer to buffer.

iSCSI exploits TCP/IP checksums, Ethernet CRC trailers, and optional iSCSI CRC-32 digests:

■ iSCSI assumes and depends on the one's complement checksum provided by TCP/IP and the CRC checks provided by the Ethernet to ensure a very substantial level of integrity checking.

■ iSCSI has defined and requires vendors to implement a supplemental integrity check called CRC-32c digests (its use is optional).

As for naming and addressing, we learned the following:

- iSCSI has developed a naming structure to support both manufacturers and customers, so that iSCSI network entities can be uniquely defined worldwide.

- iSCSI supports both IPv4 and IPv6 network addressing structures.

- iSCSI provides a convenient way for the naming and addressing to be written unambiguously, called a URL for use in human communication and for use with administrative applications.

# 5 Session Establishment

## To the Reader

This chapter provides a general introduction of the login process followed by a much more detailed discussion. If you only want a high-level view, I suggest you read the introduction to the login process, and then skip to the diagrams of the login request PDU and the login response PDU to see their general layout. After that, you can jump to the Chapter Summary to pick up the highlights.

If you need a more in-depth understanding of iSCSI, read the entire chapter.

We will address session establishment in several ways:

- A general introduction to the login process (in this chapter)

- A much more detailed description of the login process (also in this chapter)

- Detailed descriptions of the login request and response PDUs, along with the exact formats (in this chapter and in Appendix A)

- Details of the keywords and their values (in this chapter and in Appendix B)

- More information about the keywords and their exchange process (explained in detail in Chapter 6)

## Introduction to the Login Process

The login process is intended to

- Start the iSCSI TCP/IP connection (which in turn can establish a secure IPsec connection).

71

- Permit authentication of the iSCSI endpoints.

- Negotiate the parameters to be used by the iSCSI endpoints.

The iSCSI TCP/IP connection thus established also establishes an iSCSI session, sometimes just called the session, which can be made up of more than one connection from an initiator system to a target system. As each connection is established, it can negotiate its own unique parameters. Note that the leading (first) connection is the one that establishes the session-wide values; subsequent connection logins can only negotiate for their own appropriate values.

The login is composed of requests and responses. This process of sending and receiving login requests and responses is handled as if it were a single task, which means that it is not completed until one side or the other abandons it and drops the connection or both agree to go to "full-feature" phase. The full-feature phase is the normal mode, which can actually send or receive SCSI commands (CDBs) in the iSCSI protocol data units (PDUs). The connection may not perform any other function until the login is complete and the full-feature phase is entered.

There will be one or more login requests, each followed by a login response from the target until the target sends the final response. That response either accepts or rejects the login.

There are two types of login sessions:

- Normal

- Discovery

Until now we have been addressing the normal iSCSI session. The discovery session will be addressed later.

The initial login must include in a field of the PDU called the `DataSegment` the login parameters in **text request format**. This format consists of a series of textual keywords followed by values. What follows is an example of login keywords that must be sent on the first command of every connection's login. These keywords are `InitiatorName` and `TargetName` (see Figure 5–1).

- Initiator Name=iqn.1998-03.com.xyc.ajax.wonder:jump

- TargetName=eui.acde48234667abcd

The login process will go through the exchange of iSCSI operational parameters as well as security authentication processes, which are intended to ensure that the initiator is valid and authorized. On the completion of the

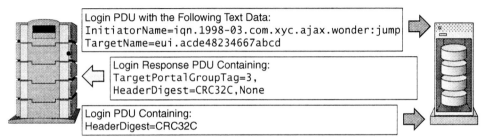

Figure 5–1 Login and login responses.

login, the connection and the session will be able to flow SCSI commands and data between the initiator and the target.

As mentioned, there is another session type, the discovery session. It is used to identify to the initiator the available iSCSI target nodes and their IP addresses and ports. These addresses and ports should be used in connecting to the nodes. The login process of the discovery session follows the same rules as for a normal login, except that TargetName does not have to be specified.

## Login and Session Establishment

Session establishment is begun when the iSCSI initiator sends a Login Request PDU to an iSCSI target. To accomplish this, the iSCSI host system first determines the name and IP address (and port) of the appropriate iSCSI target. (The techniques needed to determine what targets the host is permitted to contact, along with their names and addresses, will be handled in Chapter 12.) When a TCP/IP connection is established at the target IP address, the initiator system will send a login PDU to that iSCSI target. The login PDU will send, in its DataSegment field, the name of the iSCSI target to which it desires connection. If such a device is located at the target IP address, the login process will continue.

Login has several phases (discussed below), one of which deals with security and authorization (covered later). For our purposes at this time, we will assume that the security is handled appropriately when required and we will focus on the other aspects of session establishment. Session establishment is primarily identification of the remote site along with negotiations to establish which set of functions (options) will operate between the initiator and the target, along with the level of support or resources that will be used.

For example, it can be determined if the target can support the shipment of data with the command PDUs. It can also be determined if the target can support the initiator shipping data (in support of a SCSI write command, for instance) without the target first soliciting the initiator for the data. Even if the target does support the "unsolicited" arrival of data, it probably has some limitations on the size of its "surprise"—that is, how much "unsolicited" data buffering capability it must reserve for surprises. Even the order of the data's arrival (in order only or out of order accepted) can be negotiated between the initiator and the target.

Generally, one side or the other may send a keyword and a single value, a range of values, or a list of values that it supports—arranged in most preferred to least preferred order—for the function represented by the keyword. The opposite side is supposed to pick the first option or value that it supports. This process continues back and forth until both sides agree that they are through with the negotiation. At that point either the connection is broken or the full-feature phase of the session is established. Then the initiator can begin sending SCSI commands to the target node. If desired, additional connections can be started and related to this one, so that an iSCSI session can be made up of multiple connections. MC/S (multiple connections per session) will be discussed later.

There are actually three modes/phases through which the session establishment (or additional connection establishment) progresses. They are

0   Security negotiation phase (**SNP**)

1   Login operational negotiation phase (**LONP**)

2   Not used

3   Full-feature phase (**FFP**)

Only after the establishment of the full-feature phase can PDUs, containing actual SCSI command CDBs, be sent and responses received. Likewise, it is only after full-feature mode is established on the leading connection that other connections can be created and made part of the session.

## Login PDUs

The initiator will request a session with the target by issuing a login request PDU, and the target will respond, using the Login Response PDU. These request and response PDUs can be issued *repeatedly,* until both sides are satisfied with the parameters that are negotiated.

## The Login Request PDU

The details in Figure 5–2 will be fully discussed in Appendix A, but some highlights will be touched on here. Notice that the figure contains a field called **CID**. This is the connection ID, which the initiator originates and sets in the login PDU when it is starting a new session connection (either in a single connection or in a multiple connection session). The CID is used by the logout (explicit and implicit) function to identify a connection to terminate. Also notice that the login PDU contains the initiator task tag (**ITT**) field. This field accompanies all command PDUs so that responses can identify the command to which they are responding. The iSCSI initiator sets the ITT, and the target responds using the same ITT when the command completes. Technically the

| Byte | 0 | 1 | 2 | 3 |
|---|---|---|---|---|
| Bit | 0 1 2 3 4 5 6 7 | 0 1 2 3 4 5 6 7 | 0 1 2 3 4 5 6 7 | 0 1 2 3 4 5 6 7 |
| 0 to 3 | . \| . \|0 0 0 0 1 1 | T\|C\|0 0\|CSG\|NSG | Version-Max | Version-Min |
| 4 to 7 | 0 | DataSegmentLength (Length of Login Parameters) | | |
| 8 to 15 | ISID | | TSIH | |
| 16 to 19 | ITT | | | |
| 20 to 23 | CID | | Reserved | |
| 24 to 27 | CmdSN | | | |
| 28 to 31 | ExpStatSN or Reserved | | | |
| 32 to 47 | Reserved | | | |
| 48 to n | DataSegment (Login Parameters in Text Request format) | | | |

Figure 5–2 Login request PDU.

login does not need ITTs since only one login command can be outstanding at any one time on any specific connection. However, it is required here to enable common code to handle both logins and normal commands.

Also within the login command are two sequence number fields (which use sequence number arithmetic; refer to Appendix A). These fields, which are initialized in the login to start things off, are the command sequence number (**CmdSN**) and the expected status sequence number (**ExpStatSN**). Normally the ExpStatSN is not specified (except when a reconnection is issued), and the CmdSN can usually be set to any value (except zero) on the initial login of a session (referred to as the leading login). However, both sequence numbers must be set with the then current values when used to start additional connections. The CmdSN will be set to the same value on each Login Request PDU throughout the leading login negotiation process.

All connections are established between what iSCSI calls "portals," which are associated with the initiator node and the target node. Portals carry an IP address and, in the case of target portals, a TCP listening "port."

Multiple connections established between an initiator and a target are between sets of portals on each. The collection of portals on an initiator or a target is called a "portal group." Groups of target portals that can contain connections for the same session are given a common ID, called the "target portal group tag" (**TPGT**). (See the sections "Keywords and the Login Process" and "Discovery Session' in this chapter for additional descriptions of portals, portal groups, and target portal group tags.)

The initiator session ID (**ISID**) is set by the initiator on the leading login to make the session unique within the initiator system. It is also used on any subsequent session connection to tie the connection to the base session.

The target session identifying handle (**TSIH**) is set in the last target response during the leading login. When a subsequent connection login is started, to be part of the same session as a previous connection it may originate from the same physical portal as that previous connection or from a different physical connection. The target portal must be in the same portal group (i.e., have the same TPGT) as the leading connection for the session. When the login for this subsequent connection is issued, the initiator will replicate to the new login PDU the ISID and TSIH fields obtained during the leading login of the session.

The version number fields (versionMax and versionMin) in the login PDU are used to ensure that the initiator and target can agree on the protocol level they support.

Now let's look at moving from one login phase/stage to another in the login process. (This topic will be revisited in Appendix A, but the information that follows should give you a flavor of the login process.)

The **CSG** (current stage) field will specify the phase that the session is currently in. The **NSG** (next stage) field will specify what phase is desired next. When the initiator or target wishes to transit between its current phase and another phase, the **T bit** (Transit bit) must be set and the desired phase set in the NSG field. NSG is only valid when the T bit is set. (See example in Figure 5–3.)

The login command is an "immediate command," which must be operated on right away. This is implied with the leading login, during which nothing else can be happening. However, on subsequent connections other things can be going on within the session on other existing connections. The immediate requirement, whether used on this command or others, is requesting immediate action and focus. An example is the case when another connection is needed to replace a failing one so the new login must be executed immediately.

The DataSegment of the login request or response contains login text requests, which will be discussed in Chapter 6. Also, details about each keyword and value will be found in Appendix B.

### The Login Response PDU

The target sends the Login Response PDU whenever it wants to accept, reject, or continue receiving the initiator's login requests. This may be a response to the initiator's initial Login Request PDU or a subsequent continuing Login Request PDU. (See Figure 5–3.)

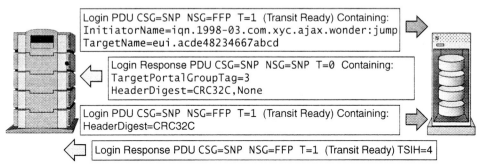

Figure 5–3 Phase transition through login and login responses.

Notice in Figure 5–4 that the login response contains fields similar to those found in the login request. These fields are the T bit, the **C bit**, the CSG and NSG, the version information (maximum and actual), the DataSegment-Length, the ISID, the TSIH, and the ITT. It also contains the **StatSN** (status sequence number), which is set on the first response and incremented by one each time a new status is returned on a specific connection.

For compatibility with normal command handling, there is an ExpCmdSN (expected command sequence number) field. On a leading login, it will have

| Byte | 0 | 1 | 2 | 3 |
|---|---|---|---|---|
| Bit | 0 1 2 3 4 5 6 7 | 0 1 2 3 4 5 6 7 | 0 1 2 3 4 5 6 7 | 0 1 2 3 4 5 6 7 |
| 0 to 3 | .\|.\|1 0 0 0 1 1 | T\|C\|0 0\|CSG\|NSG | Version-Max | Version-Act |
| 4 to 7 | 0 | DataSegmentLength (Length of Login Parameters) | | |
| 8 to 15 | ISID | | TSIH | |
| 16 to 19 | ITT | | | |
| 20 to 23 | Reserved | | | |
| 24 to 27 | StatSN | | | |
| 28 to 31 | ExpCmdSN | | | |
| 32 to 35 | MaxCmdSN | | | |
| 36 to 39 | Status-Class | Status-Detail | Reserved | |
| 40 to 47 | Reserved | | | |
| 48 to n | DataSegment  (Login Parameters in Text Request format) | | | |

Figure 5–4  Login response PDU.

the same value each time it responds during the leading login sequence, since it will expect the next CmdSN to be the same as the previous one (because CmdSN does not change during the leading login). (*Note:* The issues and approaches dealing with sequence numbers will be addressed in Chapters 7 and 8.)

One of the important things the target specifies in the last response to the leading login is to pick a TSIH and return it to the initiator. On the first login request of the leading login, the TSIH will be zero, but on the last response the target will create that unique value for the session. During the login process both the initiator and the target will continue to reflect back to each other, in the login request and login response PDUs, the ISID, and TSIH fields. Also, the first login response PDU should carry, in its DataSegment, the text field that identifies the target portal group tag (TPGT) to which the initiator is connected.

The most important item in the Login Response PDU is the return code found in the status-class and status-detail fields, which represent one of the results listed in Table 5–1. (*Note:* Refer to the IETF specification for the current codes settings.)

## TABLE 5–1 LOGIN RESPONSE RETURN CODES

| Status | Description |
| --- | --- |
| Success | Login proceeding OK |
| Target Moved Temporarily | Requested target node moved temporarily to address provided |
| Target Moved Permanently | Requested target node moved permanently to address provided |
| Initiator Error | Miscellaneous iSCSI initiator errors |
| Authentication Failure | Initiator not authenticated |
| Authorization Failure | Initiator not allowed access to target |
| Not Found | Requested target node not at this IP address |
| Target Removed | Requested target node removed, no address |
| Unsupported Version | Supported version not in range requested |
| Too Many Connections | No more connections accepted in this session |
| Missing Parameter | Missing parameter |
| Can't Include in Session | Cannot span to this address |
| Session Type Not Supported | Target does not support this type of session |
| Session Does Not Exist | Attempt to add a connection to a nonexistent session |
| Invalid During Login | Invalid request type during login |
| Target Error | Target hardware or software error |
| Service Unavailable | iSCSI target or service not currently operational |
| Out of Resources | Target has insufficient session, connection, or other resources to support this connection |

## iSCSI Sessions

Sessions in iSCSI can have single or multiple connections. Let's first examine the single-connection session.

Single-connection sessions start out with the establishment of the TCP/IP connection at a TCP/IP address and port obtained via an administrative or discovery process. This connection is established via a normal socket call. ("Socket" is a TCP/IP term for a software application programming interface, or API.) Based on this socket call, the TCP/IP layer will not only establish a TCP/IP connection but may also engage the IPsec functions, which in turn invoke the Internet Key Exchange (**IKE**). IKE will perform the appropriate certificate or key exchange and then return control to IPsec. IPsec determines the degree of security the initiator requires and the degree of security the target requires; based on the negotiation between the endpoints, it establishes the most rigorous security environment that either side requires.

With the establishment of a working connection, the initiator is given back control and can start the iSCSI login. Part of this login request is a text field (within the DataSegment) containing the iSCSI initiator name and the iSCSI target name. The target first checks to be sure that the iSCSI target name, sent as part of the login, is in fact its own name. If not, the login is denied and the connection is dropped. If the target name is appropriate, the target checks to see if the iSCSI initiator name is authorized to log in; if not, again the login is denied and the connection is dropped.

This "To-From" verification is the way all sessions begin and is part of the security phase of login. Depending on the iSCSI authentication mode chosen, there may have to be a further exchange of information, such as a user ID, and a form of password or a certificate that can be verified by a third party. The user ID can be either the iSCSI initiator name, already sent, or a true user ID. It is recommended that installations use the existing iSCSI initiator name as the user ID if at all possible, since this will reduce the administrative load and keep the environment a little less confusing.

The iSCSI storage controllers need to keep their authorized user IDs in sync with the iSCSI initiator names. Therefore, there needs to be a table within the iSCSI target device that says, for example, "user ID Frank" is authorized to use the iSCSI node `iqn.1998-03.com.xyc.ajax:wonder:jump`.

It is also possible for the user ID to have a one-to-many (or a many-to-one or even a many-to-many) relationship with iSCSI initiator node names, depending on the sophistication of the implementation. The important thing is that it must have a defined relationship to the iSCSI initiator name, which is used at the beginning of the same login.

If the installation can avoid user IDs, it probably can reduce its storage administrator's load. This is because the administrator will not have to deal with managing the relationship between the ID and the iSCSI initiator names.

### Authentication Routines

The authentication routines that iSCSI requires (must implement) and those it permits (should/may implement) are listed below:

- **CHAP** (Challenge Handshake Authentication Protocol)—must implement

- **SRP** (Secure Remote Password) protocol—may implement

- **Kerberos version 5** (a third-party authentication protocol)—may implement (For what it is worth, in Greek mythology Kerberos is the three-headed dog that guards the entrance to the underworld.)

- **SPKM-1** or **SPKM–2** (Simple Public Key Mechanism)—may implement

The above protocols are defined by their own IETF standard documentation RFCs (Requests For Comment). SRP is defined in [IETF RFC2945]; CHAP, in [RFC1994]; SPKM in [RFC2025]; and Kerberos v5, in [RFC1510].

SRP, though only a "may implement," is being included by many vendors because of its fairly secure method of authentication even when used on links that are not protected by IPsec. CHAP was chosen by the IETF because of its lesser entanglement with intellectual property rights (**IPR**), that is, patents. It is not as secure as SRP but can be made adequately secure by using a minimum 96-bit CHAP secret or by incorporating IPsec in the underlying connection. The login command/response process is the method for exchanging the information required for these protocols.

## Login Keywords

iSCSI keywords are actually made up of something we call the key=value pair (even when the value is a list). These characters are encoded in UTF-8 Unicode. The key part of the pair must be represented exactly as shown in the iSCSI specification. Upper case and lower case are required in the key, as shown in Appendix B (it is case sensitive), and there are no blank (white space) characters or nulls. The = sign must immediately follow the key part, without any blanks. The value(list) string must follow the = and is made up of letters or numbers. The key=value pair is terminated by a null character (hex 00). The numeric numbers can be represented by either decimals or hexadecimals. Hexadecimal numbers are indicated by a leading 0x set of characters. An example is 0xFA154c2B.

Very large bit strings can be represented in base-64 encodings indicated by a leading 0b set of characters. (See Appendix D.)

The key=list form of the key=value pair can be made up of several values separated by a commas. Values should not exceed 255 characters, unless expressly specified by the keyword writeup. This 255-character limitation applies to the internal value, not the string used to encode the value in the text field. For example, the hex value expressed externally as 0x2a579b2f will take up 4 bytes of internal representation, not 10.

In addition to the iSCSI specification of standard key=value items, there is a special key=value pair intended to permit vendors to add something unique to their implementations. This is X-*, where the * is replaced by the vendor's reverse DNS name and an action key. For example, X-com.acme. var.foo.perform_xyz_function=10011100

It is also possible for a vendor to use the form X#** where ** is replaced by a character string registered with INIA (Internet Assigned Numbers Authority). For example, X#ActionKeyNumber=25

When the key=list form is used, it is supposed to have the values in the list arranged in most preferred order. Say the list is made up of value1, value2, and value3, with value3 the most preferred and value1 the next most preferred; the key=list should be shown as key=value3,value1, value2. In this way, the other side will pick the first value in the list that it wants to support.

It is also possible for the key=value pair to specify a range. In this case the values in the list may be the minimum and maximum separated by the tilde (~). It is expected that the other side will respond with a key=value pair made up of a number between (or equal to) these minimum and maximum values. In the iSCSI spec, and henceforth in this book, the syntactical notation key=<something> denotes that "something" is a variable that may be used with the corresponding key but without its surrounding angle brackets (< >).

## Keywords and the Login Process

With all that in mind, we will look at examples pulled from the iSCSI standard specification. The specification includes flag bit settings and the like.

However, only the general ideas will be presented here. For more details see Appendix A; the values themselves are shown in Appendix B. Note that in the description I-> indicates that the initiator sends what follows and T-> means that the target sends what follows. The quoted strings are comments that will not flow on the wire.

Before we get into the examples, let's list some of the key=value items that are important to the initial login PDU of any connection:

- InitiatorName=<iSCSI Initiator Name> (always required)

- AuthMethod=<List of Authentication Methods Supported> (if CSG=SecurityNegotiation)

- SessionType=<discovery|normal> (optional; default is normal)

- TargetName=<iSCSI Target Name> (required if SessionType=normal)

It should be noted that secondary connection logins must have the same InitiatorName=value and the same TargetName=value as those of the first connection in an iSCSI session.

The login normally starts in the security negotiation phase. In that case the initial login PDU will have its CSG field set to the value that specifies security negotiation phase (SNP) in progress. It should also set the NSG field to a value that specifies that either the next phase should be login operational negotiation phase (LONP—if the initiator has additional values to negotiate/ declare) or full-feature phase (FFP). It is expected that the target will decide whether to move into login operational negotiation phase (or full-feature phase) or stay in the security negotiation phase.

If the initiator does not want to negotiate security, it can initially set its CSG to login operational negotiation phase (LONP), and its next stage to either the same, or full-feature phase (FFP). However, if the target is unwilling to operate without security, it may just end the session by returning a login reject response (with an Authentication Error), and drop the connection. (See Login Response PDU in Appendix A.)

Perhaps a better approach for an initiator that wants to operate without security, but is willing to negotiate security if required by the target, is to set the CSG to security negotiation phase, but then just not send any security parameters. It will then be up to the target to offer its preferred set of security parameters and have the initiator make the appropriate selection.

The general rule for phase moves is that the initiator can request a transition from one phase to another whenever it is ready. However, a target can respond with a transition only after it is offered one by the initiator.

If the header digest and/or the data digest are negotiated and accepted (during login operational negotiation phase), every PDU beginning with the first one sent after the start of the full-feature phase must have the appropriate header and/or data digests.

The following example attempts to show not only the login processes dealing with key=<values> but also how the security authentication process works.

In the example below, I-> indicates that the initiator sends; T-> indicates that the target sends. Also, the target, via SRP, authenticates only the initiator.

I-> Initial Login Request PDU with CSG set to SecurityNegotiation and NSG set to LoginOperationalNegotiation (with the T bit set). "The PDU also contains the following keys in the data field (comments are enclosed in quotation marks):"

■ InitiatorName=iqn.1999-07.com.os.hostid.11—"name of the iSCSI initiator node"

■ TargetName=iqn.1999-07.com.acme.diskarray:sn.88—"name of the desired iSCSI target node"

■ AuthMethod=KRB5,SRP,None—"initiator can support Kerberos (preferred) or SRP"

T-> Login response from target with NSG set to SecurityNegotiation and T bit set. "The PDU also contains the following key in the data field:"

■ TargetPortalGroupTag=3

■ AuthMethod=SRP—"target will use SRP for authentication"

I-> Login command (continuing in security phase of login using SRP processes). "And the following keys:"

■ SRP_U=<user>—"user name is sent, if <user> isn't equivalent to iSCSI initiator name; otherwise, U= isn't sent"

■ TargetAuth=No—"no need to authenticate the target"

T-> Login response (target responds using SRP security processes):

■ SRP_GROUP=<G1,G2 ...>

■ SRP_s=<s>

I-> Login command (initiator continues the SRP security interactions):

- SRP_A=<A> SRP_GROUP=<G>

T-> Login response (target continues with SRP security responses):

- SRP_B=<B>

I-> Login command finishes with the SRP security protocols and sets NSG to LoginOperationalNegotiation with the T bit set:

- SRP_M=<M>—"if the initiator authentication is successful, the target proceeds with:"

T-> Login response (ending security phase), setting the NSG to LoginOperationalNegotiation and with the T bit set.

I-> Login command (host indicates it's current phase by setting CSG to LoginOperationalNegotiation but with the T bit not set):

- HeaderDigest=CRC-32C,None—"initiator wants to use CRC-32c but will accept no header digest"

- DataDigest=CRC-32C,None—"also wants CRC-32c for data"

- ... Other iSCSI key=value parameters

T-> Login response (continues to exchange negotiations on parameters) with the T bit not set:

- HeaderDigest=CRC-32C—"willing and able to support CRC-32c"

- DataDigest=CRC-32C—"will also support CRC32c on data"

- ... Other iSCSI key=value parameters

**And at the end of parameter negotiations:**

I-> Login command (host indicates willingness to end the login process by setting the NSG to FullFeaturePhase with T bit set):

- ... Other iSCSI key=value parameters

T-> Login (target indicates it's willing to go into full-feature phase by setting the NSG to FullFeaturePhase with the T bit set), sets the TSIH and replies with an empty DataSegment.

At this point the login is complete and the session enters its full-feature phase, in which commands and data will be sent from the initiator to the target for execution by the appropriate LU. From this point on, any PDU on this connection must have CRC-32C digests for the header and data.

You can see from the example that the login phase can be very chatty. Each side exchanges its key=value pairs and receives the key=value pairs from the other side. In spite of this verboseness, the base concept is very simple. Since the sessions are very long lived, the overhead in this process is hardly noticeable. However, since many of the key=value pairs can be included in one request or response, and since there are many defaults, often the complete login is accomplished with one exchange.

We have just described a leading login process, so named because there can be parallel connections established within the same session between the same iSCSI initiator endpoint (the SCSI initiator port) and the same iSCSI target endpoint (the SCSI target port). Now we will describe how these non-leading logins are processed in order to establish a secondary connection in a session.

First, the initiator finds an appropriate TCP/IP address and port on the target, which is associated with the connection used to establish the "leading login" (within the same target portal group). (See SendTargets in the Discovery Session section to come.) Once the appropriate TCP/IP address and port are determined, the initiator starts a new TCP/IP connection. The new connection may originate either from a different physical network connection on the initiator or from the same physical connection. In this way there can be parallel connections from the host to the storage controller. If all the connections in this set use different physical network connections, the total bandwidth of a session will equal the sum of the individual connections.

A new connection within an existing session is started just like the original connection—that is, via a socket call, which in turn causes the establishment of the IPsec coverage, and so forth. The initiator then sends a login PDU to the target. The PDU will also contain a new CID (connection ID), created by the initiator, so that the different connections within the session can be identified. The initiator will insert the current session-wide CmdSN into the Login Request PDU, along with the session's ISID and TSIH. The initiator name, ISID, and TSIH will indicate to the specified target the session to which this connection belongs. All the other PDU fields and processing required as parts of the "leading connection" authentication are repeated for the secondary connection. The initiator and the target must still go through authentication via the exchange of login key=value pairs for the secondary connection, even if that was already done on the leading connection.

Any values that were negotiated on the leading connection will apply unless reset by key negotiations on the secondary connection. Some key=value pairs can be set only during the leading login; some, only during the full feature phase; and others, in all phases.

All the authentication keywords are legal only during the login security phase.

In addition to the key=value pairs associated with the security phase, the login on a secondary connection can exchange key=value pairs that are not reserved to the leading connect phases. The entire list of valid key=value pairs can be found in Appendix B.

It is not a requirement that subsequent logins be on different physical network connections, either on the initiator or the target. Though it seems strange, there are situations that make this reasonable. One is where a target physical network attachment might have two 10 Gb/s physical connections while its initiators might each have four 1 Gb/s physical connections. In this case the target connections have more bandwidth than initiator connections, so it makes sense to share a target's physical connection by letting the initiator log in several of its physical connections to the same target physical connection.

Another situation has to do with the initiator transmitting commands while simultaneously assembling a large data PDU. In this case the physical connection needs multiple logical connections so it is not slowed down by long data assembly processes from the initiator's main memory to the HBA. This is because other logical connections can be sending short commands during the long assembly process. It is sufficient to say that there are reasons for logical MC/S as well as physical MC/S.

Several vendors are making iSCSI HBAs that will be able to support the spanning of secondary session connections across multiple HBAs. Others will have multiple physical network connections mounted on the same HBAs and will support secondary connections across those physical network connections. Still others will support secondary connections both on their multi physical connection HBAs, and across multiples of those HBAs. And for each physical connection there could be multiple logical connections.

At this point it is appropriate to repeat the name given to the connection point (the IP address and the TCP listening port on the target). iSCSI calls this a **portal,** and it can be **logical** or **physical.** A collection of portals that are used by an iSCSI initiator or an iSCSI target is called a **portal group.** (Figure 5–5 shows these portals and their addresses along with iSCSI initiator/ target names.)

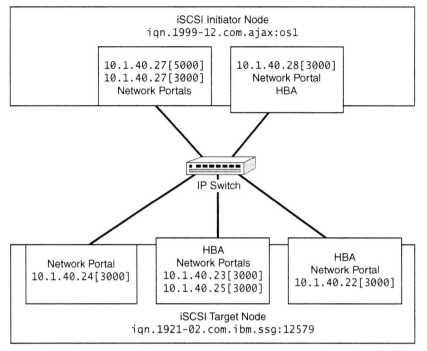

Figure 5–5  Addresses and portals.

## Discovery Session

In this section we will cover the iSCSI discovery session and the information that can be obtained from it. It should be understood that several different techniques can be deployed as part of discovery and the discovery session is only one of them. I cover it extensively here because it is a basic part of the iSCSI protocol. The other types of discovery are only companion processes that can be optionally implemented within iSCSI devices. A more extensive review of the alternatives is offered in Chapter 12.

The discovery session is established like any other iSCSI session; however, the initiator must send the key=value pair of SessionType=Discovery, which must be in the initial login PDU of the session.

The discovery session may or may not be covered by IPsec and/or session authentication. That decision depends on the installation. Like any iSCSI session, it requires implementers (vendors) to support IPsec and session authentication in their products. However, it is an installation's decision whether to use this form of security. Some installations may decide that it is not important to secure discovery sessions, which only provide the name and address of iSCSI target devices. The iSCSI specification is silent on this issue. The installation should bear in mind that security is always a set of fences, and it is sometimes useful to set a fence that hides even information about locations from potential intruders.

It is a requirement that any iSCSI device that contains targets support a discovery session on all its IP addresses. Therefore, if an IP address supports IPsec and authentication on its normal sessions, it will automatically be able to support IPsec and authentication on discovery sessions. The customer may not actually use these security functions on a discovery session if the vendor offers a way for the installation to explicitly disable them.

After entering the full-feature phase on the discovery session or on a normal session, the SendTargets command may be issued via the text request PDU (see Chapter 6 and Appendix A). The following key=value pair will be sent in the DataSegment of the Text Request PDU issued by the initiator to the discovery target:

```
SendTargets=<All | <iSCSI-target-name> | <nothing>
```

The values of All or of a specific iSCSI target name *must* be supported on discovery sessions; however, All *may not* be sent on normal sessions. In contrast, the null value (<nothing>) *must* be supported on normal sessions.

The <iSCSI-target-name> value *may* be supported on normal sessions, and null (<nothing>) *may* be sent on the discovery session. However, neither *must* be supported in those environments.

**Therefore, if we want to ensure that SendTargets works from an initiator to any target, we should avoid using the null value on discovery sessions and avoid "All" and <iSCSI-target-name> values on normal sessions.**

The following is the syntax of the response strings in the DataSegment of the Text Response PDU for the SendTargets text request.

```
TargetName=<iSCSI-target-name>
TargetAddress=<ip-address>[:<port>],<portal-group-number>
[<additional-number-of-TargetAddress-text-responses>]
    .
    .
    .
[<additional-TargetName-text-response>]
[<additional-number-of-TargetAddress-text-responses>]
```

.
.
.

(*Note:* The iSCSI default TCP/IP port is currently 3260; if it is used, the port number field can be eliminated.)

If an `all` parameter value is used in the text request, the response will include the `TargetName` response string for each `TargetName` known to the discovery target (which the initiator is permitted to access). Following each `TargetName` will be a list of all IP addresses (and ports) in the form of `TargetAddress` response strings, which can be used to address that target.

On all `TargetAddress` strings there will be a <portal-group-number>. This is a tag (the TPGT) used to relate one `TargetAddress` string to another, such that the initiator systems know what IP address to use in order to obtain MC/S on different IP addresses.

It is of course possible to have a multiple-connection session to the same IP address, but unless the target connection has bandwidth equal to that of the combined initiator connections, the throughput advantages of MC/S will be reduced proportionally to the bandwidth of the target portal.

When the `SendTargets` text request is issued on a normal session, with either the null parameter value or the iSCSI target name value, only the information about the implied/specified target is returned. The implied target for the null request is the current target (the one sustaining the normal session). The implied/specified target will have its and only its target name, target addresses, and TPGTs returned in the `DataSegment` of the Text Response PDU.

The part of the discovery process just described is directly supported by iSCSI and an iSCSI session (the discovery session). However, iSCSI has defined not only this capability within its own protocol but also how other IP protocols can be used in a more comprehensive discovery process. More information on the discovery process is provided in Chapter 12.

 ## Chapter Summary

This chapter introduced the process of establishing an iSCSI session.

- It was shown how to use the Login Request and Login Response PDUs to begin the session and related connections.

  - ➢ An iSCSI session is started by a Login Request PDU with text key=value data that is used to negotiate with the target.

➤ A target responds with a Login Response PDU and its own key=value pairs.

➤ A series of interactions continues until all negotiated key=value pairs are agreed on.

■ Also discussed was how to handle the exchange of parameters:

➤ With key=value pairs

➤ Until both sides go to full-feature phase

■ Examples were given to explain the give and take that occurs during parameter negotiation.

■ The concepts of portal, portal group, and target portal group tag (**TPGT**) were defined.

➤ A portal is a TCP/IP connection to the network.

➤ A portal group is a collection of portals that can be used in a multiple-connection session.

➤ A TPGT is a number attached to a target portal group that distinguishes the group from other target portal groups.

■ The process of establishing a discovery session was also defined. A requestor may obtain the following information needed to establish a normal iSCSI connection:

➤ The names of the available (and authorized) iSCSI target nodes

➤ The TCP/IP addresses and ports

➤ The iSCSI target portal group numbers/TPGTs

# 6

# Text Commands and Keyword Processing

## To the Reader

This chapter contains very detailed information concerning how text commands and key=value pairs are negotiated. If you are not interested in the details of this process, skip to the chapter summary.

The iSCSI protocol includes a method to send non-SCSI commands from the initiator to the target. It also has a technique for negotiating values between the two sides. This is the same process and negotiating routine that is part of the login process—even the syntax is the same. (See Chapter 5, the section Keywords and the Login Process.)

## Text Requests and Responses

The Text Request PDUs and the Text Response PDUs permit the iSCSI initiator and target to exchange information that is unavailable to the SCSI layer. An example of this is the SendTargets command, which the initiator sends to the target via the Text Request PDU. The target responds to it via the Text Response PDU. The text request and response PDUs permit new standard extensions to iSCSI, and they permit vendors to provide additional value-added functions.

The text field is in the DataSegment of the text request or response PDU. It must be in the key=value format as detailed below (similar to the login text field). The initiator initiates all requests. The target can respond only with a Text Response PDU. The target can, however, signal the initiator within Asynchronous Message PDU that it wants to begin a text exchange. The exchange process can continue across several text request and response PDUs in a sequence.

**PDU Fields**

The text request and response PDUs have four fields that control the semantics of the exchange process (see Appendix A for PDU layouts). These are:

- The F bit (the final bit)

- The C bit (the continue bit)

- The initiator task tag (ITT)

- The target task tag (**TTT**)

The initiator always assigns an ITT to each new task (SCSI or iSCSI) that it starts. Each new Text Request PDU sequence will have an ITT assigned to it that is unique across the session and which the target will return in its responses. In this way requests and responses are clearly coordinated.

Text requests and responses can have more key=value pairs than fit within a single PDU. This means that the pairs may continue on a subsequent PDU, in which case the request or response PDU will have its F bit set to zero to indicate that it is not the final PDU. When the F bit is set, the text request or response is signaling that it has reached the end of its text entry and/or that the negotiation is complete.

If it happens that a key=value pair spans a PDU entry, the sender must set the C bit in its text request or response. The receiver of such a PDU must only respond with empty text PDUs until it receives one with the C bit cleared. Things may then continue as normal.

Whenever it seems the text response may solicit additional related comebacks, it will have its TTT set to some value that is useful to the target. Upon receiving a TTT, if the initiator has any additional text to send, it will return that same TTT to the target via its Text Request PDU.

Each side is required to send an appropriate text request or response to the other side, as long as the other side has not set the F bit to 1 (meaning that it has not yet sent the final piece of text). The normal technique for completing a text interaction is that both sides have the F bit set.

The initiator will determine when the text communication is at an end. It does so either by sending no more Text Request PDUs following a text response with the F bit set, or by sending a new text request with the TTT set to its reserved value of hex FFFFFFFF. Likewise, when the target believes the appropriate response is at an end, it should set the F bit to 1 and send a TTT of hex FFFFFFFF on its final response. The target is more limited in its ability to end a communication, however, since it can set the F bit to 1 only if the initiator has given its permission by setting its own F bit to 1 in the previous Text Request PDU.

The target will assume that any text request received with a TTT of hex FFFFFFFF is the beginning of a new request series and will reset all its internal settings (if any) for the ITT specified. Since there can be only one text request outstanding on a connection at any time, the target can also clear any internal settings it has regarding *any* ITT used for a previous text request on that same connection.

The `SendTargets` command is an example of a text request that may have a long text response. The following shows how that should be handled. (`I ->T` means that the initiator sends to the target; `T->I` means that the target sends to the initiator. Also `0x` is the string symbol that leads a hex string.)

```
I->T Text SendTargets=All (F=1,TTT=0xffffffff)
T->I Text <part 1> (F=0,TTT=0x12345678)
I->T Text <empty> (F=1, TTT=0x12345678)
T->I Text <part 2> (F=0, TTT=0x12345678)
I->T Text <empty> (F=1, TTT=0x12345678)
...
T->I Text <part n> (F=1, TTT=0xffffffff)
```

In summary, the iSCSI initiator can send commands to the iSCSI target using the Text Request PDU. The target can respond to the initiator with some value in the Text Response PDU. The flow of messages is controlled by use of the F bit, the C bit, the ITT, and the TTT. The text in the request and response PDUs are in key=value format, which is further explained in the next section.

## Text Keywords and Negotiation

The format for the text field in the login and in the text request and response PDUs is the key=value pair, which can be either declared or negotiated. The format of a key=value declaration (where -> means that the following string is sent) is

```
Declarer-> <key>=<valuex>
```

The format of a negotiation is

```
Proposer-> <key>=<valuex>
Acceptor-> <key>=<valuey>|NotUnderstood|Irrelevant|Reject
```

The proposer, or declarer, can be either the initiator or the target, and the acceptor can be either the target or the initiator. Target requests are not limited to responses to key=value pairs proposed by the initiator but may propose their own key=value pairs.

**Rules for Key=Value Pairs**

1. They are encoded in UTF-8 Unicode and are case sensitive.

2. They have various fields and character sets (defined in Appendix D).

3. Their fields are made up of

   ■ A key-name (the name of the key=value pair)

   ■ A value (the value of the key=value pair), which can be one or more of the following:

   ➤ Text-value (a string of characters)

   ➤ iSCSI-name-value (the name of the iSCSI node, a special text-value. See Appendix D.)

   ➤ iSCSI-local-name-value (an alias for the iSCSI node, a special text-value. See Appendix D.)

   ➤ Boolean-value (example: `Yes, No`)

   ➤ Hex-constant (example: `0xffffffff`)

   ➤ Decimal-constant (example: `12345`)

   ➤ Base64-constant (example: `0b1w7aF81A`)

   ➤ Numerical-value (hex, decimal; example: `128`)

   ➤ Large-numerical-value (hex or base64-constant; example: `0x6a90fa7c1f09fe34abec72fe`)

   ➤ Numeric-range (numerical-value~numerical-value; example: `50~125`)

   ➤ Regular-binary-value (decimal, hex, or base64 constant; example: `0xffffffffffffffff`)

   ➤ Large-binary-value (hex, base64-constant; example: `0xffffffffffffffffffffffff`)

&gt; Binary-value (regular-binary-value, large-binary-value)

&gt; Simple-value (text-value, iSCSI-name-value, Boolean-value, numeric-value, numeric-range, binary-value)

&gt; List-of-values (text-value, text-value, text-value; example: 3,5,7)

■ Key-name and value separated by and equal "=" (hex 3d)

4. They may have many, various instances included in the same text field of a Login Request, Login Response, Text Request, or Text Response PDU. Each instance must of course be unique and separated by at least one null (hex 00).

5. They must not permit their key names to exceed 63 bytes.

6. By default they have a maximum length of an individual value (not its encoded representation) of 255 bytes, not including the delimiter (comma or null). Values can be longer than 255 bytes; however, the specification must explicitly specify the maximum length.

7. They can span text request or response boundaries (i.e., can start in one PDU and continue in the next).

8. If they are split between PDUs, the sending side must set the C bit, and the receiving side must not respond with any text value until it receives a PDU with the C bit cleared. (During that time, null PDUs are acceptable responses to the proposer.)

The data lengths of a text field in request or response PDUs must not exceed MaxRecvDataSegmentLength, a per-connection and per-direction declared parameter. See Appendix B for details on this value. Text operations are usually meant for parameter setting/negotiations but can also be used to perform some long-lasting operations. The DataSegment in login and text request/response PDUs, which are likely to take a long time obtaining a response, should be placed in their own text request.

### Rules for Keyword Value Negotiation

1. All negotiations start out stateless; that is, the results are based only on newly exchanged values. Each side keeps state during the negotiations.

2. Not proposing a key for negotiation is not equivalent to proposing the current (or default) value. A default remains a default only if not offered by either party.

3. A value should be proposed if unsure of the other side's default.

4. In literal list negotiation, the proposer sends—for each key—a list of options (literal constants, which may include None) in its order of preference.

5. The accepting party answers with the first value from the list it supports, and is allowed to use for the specific proposer.

6. The constant None is used to indicate a missing function. However, it is a valid selection only if it is explicitly offered.

7. If an acceptor is not supporting or not allowed to use—with a specific proposer—any of the proposed options, it may use the constant Reject.

8. For non-Boolean single-value negotiations:

   ■ For numerical values the accepting party responds with the required key and the value it selects. This is based on the results function specific to the key and becomes the negotiation result.

   ■ Nonnumeric strings are primarily used for declarations.

   ■ Selection of a value not admissible under the selection rules is considered a protocol error (see the section Rules for Negotiation Failure to come).

9. All Boolean keywords have a result function, the value of which (specified in Appendix B) is either AND or OR.

10. For Boolean negotiations (keys taking the value Yes or No) the accepting party responds with the required key and the chosen value, or responds with nothing if the result can be determined by the rules of that keyword. The last value transmitted becomes the negotiation result.

11. The rules for selecting the value to respond with are expressed as Boolean result functions (AND/OR) of the value received and the value that the responding party would select in the absence of knowledge of the received value. (See rule 12 and Appendix B for the keywords' appropriate Boolean result functions.)

12. Based on rule 11, the two cases in which responses are optional are

- When the Boolean function is AND and the value received is No. (This makes the automatic outcome of the negotiation No and no response is required.)

- When the Boolean function is OR and the value received is Yes. (This makes the automatic outcome of the negotiation Yes and no response is required.)

13. Responses are required in all other Boolean cases, and the value chosen and sent by the acceptor becomes the outcome of the negotiation.

14. For list value negotiation, the proposer arranges the values in the order it prefers, and the acceptor chooses the first value in the list that it prefers. The value chosen by the acceptor becomes the result of the negotiation.

15. If a specific key is not relevant to the current negotiation, the acceptor may answer with the constant Irrelevant for all types of negotiation.

16. The acceptor, without affecting basic function, may ignore any key not understood. However, it must send back <key>=NotUnderstood.

17. The constants None, Reject, Irrelevant, and NotUnderstood are reserved for the functions described here.

## Rules for Negotiation Flow

1. Operational parameter negotiation may involve several request–response exchanges, which are started and terminated by the initiator and use the same initiator task tag.

2. The initiator signals its intention to end the negotiation by setting the F bit (final flag) to 1.

3. The target sets the F bit to 1 on its last response.

4. When the initiator sends a text request that has the final flag set to 1:

   - If the target has only one response, it should set its final flag to 1.

   - If the target has more than one response, it should set the F bit to 0 in each response except the last, and set the F bit to 1 on its last response.

- The initiator—if it has no more to negotiate—must keep sending the text requests (even if empty) with the F bit set to 1 until it gets the text response from the target, with its F bit set to 1. (Responding to a text request whose F bit is set to 1 with an empty response {no key=value pairs} whose F bit is set to 0 is not an error but is discouraged.)

5. Targets must not submit parameters requiring an additional initiator text request when the target is responding with the F bit set to 1.

6. Text request sequences are independent of each other. Thus, the F bit settings in one pair of text requests–responses have no bearing on the F bit settings in the next pair.

7. An initiator that has set the F bit to 1 in a request:

   - Can be answered by the target with an F bit setting of 0, in which case the initiator may further respond with a request PDU that

     > has F=0 (indicating a response that has multiple text request PDUs)

     > has F=1 (indicating that its response sequence is done).

   - Can be answered by the target with an F bit set to 1 (indicating that the target's response sequence is completed).

8. Whenever parameters' actions or acceptance are dependent on the actions of other parameters, the dependent parameters must be sent after the parameters they depend on.

9. When dependent parameters are sent within the same command, a response for one parameter might imply responses for the others.

10. Whenever the target responds with the F bit set to 0, it must choose and set the TTT to a value other than the default hex FFFFFFFF.

11. A reset of an operational parameter by an initiator issuing a text request with the TTT set to the value of hex FFFFFFFF after having received a response with the TTT set to a value other than hex FFFFFFFF. (This works since the target is expecting its TTT back,

and this response is clearly an alert of a change/reset.) A negotiation reset can also be signaled by a target issuing a `Reject` PDU with a reason code of `Negotiation Reset`. (See Appendix A.)

12. No parameter should be negotiated more than once during any sequence without an intervening reset. The values `Reject`, `Irrelevant`, and `NotUnderstood` are considered completed responses, so sending the key=value again is a renegotiation and not permitted.

13. Key=value pairs may span PDU boundaries. An initiator or target that is about to send a partial key=value text within a PDU must so indicate by setting the C bit to 1. A target or initiator receiving a text request or response with the C bit set to 1 must answer with a response or request PDU that has no data segment (`DataSegmentLength=0`). A PDU having the C bit set to 1 must not have the F bit set to 1 as well. This rule also applies to Login Request and Login Response PDUs.

14. If multiple negotiations of the same parameter, without a reset, are detected by:

   ■ The target, then the target must send a Reject PDU with a reason of `protocol error` (see Appendix A). During login, however, the Login Response PDU should reflect the error and the connection should then be terminated.

   ■ The initiator, then the initiator must reset the negotiation in FFP, but during login it must terminate the connection.

## Rules for Negotiation Failure

1. During login, any failure in negotiation is considered to be a failure of the login process. The login phase and its connection must be terminated. If the target detects the failure, it will terminate the login with the appropriate login response code and then drop the connection. If the initiator detects the failure, it will just terminate the connection.

2. A failure of negotiation in a Text Request or Text Response PDU process requires the termination of the entire negotiation sequence. The operational parameters of the session or the connection will

continue to be the values agreed upon during an earlier successful negotiation or will be the defaults. Any partial results of this unsuccessful negotiation must be undone.

 ## Chapter Summary

In this chapter

- We explained the process of handling Text Request and Text Response PDUs.

- We explained the syntax of key=value pairs, which are the basic element of exchange.

- We explained how the text requests and responses could be used as a command–response sequence, as in the case of SendTargets, or to negotiate operational parameters.

We also covered

- Rules for negotiating the various values a parameter might use.

- Rules governing the handling of multiple response sequences (for example, the response from SendTargets).

- Negotiation failure rules:

  ➤ Terminate the login.

  ➤ Terminate the text command negotiation and reset.

Individual keywords are described in Appendix B.

# 7 Session Management

## To the Reader

This chapter details the management of iSCSI sessions. Once again, skip ahead to the Chapter Summary if you don't want an in-depth treatment of this subject.

The iSCSI session endpoints are dynamically created constructs, which conceptually map to a SCSI entity known as a "SCSI port." The SCSI port has a variant for each end, an initiator SCSI port and a target SCSI port. To show this endpoint relationship to both iSCSI and SCSI, I will often call the endpoints of an iSCSI session the iSCSI (SCSI) initiator port and the iSCSI (SCSI) target port.

The iSCSI session begins with the login process described in Chapter 5 for the main (first) connection. The initiator will set a unique connection ID (CID) in the initial login PDU for the connection and set a new CID for each of the connections that follow. The CID is a "handle" that the target and initiator can use to queue various connection-related items. It will be presented not only with each connection login, but also with each logout.

## Initiator Session ID

In addition to the CID, the initial login sends the initiator session ID (ISID), a 48-bit field made up of the vendor ID and a unique qualifier that the vendor assigns. Figure 7–1 is a general depiction of the ISID field. Figure 7–2 shows the three ISID layouts that have been defined. The vendor type field is located in byte 0, bits 0 and 1, of the ISID. Notice that the layout of the 6-byte ISID depends on the setting of the vendor type field, as shown in Figure 7–2.

| Byte in PDU | 0 | 1 | 2 | 3 |
|---|---|---|---|---|
| Bit | 0 1 2 3 4 5 6 7 | 0 1 2 3 4 5 6 7 | 0 1 2 3 4 5 6 7 | 0 1 2 3 4 5 6 7 |
| 8 to 13 | ISID | | | |

Figure 7-1  ISID field in the login request and login response PDUs.

| Byte in PDU | 0 | 1 | 2 | 3 |
|---|---|---|---|---|
| Bit | 0 1 2 3 4 5 6 7 | 0 1 2 3 4 5 6 7 | 0 1 2 3 4 5 6 7 | 0 1 2 3 4 5 6 7 |
| 8 to 11 | 0 0   22-Bit OUI | | | Qualifier Part 1 |
| 12 to 13 | Qualifier Part 2 | | | |

| Byte in PDU | 0 | 1 | 2 | 3 |
|---|---|---|---|---|
| Bit | 0 1 2 3 4 5 6 7 | 0 1 2 3 4 5 6 7 | 0 1 2 3 4 5 6 7 | 0 1 2 3 4 5 6 7 |
| 8 to 11 | 0 1   0   IANA Enterprise Number | | | |
| 12 to 13 | Qualifier | | | |

| Byte in PDU | 0 | 1 | 2 | 3 |
|---|---|---|---|---|
| Bit | 0 1 2 3 4 5 6 7 | 0 1 2 3 4 5 6 7 | 0 1 2 3 4 5 6 7 | 0 1 2 3 4 5 6 7 |
| 8 to 11 | 1 0   0   Random Number | | | |
| 12 to 13 | Qualifier | | | |

Figure 7-2  Three ISID layouts.

**TABLE 7-1  ISID LAYOUT**

| Vendor Type Value | Layout of Bits and Bytes in the ISID |
|---|---|
| 0 | 22 bits follow, i.e., the lower 22 bits of the IEEE OUI* (Organization Unique Identifier) a.k.a. company ID. The remaining three bytes are a unique qualifier. |
| 1 | 6 bits of zeros follow, then 3 bytes of an IANA enterprise number (**EN**), and then a 2-byte unique qualifier. |
| 2 | 6 bits of zero follow, then a random 3-byte value and a 2-byte qualifier. |
| 3 | Reserved. |

*The OUI is actually 24 bits, but only the lower 22 are of use here.

The important thing to understand is that the full ISID is made up of the vendor ID and any additional qualifier that will create a unique identifier within any host initiator system. Therefore, when the full ISID is concatenated with the iSCSI initiator node name, it creates a unique name in the world, which represents the iSCSI (SCSI) initiator port.

Unlike Fibre Channel, in which each FC HBA relates one to one with a SCSI port, the iSCSI (SCSI) initiator port may actually span multiple HBAs. Therefore, the initiator side of an iSCSI session can use more than one initiator HBA. In fact, the iSCSI initiator may use several HBAs or portals within various HBAs to support multiple connections in a single session.

iSCSI's architects wanted to avoid what seemed to be a mistake in Fibre Channel, which was linking the physical HBA tightly to the logical concept of port and often to the concept of node. Therefore, they established rules to ensure that any iSCSI (SCSI) initiator port which has its ISID tied to a hardware identity is not required to keep that ISID permanently. The ISID can be used for various bringup or initialization purposes (such as initial boot), but may need to be automatically adjusted if used in a portal group (since there is more than one HBA and thus more than one potential ISID). In any event, it needs to be configurable to values that the installation considers appropriate.

If the ISID is derived from something assigned by the factory, as a preset default value, there must be a way for it to *automatically change* to a new value if it is part of a portal group. Also, any preset default value needs to be configurable so that the administrator or the management software can choose a different ISID. This configured ISID

- May be applied to a portal group of more than one HBA.

- Can be used instead of the preset default value so that the preset default value does not need to be the ongoing value of the ISID.

- Can become the ongoing ISID, but must be made persistent across the following:

  - ➤ Hot-swap with another HBA (in theory even from another vendor but at the least from the same vendor)

  - ➤ Reboot

  - ➤ Power down, swap-out old HBA, swap-in new HBA, and reboot

When an HBA is placed in a system in which the vendor's device driver supports portal groups for multiple connections per session (MC/S), the resultant session's ISID must apply to the total portal group regardless of the factory default values that may be part of any specific HBA. Techniques such as using the hardware defaults of the first HBA detected by the device driver meet the automatic change requirement for each HBA. However, the results must be made persistent and must remain the same, even if the HBAs that are members of the MC/S group are rearranged, replaced, or deleted.

## Connection Establishment

In order to take advantage of the ISID identity, the iSCSI initiator establishes its first connection with the target by sending a Login Request PDU. In this PDU the initiator places the appropriate values in the CID and the ISID fields, as well as in the text field. The text field will contain, among other things, the name of the iSCSI initiator node and the name of the target node. The iSCSI target responds appropriately and, on the last login response—of the leading login of the session—includes the unique (nonzero) target session identifier handle (TSIH). The TSIH must be unique within the target node for each session with the same named initiator. The implementation may assign to the TSIH any value other then zero.

After the TSIH is returned to the initiator, the session is considered established and in the full-feature phase (FFP). The initiator must then use that

TSIH when starting a subsequent connection with the target for the same session.

A session identifier (**SSID**) is unique for every session an initiator has with a given target. (See Figure 7–3.) It is composed of the ISID and the TPGT.

When a target node sees that an initiator is issuing a login for an existing SSID (with a nonzero TSIH), it assumes that the initiator is attempting to start a new connection (or reestablish an old one, as discussed below). Once the multiple connections are started, the initiator may send commands on any free connection. The data and status responses related to a command must flow on the same connection on which the command travels. This is known as connection allegiance.

Note that, when the Login Request PDU is received by an iSCSI target, it first checks to see if the TSIH is zero. If so, the target checks to see if the initiator node name and ISID are currently active on that target. If they are, the login forces a logout of the existing session and the establishment of a new session in its place. In that case any tasks active on the old session are internally terminated at the target and the new session starts fresh. (See Chapter 11 for more details on handling session restarts.) However, if the session was terminated some time before and all its tasks are now clear, a new session will just be started. If the target has retained any "persistent reserves" from that previous session, they will be associated with the new session.

If the initiator's Login Request PDU contains a nonzero TSIH, the target assumes that it is a request to establish an additional connection to an existing session. If that session is active and the new login request has a unique CID, the request will be granted and the new connection will be started. If the CID is the same as an existing CID, the current connection with the same CID will be terminated. Any existing tasks assigned to that connection will be put on suspension (if `ErrorRecoveryLevel=2`) until the initiator can get them reassigned

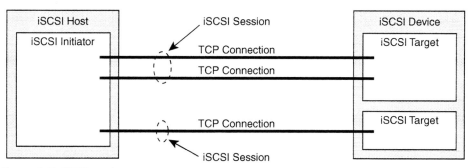

Figure 7–3  iSCSI session.

to this new connection or to another connection. It does this through the Task Management Request PDU. (See Chapter 11.) If the error recovery level is less than 2, the tasks associated with the terminated connection are just terminated.

This capability of reconnection is useful in case of a network link failure or some other transient condition that causes the TCP/IP connection to be lost. It is also useful in an error recovery situation, in which the only safe recovery method is to bring down the connection and reinitiate it. This will permit iSCSI to resume its transport duties without disturbing the SCSI layers above it.

## Data Travel Direction

The data may be write data, which is sent from the initiator:

- With the command PDU, as immediate data.

- In separate Data-Out PDUs, as unsolicited data.

- In separate Data-Out PDUs in response to an **R2T** (ready-to-transmit) PDU from the target as solicited data.

Or the data may be read data, in which case it is sent from the target to the initiator within a Data-In PDU. In all cases the data is sent on the same connection on which the command was sent. This connection is also used for

- R2T PDUs, which the target uses to request that the initiator transmit the write data.

- Command-status response PDUs, which are generated at the target and sent to the initiator.

In iSCSI there is a concept known as the **iSCSI transfer direction**. This is a direction defined with regard to the initiator. Outgoing transfers leave the initiator and go to the target, whereas incoming transfers arrive at the initiator from the target. You saw this concept earlier with data PDUs referred to as data-in or data-out depending on the direction of travel (read or write).

## Sequencing

The connection will have sequence numbers that it uses to keep track of the flow within the connection. The primary connection-level sequence number is the status sequence number (StatSN), a counter maintained per connection that tallies the count of status response PDUs sent from the target to the initiator. There are also sequence numbers dealing with the Data-In, Data-Out, and R2T PDUs that flow between the initiators and the targets. The Data-In/Out PDU and R2T PDU sequence numbers are all associated with commands, so they start counting at zero for each command.

There are also sequence numbers that apply to the commands themselves. Commands are sequenced across all connections within the session. Therefore, the command sequence number (CmdSN) is a counter that applies across the entire session (and any multiple connections therein as well). This sequencing of commands enables the target to deliver them in order to the SCSI level of processing in the target, regardless of the connection on which the command traveled. CmdSN is the only counter maintained across the different connections within a session.

It should be noted that the protocol maintains expected values for all these counters. For example, the CmdSN has a corresponding expected command sequence number (**ExpCmdSN**) counter. The various expected values are used by the responder to acknowledge receipt of the various sequenced items, up to but not including the next expected sequence number. Through the use of the expected values, it is not required that a separate acknowledgment (**ACK**) of the safe arrival of an individual PDU be sent. The responder may instead "piggy-back" all previous arrival acknowledgments with the next command or status response message. For example, the initiator can tell the target not only what command number it is sending but also what it believes should be the next status sequence number (StatSN) returned by the target. The target then knows that the initiator has received all status responses up to that point. This approach is especially useful given that an error seldom occurs that is not detected and fixed by TCP/IP. Therefore, network bandwidth is not consumed by acknowledgments that are almost never needed.

The SCSI Response PDU, which is sent by the target to acknowledge the completion of a command, will not only contain its own StatSN but also will contain the ExpCmdSN, thus informing the initiator of not only the status of the specific command but also the safe arrival of all the commands up to the ExpCmdSN.

The target has two ways to return ending status to the initiator. The normal method is via the SCSI Response PDU; the other is via the last Data-In PDU (if any). For example, if a read command completed successfully without any exception conditions, that fact can be signalled in the ending

Data-In PDU without having to send a separate response PDU. This technique is called "phase collapse," because the normal SCSI response phase is collapsed into the PDU that ends the data transfer. In any event, the SCSI Response PDU's StatSN field holds the count of all status responses, whether on ending Data-In PDUs or as part of the SCSI Response PDUs (also called status PDUs), sent on this connection.

The various PDUs that travel from the initiator to the target will return a value in a field called ExpStatSN. This field is generally one higher than the last StatSN value received by the initiator. The target can free up all resources for commands whose StatSN is less than ExpStatSN.

At this point let's recap the above. The CmdSN is what the initiator uses to tell the target the current sequence number for a command; the ExpStatSN is what the initiator uses to tell the target what status response it thinks is next. The target, via the StatSN, tells the initiator what status response it is on and, via ExpCmdSN, what command PDU sequence number the target thinks is next. All this is a means of sending acknowledgments of received commands or responses without having the overhead and latency of individual acknowledgments for each PDU. Acknowledgments just become part of other commands or responses, so there could be a number of commands received before an acknowledgment is sent. Therefore, by sending the value that the target thinks should be the next ExpCmdSN whenever it has a response to issue, the target implicitly acknowledges the receipt of all commands up to that number and does not need to acknowledge each command.

If there are no pending response messages for a period of time, the responder should generate a **NOP** (no-operation) message (either NOP-In, or NOP-Out) and specify the next expected sequence number.

The CmdSN not only has a corresponding ExpCmdSN, it also has another related field, the maximum command sequence number (**MaxCmdSN**). The combination of ExpCmdSN and MaxCmdSN are included in every PDU sent from the target to the initiator and can be used to provide a "windowing" technique for the acceptance of new commands.

When the MaxCmdSN plus 1 is equal to the ExpCmdSN, the command window is closed* and the initiator must not send any more commands until

---

*By its definition, serial-number arithmetic has no operation defined for subtraction, so the technically correct way to determine if the window is closed is to compare MaxCmdSN +1 to ExpCmdSN to determine if they are equal (see Appendix A for a description of serial-number arithmetic).

the window opens, an event signaled by a difference between the MaxCmdSN plus 1 and the ExpCmdSN. This is also a time when the NOP-In message, if no other PDUs are pending, can be used by the target to signal the increase in the MaxCmdSN. Whether a NOP-In or some other target-to-initiator PDU technique is used to inform the initiator that the window is open, it will signal that resources at the target have been freed up and that the target can begin accepting additional commands. It should be noted that the window need not go from full open to full close, but instead can be used to control the number of concurrent commands, which are in flight at any time from a specific iSCSI (SCSI) initiator port. This is done by keeping the difference between the current or expected CmdSN within *n* of the MaxCmdSN.

As explained previously, in addition to the command sequence numbers and the status sequence numbers, there are data sequence numbers and R2T sequence numbers. Figure 7–4 depicts the use of the various sequence numbers. The data sequence number (**DataSN**) starts at zero for each related command, so, if 10 different data PDUs are sent in relation to a specific (read

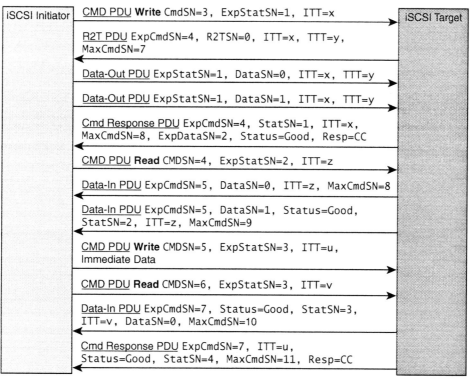

Figure 7–4 Sequencing.

or write) command, it will increment from 0 to 9. Then, some time after the completion of the data transfer operations, the SCSI command will complete and a status message will be issued from the target to the initiator. In case of a read operation, as specified above, this message will contain an expected DataSN (**ExpDataSN**) that will be one higher than the last DataSN sent for the corresponding command. The initiator can then determine if it has received all the data the target sent. It does this by making sure that the corresponding numbers of Data-In PDUs, specified in the status response PDU, have actually been received. A similar thing happens if a phase collapse has permitted the last Data-In PDU to return a good ending status. In this case, however, the last DataSN is in the ending Data-In PDU and does not have to be sent in the ExpDataSN field of a response PDU.

## Resending Data or Status

If the initiator has not received all the data, it may request that the target resend the missing Data-In PDUs. To request the resend, the initiator must issue a **SNACK**\* (selective negative acknowledgment) PDU to the target.

A SNACK is the only method that the initiator can use to request that the target resend the missing Data-In or status PDUs. It is intended for environments operating at `ErrorRecoveryLevel>0`. At that level, the missing Data-In PDUs must be resent by the target exactly as they were sent originally, except that the ExpCmdSN and the MaxCmdSN must be current.

The initiator will not know that Data-In PDUs are missing until the status response occurs. This is important to understand. In normal operation, TCP/IP will perform all error recovery and retransmission. It is only when iSCSI adds a CRC digest that it can tell that it has detected an error that slipped by TCP/IP error detection. If it turns out that the error was detected in the data part of the PDU via the data CRC digest (meaning that the header passed the CRC correctness test), the initiator or target can tell enough about the data PDU to ask for the data to be retransmitted. As mentioned above, the initiator does this by issuing the SNACK PDU and requesting the retransmission of the corrupted data. The target, on the other hand, deals with the CRC data digest error by issuing a Reject PDU and then sending a recovery R2T. (The details of the various SNACK modes can be found in Appendix A in the section on SNACK PDU.)

---

\*This PDU is also called "sequence number acknowledgment."

However, if the digest error is in the header of the PDU, the initiator cannot trust the information in the header and therefore cannot immediately ask the target to resend the appropriate Data-In PDU. In fact, it cannot be sure even that it was a Data-In PDU. Only the arrival of the status response PDU or a command's last Data-In PDU with phase collapse status permits the initiator to detect that a Data-In PDU is missing. Likewise, the receipt of any other PDU from the target that has the StatSN value will let the initiator know that there is a missing Data-In or SCSI Response PDU. As specified above, it then has the missing PDU retransmitted by making the request via the SNACK PDU. A similar process occurs on the target side with Data-Out PDUs; the only difference is that the target issues the R2T PDU (instead of a SNACK) to request the missing data, and lets the initiator detect and retransmit missing commands.

It is important to understand at what point the target can free up the buffers for an operation. The target needs an indication that the initiator has successfully received the status response as well as all the data the target sent. To do this, it checks the values in the next PDU sent on the connection from the initiator. If the ExpStatSN is what the target thinks it should be, the target can then free the buffers without a lot of handshaking and round-trip delays. This acknowledgment is accomplished via any PDU sent from the initiator to the target during full-feature phase.

If the traffic from the initiator to the target is inactive, the target can issue the NOP-In PDU (in "ping" mode). In a normal situation the initiator will return the "ping" (in a NOP-Out PDU) and contain the latest values for the CmdSN and ExpStatSN. Also in a normal situation, all values will be correct and things will continue.

Now let's follow a situation that is not exactly normal. In this case, when the target wants to check on the health and status of an initiator, it may send a NOP-In PDU. The NOP-In will contain the StatSN value that the target plans on issuing next. The initiator must then check to see if it is missing a status response PDU (detected by the fact that its own StatSN count is behind the value in the StatSN field of the NOP-In PDU).

If the initiator detects a missing response, it issues a SNACK PDU. This SNACK will request that the target resend the missing status response PDUs. As it receives these PDUs the initiator may find that other things are missing, such as Data-In PDUs. The initiator should then issue the SNACK and request the missing Data-In PDUs. Figure 7–5 depicts this sequencing and recovery after a CRC-detected header error.

The use of a NOP-In (ping), permits the target, on an inactive link, to confirm that the initiator has received all the status responses up to that

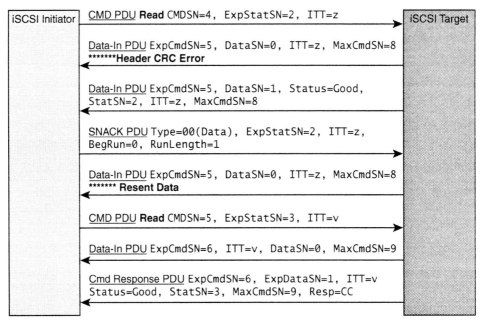

Figure 7–5  Recovering Missing Data.

point. The target may then free up the resources held for all those completed commands.

We might think that, if the link is not actively sending commands or data, there is no harm in tying up the target resources with unacknowledged status responses until the link becomes active again. However, even if this connection or session is currently inactive, other sessions may be active and probably need the resources.

Let's now examine the write operation. Assuming that the target was sent a write command earlier, it needs to ensure that it has received all the data required for the command's execution. If not, the target will request from the initiator any needed data that it has not received. Even if the data was originally sent via unsolicited Data-Out PDUs, the target can request any missing data via R2T PDUs. Therefore, if the unsolicited Data-Out PDU was discarded because of a header digest error, the target can have it resent via the R2T (called a recovery R2T).

If solicited or unsolicited data is detected with an error in the data section of the PDU (via an error in the data digest), the target is required to explicitly send a Reject PDU with the reason code of "Data (payload) Digest Error" and discard the in-error PDU. Then it can explicitly request the retransmission of the data via an R2T PDU.

Tables 7–2 through 7–4 are examples of normal read and write operations along with the settings of the various sequence numbers and the Final bit (F bit).

### Recap

Session management is the handling of the one or more connections that make up a session. It involves dealing with the sequence numbers that permit multiple connections to manage the delivery of SCSI commands and data as if they were all on a single TCP/IP connection.

Because there can be header digest errors as well as data digest errors, the sequence numbering of StatSN, ExpStatSN, DataSN, and R2TSN permits the initiator and the target to precede normally without extra acknowledgments for each data, status, or request exchange. Yet when a digest error does exist, sequence number management permits recovery from both error types.

---

**TABLE 7–2  READ OPERATION DATA SEQUENCING**
**(NOTE: <<< OR >>> DENOTE DIRECTION OF**
**TRAVEL.)**

| Initiator Function | PDU Type | Target Function |
|---|---|---|
| Command request (read) | SCSI command (read)>>> | Prepare data transfer |
| Receive data | <<< SCSI Data-In | Send data |
|  | DataSN=0, F=0 |  |
| Receive data | <<< SCSI Data-In | Send data |
|  | DataSN=1, F=0 |  |
| Receive data | <<< SCSI Data-In | Send data |
|  | DataSN=2, F=1 |  |
|  | <<< SCSI Response | Send status and sense |
|  | ExpDataSN=3 |  |
| Command complete |  |  |

## TABLE 7–3  WRITE OPERATION DATA SEQUENCING (A)

| Initiator Function | PDU Type | Target Function |
|---|---|---|
| Command request (write) | SCSI command (write) >>> with immediate data | Receive command and queue it |
| | Data-Out (write) >>> unsolicited data DataSN=0, F=0 | Process old commands and receive unsolicited data for write |
| | Data-Out (write) >>> unsolicited data DataSN=1, F=1 | Process old commands and receive unsolicited data for write |
| | <<< R2T R2TSN=0 TTT=x | Ready to process write command, request part of remaining needed data |
| Send all data for R2TSN 0 | SCSI Data-Out >>>> DataSN=0, TTT=x F=1 | Receive data |
| | <<< R2T R2TSN=1 TTT=y | Buffers ready for more data |
| | <<< R2T R2TSN=2 TTT=z | Additional buffers ready to receive even more data |
| Send data for R2TSN 1 | SCSI Data-Out >>>> DataSN=0, TTT=y F=0 | Receive some data for R2T request 1 |
| Send data for R2TSN 1 | SCSI Data-Out >>>> DataSN=1, TTT=y F=1 | Receive rest of data for R2T request 1 |
| Send data for R2TSN 2 | SCSI Data-Out >>>> DataSN=0, TTT=z F=1 | Receive data for R2T request 2 |
| | <<< SCSI response | Finish processing write command and send status (and sense if needed) |
| Command complete | | |

## TABLE 7–4  WRITE OPERATION DATA SEQUENCING (B)

| Initiator Function | PDU Type | Target Function |
|---|---|---|
| Command request (write) | SCSI command (write) >>> | Receive command and queue it |
| | | Process old commands |
| | <<< R2T R2TSN=0 TTT=x | Ready for data |
| | <<< R2T R2TSN=1 TTT=y | Ready for more data |
| Send data for R2TSN 0 | SCSI Data-Out >>>> DataSN=0, TTT=x F=0 | Receive part of data for R2T 0 |
| Send data for R2TSN 0 | SCSI Data-Out >>>> DataSN=1, TTT=x F=1 | Receive the rest of data for R2T0 |
| Send data for R2TSN 1 | SCSI Data-Out >>>> DataSN=0, TTT=y F=1 | Receive all data from R2T 1 |
| | <<< SCSI response | Finish processing write command and send status (and sense if needed) |
| Command complete | | |

## Chapter Summary

In this chapter we discussed how a session's flow of commands and data is managed:

- How iSCSI keeps track of the various connections that make up a session (via the CID)

- How iSCSI identifies sessions by creating a session ID called **SSID** (made up of ISID and TPGT)

- How the ISID is created (via IEEE OUI or IANA EN)

    We also learned

- How each command is identified during transit via a command sequence number (**CmdSN**).

- How the Data-In and Data-Out PDUs are ordered with data sequence numbers (**DataSN**s).

- How the resultant status from a command has a status sequence number (**StatSN**) carried in the SCSI response PDU.

- How the PDUs that originate from the initiator generally carry a CmdSN or a DataSN, along with the expected status sequence number (**ExpStatSN**) to be received on the next response from the target.

It was explained that the iSCSI process

- Keeps track of the missing pieces on each side.

- Only flows the acknowledgment of reception when it can be "piggy-backed" onto other PDUs that are flowing between the initiator and the target.

- Initiator uses the status negative acknowledgment (**SNACK**) PDU to request a resend of missing PDUs (PDUs discarded because of a CRC-detected error).

The chapter also discussed

- The receiving and sending of data (data being read and written).

- The concept of unsolicited data, including "immediate" data sent as part of a write operation.

- The concept of a target soliciting the initiator for data needed for a write operation and how the request to transfer (**R2T**) PDU was used for that purpose.

- The use of NOP-In and NOP-Out to ensure that the expected counts including those used for "window size" management are received and synchronized between the initiator and the target, especially when link activity is too low to piggyback the counts on other PDUs.

Examples were given of

- Data PDU flow.

- Setting the "Final" flag (F bit).

Finally it was explained that the main purpose of these sequence fields (with the exception of MaxCmdSN) is to address the loss of a PDU because of a header digest error or the loss of data because of a data digest error.

# 8

# Command and Data Ordering and Flow

## To the Reader

This chapter will present the details of flow control for both commands and data. It will take the concepts introduced in Chapter 7 and expand them. As always, if you desire just an overview, skip to the Chapter Summary.

## Command Ordering

Commands such as read and write are sequenced by iSCSI initiators so that the iSCSI target can present them to the target SCSI layer in the order in which they were sent. As specified in Chapter 7, to do this each command is given a unique number, called the command sequence number (CmdSN), which is placed in the header of the various request PDUs sent from the initiator to the target, starting with the initial login request of the first connection within a session. The next sequence number is assigned to the *second* nonimmediate request PDU following the final login message from the initiator. The first request (command) PDU sent in full-feature phase (FFP) contains the same CmdSN as the login request itself.

The thing to be understood here is that the login process is considered a single immediate command, regardless of how many login messages are exchanged. The login on any one connection can only have a sequential exchange of login parameters with no overlapping of other commands or data in that connection, before the process ends (when full-feature phase is reached on the connection). Therefore, there is no need to increment the CmdSN until after the login is complete, and, because it is considered to be an immediate command, the CmdSN is not incremented even then. However, after the initial login, for all nonimmediate commands from that point forward, the CmdSN is increased by 1, regardless of the connection on which the command is actually sent. The CmdSN is a global value, maintained throughout the entire session across all connections.

As specified in Chapter 7, it is expected that the target will return to the initiator—whenever it has a response of any kind—an indication of the highest value of CmdSN that has been delivered to it (without a PDU header error). This value—the expected command sequence number (ExpCmdSN)—is always 1 higher than the highest CmdSN value received. Based on the ExpCmdSN, the iSCSI initiator may discard from its transmission buffers any copies of commands that have been received at the target.

If there is a large absolute difference between what it thinks is the next CmdSN and the last received ExpCmdSN, the initiator may have a problem with the error-free reception of all its commands at the target. To verify this or to detect a clog in the network, it may send a NOP (no-operation) PDU to the target and request a response (a **ping**). If no response is received for a long period of time, the network or target may be in distress. However, if the ping comes back, it will also contain the latest ExpCmdSN as seen by the target. If this value is lower than the initiator thinks it should be, the initiator may assume that one or more commands have been lost, and then begin by resending the commands starting with the command that has CmdSN equal to the returned ExpCmdSN. This process can continue until the ExpCmdSN that matches what the initiator thinks should be its value is returned by the target. (More information on this is given in Chapter 11.)

Ignoring the error case, there is a potential exception to the in-order delivery of commands, especially on a single-connection session. Let's focus on the single-connection case, in which the iSCSI initiator HBA is given one command (perhaps a write) that includes immediate data, and another command so close behind the first, that the second command is ready to be sent before the write command is ready. This can happen when the first command is still gathering the immediate data across the PCI bus, as the following command (perhaps a read) arrives and is ready to be transferred across the PCI bus to the HBA. If the commands were numbered before they were sent to the HBA, the second command could actually be ready to be sent on the link before the first command completed gathering all the data onto the HBA. If commands were sent in this out-of-order manner, the physical link would be more completely utilized; however, it would seem to the iSCSI target that the first command was lost (as if it had experienced an iSCSI header digest error). Therefore, this potential exception to the command ordering rules has not been accepted.

To prevent this error-processing trauma, and yet fully utilize the capacity of the link, it is expected that many HBA vendors will open one or more additional "logical" connections on the same physical link, so that commands can be sent out immediately when they are ready without having to wait for long data-related PDUs.

This same type of issue exists even when multiple physical links are used in the same session—each physical link/HBA may face a similar problem. Therefore, it is expected that some vendors will utilize both multiple physical links and multiple logical connections per physical link within the same iSCSI session. In this way they not only will be able to increase the bandwidth available to each session, but also will be able to fully utilize the bandwidth of each physical link.

Independent of the order in which the iSCSI target receives the command PDUs (across several connections within a session), it is the job of the iSCSI target to deliver the commands in CmdSN order to the SCSI target layer. Many folks believe that SCSI only demands in-order delivery to the LU (logical unit) from any specific SCSI initiator. However, if the iSCSI and SCSI layering are kept completely isolated, the iSCSI layer will not understand the LUN (LU number) received with the SCSI command. Therefore, the simplest thing for any iSCSI target to do is ensure that the commands turned over to the SCSI layer are delivered in CmdSN order. This way iSCSI will also be sure that the LU ordering is maintained, and keep the iSCSI to SCSI processing as simple as possible.

The CmdSN is set in all request PDUs sent from the initiator to the target, except for the SNACK Request PDU. This means that the following PDUs sent from the initiator to the target contain the CmdSN:

- SCSI (command) Request

- Task Management Function Request

- Text Request

- Login Request

- Logout Request

- NOP-Out

The ExpCmdSN value is returned in the following PDUs:

- SCSI (command) Response

- Data-In

- Request to Transfer (R2T)

- Asynchronous Message

- Text Response

- Login Response

- Logout Response

- Reject

- NOP-In

- Task Management Function Response

In other words, all PDUs that flow from the target to the initiator will have the ExpCmdSN value set. Therefore, every target response will be able to acknowledge commands previously sent by the initiator. The value set in the ExpCmdSN is equal to the last CmdSN sent to the target SCSI layer plus 1. This statement reflects the following important concept:

> iSCSI requires the iSCSI layer to deliver the commands to the SCSI layer *in order*. By implication, if a "hole" exists in the CmdSN sequence, the commands that have a CmdSN higher than the "expected value of the hole" cannot be delivered to the SCSI layer until the missing commands are received by iSCSI.

## Command Windowing

The MaxCmdSN is another value associated with the CmdSN. It is returned in the same PDUs that contain the ExpCmdSN (listed previously).

As discussed in Chapter 7, the combination of ExpCmdSN and Max-CmdSN defines a window that controls the arrival of commands at the target. Lowering the absolute difference between the ExpCmdSN and the Max-CmdSN (plus 1) will reduce the amount of memory the target needs for servicing the initiator requests. As the absolute difference becomes smaller, fewer commands can be sent without rechecking the MaxCmdSN value. Thus, when the window gets small—say to a 1-unit difference—the initiator must wait after it sends a command to ensure that a response is received showing that the window is still open. If the window closes (MaxCmdSN equals CmdSN), the initiator must wait until it receives a response or data PDU with the absolute difference between the ExpCmdSN and the MaxCmdSN (plus 1) larger than zero. MaxCmdSN is returned on the same PDUs that carry ExpCmdSN (listed previously) so the difference can be determined immediately.

Now, this form of resource management is actually a rather gross form of buffer management, because the number of buffers at the target needed to handle any specific number of tasks can only be guessed at. This is especially the case when the initiator can send both immediate and unsolicited data to the target. Therefore, the implementation will need to set up some rules of thumb to detect when the buffer pool is being depleted at an unsustainable rate. In such a case, the target should dynamically reduce the absolute difference between the ExpCmdSN and the MaxCmdSN (plus 1)—which together make up the "command window."

Lowering to one the absolute difference between MaxCmdSN relative to the ExpCmdSN reduces the uncontrolled flow of commands into the target—and will cause the initiator to stop sending commands. However, as buffers are freed up by the completion of previous commands, the MaxCmdSN value can be raised (relative to the ExpCmdSN), which will raise the command window and permit more commands to flow. This value should be monitored continuously in order to prevent the oversubscription of commands to the available target buffers.

Even though the iSCSI command window management is not precise, it can work very well in throttling back buffer consumption. In general, iSCSI storage controllers have more open sessions/connections than Fibre Channel (FC) storage controllers have. This is because there will often be not only servers interconnected to the storage controllers but also desktop and laptop systems. Therefore, the iSCSI sessions will have a lot of inactive connections. This might be a problem for Fibre Channel but probably is not a significant issue for iSCSI. In Fibre Channel the storage controller needs to advertise the "buffer credits" that can be used by each connected initiator, which often means a lot of underutilized memory. These credit values are maintained by acknowledgments that, if employed "at distance," would degrade overall throughput.

iSCSI does not advertise credits or guarantee buffers. Instead, it uses its own iSCSI windowing capability to slowly reduce the volume of commands received. When that is not enough, it exploits the TCP/IP connection windowing capability to reduce the total flow of bytes (data and commands) between initiators and targets by applying "back pressure" on the devices between them. This can be done because TCP/IP is, in general, a store-and-forward technology and so its windowing capability is used as "the final gate."

iSCSI, unlike Fibre Channel, has to deal with large distances between initiators and targets. As mentioned previously, techniques for managing buffers that employ the fine-grained control permitted by FC credits will not be as useful in at-distance iSCSI networks, because there is a long turnaround associated with larger distances. This causes significant latency in Fibre Channel's continuous credit-response approach, and that latency in turn reduces the total effective line utilization. Therefore, approaches that do not guarantee buffers and have a large control granularity seem to be the best fit for these environments, especially when backstopped with the back pressure approach available to TCP/IP.

What all this means is, when the iSCSI storage controllers overcommit their storage, they have windowing methods that reduce the command flow when buffers are short.

## Initiator Task Tag

There is another item included with the SCSI command PDU that is of major importance, especially when it comes to buffer control on the HBA. That item is the initiator task tag (ITT)—a handle used to identify an active task within a session. When the data arrives from the target, the ITT can be used by an HBA to place the data directly into the target host buffers without extra moves or additional staging buffers (see additional comments on direct memory placement, to come). This quickly frees up the critical HBA buffers for reuse by other tasks. In order for this to work, the target must place the ITT of the command into the corresponding Data-In PDUs, response PDUs, and so forth. (Refer to the design example, which follows.)

The ITT can be reused when a command is completed unless, of course, the command is part of a linked set of commands (see Chapter 10, Task Management, for more information on linked commands), in which case the initiator must keep the ITT pending for reuse by the next command in the task chain. Sooner or later, however, at the completion of the last command in the chain, the ITT can be reused. That means it can be a pointer or a handle that the initiator and the target can use to track a command and its related data and status.

One other point about the ITT is that it should be unique within the session, not just within the connection. This is because, via task management PDUs, the initiator can move a command and its allegiances from a failing connection to a healthy connection within the same session, or perhaps even to a different HBA. (See Chapter 10 for more information on command and allegiance connection reassignment.)

### Design Example: Direct Host Memory Placement

Imagine that a host device driver creates and enqueues an entry for a "command queue" that contains a partially completed iSCSI read request PDU. Also suppose that the entry has, among other things, pointers to the host buffers in which the data, when read from the target, can be placed. The address of this command queue entry (**CQE**) can be given to the HBA. The address of the HBA's copy can become the value of the ITT. The HBA might place a copy of the command queue entry in its own memory by **DMAing** (Direct Memory Accessing) it from the host memory. This copy is made up of the partially completed PDU, the addresses of the input buffers, and so forth.

Thus, as soon as the HBA fills out the rest of the read request PDU, it can send the command on its way to the target. Then, when the target responds with Data-In PDUs, the HBA can extract the ITT from the PDUs' headers and perform a lookup based on the ITT pointer. This will enable the HBA to find its copy of the CQE and use the host buffer address found therein to place the incoming data directly in the appropriate host buffers. In this way the host will not need to move the data an additional time.

Figure 8–1 shows the read data sent from the target storage controller in a Data-In PDU that is broken across two TCP segments. The header contains the ITT value of 8192, which the initiator HBA uses as a displacement into

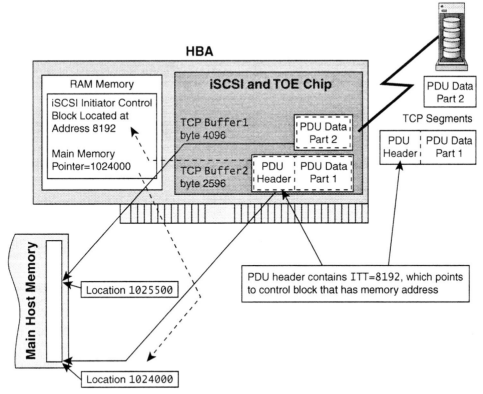

Figure 8-1 Direct initiator memory placement.

its RAM memory where it finds its copy of the CQE with the locations for the data in the actual host memory. Then the data from the PDU can be placed directly into those locations. Note that in this figure the second TCP/IP segment arrives before the segment with the PDU header, so it cannot be placed until the segment with the header arrives. This is because the header has the ITT pointer. Also, since each segment identifies the TCP byte stream displacement, it is a straightforward calculation to determine where the various data pieces are placed in the host memory.

This design example shows that, by carefully picking the values placed in the ITT, an engineer can create an HBA that does not require additional host CPU cycles to move or place storage data directly in the final host I/O buffers. This example assumes that the data will be laid into host memory following the PDU header. It is also possible to send the header one place and the data another (with additional information in the CQE).

One other consideration regarding this use of the ITT is linked commands—the same ITT value needs to be used by each of the linked commands as they are sent. In those cases, the ITT value will need to be around for a long time. For that reason (and in order to support MC/S across HBAs), the vendor may want the ITT to be created by the HBA device driver; then the HBA can use it as an indirect pointer to the HBA's version of the CQE. In that case the ITT value can be a pointer to an entry on an HBA "hash" lookup table and that entry can point to the HBA's copy of the CQE (based on the ITT value).

If HBA RAM space is needed, it is even possible to free up the CQE copy on the HBA after the command is sent. The CQE can be fetched back when the pointers to main memory data locations are needed. Of course, the main memory version of the CQE will contain the ITT and other values needed to relate the linked commands to each other as they are passed down from the SCSI layer.

What all this means is that with appropriate use of the ITT there are a number of ways to implement direct data placement (**DDP**) in the initiator's main memory.

## Data Ordering

The data sent to the target can be located in the SCSI command PDU that contains the write request. It may also be sent to the target in an unsolicited Data-Out PDU. Unsolicited PDUs contain the data to be written to the target device and are sent without solicitation from the target. It is also possible for the target to request the data needed for a write command from the initiator. To do this it sends the request to transfer (R2T) PDUs to the initiator when it is ready to accept the data.

At login, the initiator and the target negotiate three values: `FirstBurstLength`, `MaxBurstLength`, and `MaxRecvDataSegmentLength`. These values limit the amount of data that can be sent or received in a transaction.

`FirstBurstLength` is the maximum number of data bytes that can be delivered unsolicited from the iSCSI initiator to the iSCSI target during execution of a single SCSI command. This is a session-wide limit that applies to all the unsolicited data, whether it is sent as immediate data with the SCSI command PDU, or sent as unsolicited Data-Out PDUs following the SCSI command PDU, or a combination of both.

`MaxBurstLength` is the maximum data payload in a sequence of Data-In or solicited Data-Out PDUs. A sequence consists of data PDUs that all have the same task tags (initiator or target) and is terminated by a "finished" flag (F bit) in the ending data PDU.

`MaxRecvDataSegmentLength` is the maximum amount of data that can be included in any iSCSI PDU. It is a connection- and direction-specific value. For a target, the limiting factor on solicited data is the smaller of `MaxRecvDataSegmentLength` and `MaxBurstLength`. For unsolicited data, the limiting factor is the lesser of `MaxRecvDataSegmentLength` and `FirstBurstLength`. The `MaxRecvDataSegmentLength` value is not really negotiated but is declared by each side according to what it can accept.

To understand why some of these values are connection specific and others are session wide, it may be helpful to understand that the receiving buffers on an HBA may be completely independent from the main memory of the host or the storage controller. The session-wide values address the limitations of main memory, while the connection-specific values address the limitations of memory on the HBA.

The immediate data is contained in the same PDU that holds the command. The maximum amount of data that can be included in a SCSI command PDU is limited by `MaxRecvDataSegmentLength`. This value also sets the limit of data in an unsolicited Data-Out PDU.

For example, if the target's `MaxRecvDataSegmentLength` has a value of 8K and the `FirstBurstLength` is equal to 64K, then the SCSI command PDU can contain 8K and be followed by seven unsolicited Data-Out PDUs each 8K in length (see Figure 8–2). If this is not enough data to meet the needs of the SCSI (write) command PDU, the target then solicits the remaining data via the R2T PDU. In this case, if the amount of data specified in the original SCSI (write) command PDU is 137K, the target needs to solicit the remaining 73K from the initiator.

This brings us to the next negotiated value, MaxBurstLength. In the example we have been using, the value negotiated for MaxBurstLength is also 64K; therefore, the target needs to send two R2T PDUs to the initiator soliciting the first 64K of the remaining data and then the final 9K.

The initiator needs to send the data in a sequence of eight 8K Data-Out PDUs (with the last one in each sequence having the F bit set). Following that is a sequence of one 8K Data-Out PDU and one 1K Data-Out PDU that has the F bit set. Figure 8–2 depicts this example.

To recap:

■ MaxBurstLength and FirstBurstLength are both negotiated to 64K.

■ MaxRecvDataSegmentLength is declared by the target as 8K.

■ The SCSI (write) command PDU specifies a total data length of 137K.

■ 8K worth of data can be sent with the write PDU.

■ Seven 8K unsolicited Data-Out PDUs ($7\times8K=56K$) can be sent to the target following the SCSI command PDU ($8K+[7\times8K]=64K$).

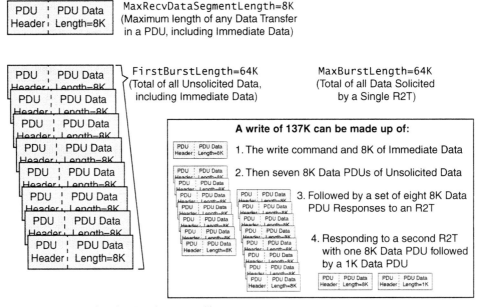

Figure 8–2  Sample of write data transfer.

■ The target replies by sending two R2T solicitations.

■ A sequence of eight 8K Data-Out PDUs (8×8K=64K), followed by
a sequence of one 8K Data-Out PDU and a single Data-Out PDU of 1K
(8K+1K=9K), results.

■ The total data written is (8K+56K+64K+9K=137K).

■ The last Data-Out PDU in a sequence will have its header's F bit
set to 1.

One other thing is important to understand: if the amount of data being
written is larger than the FirstBurstLength (the negotiated maximum amount
of unsolicited data the target will accept), the initiator *must* send the maximum length of unsolicited data or *only* the immediate data. This permits the
target to determine where the R2Ts should begin asking for data. For instance, given that the target knows what the FirstBurstLength is, if the
amount of data to be written is greater than that, then:

■ If the F bit is set in the command PDU, it means that no unsolicited data
follows this PDU and only the data with this PDU (immediate data) is
being sent without an explicit R2T. Therefore, the R2T can begin with
the offset, which follows the immediate data, if any.

■ If the F bit is not set, then the target knows that the initiator must send
FirstBurstLength of data, so the target can immediately begin sending
R2Ts starting with the offset, which follows the FirstBurstLength.

■ In either case, the target can send the R2Ts as soon as it decodes the
command PDU.

A couple of other negotiated values have a bearing on the sending of
data. One is called DataPDUInOrder, and it can be set to Yes or No. If No, the
data PDUs in a sequence can be in any order. If Yes, the data PDUs in
a sequence must be sent in continuously increasing address order. This is a
session-wide value and applies to both the sending and receiving of data.

Since the value of Yes for DataPDUInOrder invokes what is probably
assumed to be the normal way to exchange data, we might wonder why there
is even a value of No. The assumption that data arrives in order, however, is
often incorrect, because extracting from or sending to a disk can be done
whenever the disk read/write head passes over the appropriate spot. Years
ago it was common for the data sectors to be interleaved on the disk media,
and a No value would be useful in that type of environment. However, that

does not apply today. Instead, a virtualized hard disk can have its data sent to or received from several different places, and those places probably are not synchronized. Sometimes one part of the data is in a cache and another part is on the hard disk. In these cases, data may be available to be transferred to or from the media out of order. That explains the need for and value of the key=value pair `DataPDUInOrder=No`. For a normal host-based initiator, this value has no bearing since the initiator will have already allocated the needed main memory; therefore, the data can be placed in that memory in any order independent of arrival time.

The other data-sequencing value that can be negotiated is `DataSequence-InOrder`, and it is used to specify whether the sequences of Data-Out PDUs can be out of order. Since the normal host initiator has to allocate the main memory space when the SCSI (read) command PDU is sent, it does not care about the arrival time order of sequences of the data. Therefore, this negotiated value usually is applicable only to Data-Out sequences. If the value is set to `Yes`, each Data-Out sequence must be in order relative to other Data-Out sequences, using a continuously increasing offset. If the value is set to `No`, the data sequences can be in any order relative to any other data sequence. As specified above, the order of the data within a sequence is controlled by `DataPDUInOrder`. A value of `Yes` with either keyword means that the data exchanged must have some linear structural order in its arrival—ordered within a sequence, or one sequence ordered relative to other sequences, or both. Since it is the R2T that controls the order of Data-Out PDU sequences, it is usually the target that cares about the `DataSequenceInOrder` value.

Another consideration is that the target must "score-board" what data has arrived and what has not. The use of these two data-ordering key=value pairs will probably reflect the sophistication of that score-boarding, which is clearly easier if the data must arrive in order.

Though we do not talk much about third-party commands (extended copy commands) in this book, in fact iSCSI does support this capability. Thus, it is possible that the initiator of a copy command will extract data from storage media that have different access capabilities, and it will need all the flexibility of `...InOrder=No` that it can get. In fact, the most flexible and useful setting is `No` for both data-ordering values. It is probably also best that the initiator normally send data (within a sequence) in order, even if the `DataPDUInOrder` value is set to `No`. In that way the target will control all of the out-of-order output decisions via R2Ts. The important thing to note is this: If the `DataPDUInOrder` value is set to `No`, the target will send the initiator Data-In PDUs in whatever order it finds convenient.

As for R2T solicited data, as mentioned above, the target might know how it wants the data delivered so that it can apply the appropriate arrival time placement to the resultant real disks and other media. Therefore, the initiator must respond to the R2T PDUs in the order they were sent. To ensure that this ordering is possible, each R2T PDU carries its own sequence number, known as **R2TSN**. This number is unique only within the scope of the command to which it applies.

It should be noted that the R2T PDUs can be sent one after the other, with no waiting for the corresponding initiator response, up to the negotiated limit in the value known as MaxOutstandingR2T.

The question remaining is whether the sequence of unsolicited Data-Out PDUs must follow the address of the last byte of the immediate data, or can they have some other displacement address. Clearly, if DataPDUInOrder has a value of Yes, the data must be in order; however, if the value is No, the initiator can make whatever displacement address it wants for the beginning point of the unsolicited PDU sequence (as long as it is within the first First-BurstLength bytes from the beginning of the buffer). Still, though this is possible there seems to be no reason that the sequence should not start with the next address following the immediate data, if any.

The use of DataSequenceInOrder=Yes has an indirect effect on Error Recovery dealing with the retransmission of data. When DataSequence-InOrder=Yes and ErrorRecoveryLevel>0 the target can only retry the last R2T sequence, and the initiator may request retransmission of only the last read data sequence. Because of the above, if DataSequenceInOrder=Yes and ErrorRecoveryLevel>0, the negotiated value known as MaxOutstandingR2T is required to have the value of 1.

We have covered the case where DataPDUInOrder=No makes sense, but we still need to understand when it might be important for the setting to be Yes. Therefore, let's consider the streaming tape controller that has only enough RAM to accommodate the time needed to send an R2T and receive a Data-Out PDU in return. In this case, DataPDUInOrder=Yes is very important, and any out-of-order data will upset the controller's ability to stream to tape, causing a tape "back-hitch"* and needless delay.

Even though the host initiator can handle out-of-order data on reads, there is no way for the tape to do so. In general, for most if not all storage controllers, if the input to the device must be in order, the output of the device probably also needs to be in order. Therefore, the ...InOrder value applies to

---

* Also known as "shoe-shining."

both directions of the data. With third-party copy commands, which have their secondary initiator function within the actual tape storage controller, the secondary initiator cannot send or receive out-of-order data. That is one more reason why the values for `DataPDUInOrder` and `DataSequenceInOrder` apply for both sending and receiving.

A rule of thumb for host initiators: Attempt to negotiate `DataPDU-InOrder=No` and `DataSequenceInOrder=No`. Then let the targets decide what they can support.

It already has been mentioned but can stand some reiteration and additional emphasis here: Data and status must be sent on the same connection as their related SCSI command PDU. Commands can be load-balanced across the various connections within a session, but the data associated with them, whether Data-Out or Data-In, must be sent on the same connection on which those commands were sent. This ensures that the HBA that carried the command will be able to correlate the data with the command. This applies whether the data is going out or coming in, and it also applies to the status/response PDUs, which also must travel on the same connection as the corresponding command.

All unsolicited data PDUs must be sent in the same order as their related commands. That is, unsolicited data PDUs for command N must precede the unsolicited data PDUs for command N+1. Command N+1, however, may precede the unsolicited data PDU for command N.

Note that there can be more than one command linked together in a single task (see Chapter 10, Task Management, for more information on linked commands). However, the allegiance of the data and status to the same connection applies only to the specific commands and not to the task. Linked commands within one task can be individually placed on any connection within the session.

We have been talking as though immediate and unsolicited data PDUs are always supported. This is not completely correct. By default, immediate data is supported and unsolicited data is not; however, this is negotiable. The initiator and target can negotiate not to support immediate data and can also decide to support unsolicited data PDUs. R2T support is always enabled.

## Target Transfer Tag

As explained previously, when a Data-Out PDU is sent to a target, it contains an ITT—the same ITT specified with the corresponding SCSI command PDU. The initiator uses this ITT to relate data to the appropriate command;

the target also uses the ITT to correlate the data to the appropriate command that it received earlier. Each SCSI command PDU sent from an initiator to a target contains an ITT that is unique within the session. The target can use it as an association anchor, on which it may queue whatever it wishes—related information, buffer pointers, state, and the like.

Often all the data that can be sent via unsolicited techniques will not be enough to satisfy the data size specified in the SCSI command PDU. In that case, the target will need to solicit the remaining data from the initiator by sending it an R2T PDU. This PDU will contain the command's ITT so that the initiator will know to which command the R2T applies. It will also contain a target transfer tag (TTT), a "handle" the target assigns and then places in the R2T PDU. This TTT has to be unique only within the current connection of the current session and remains valid only as long as the corresponding command is active. In order to make some error recovery easier across connections in a multiple-connection session, the target may make the TTT unique within the session, but that is an implementation decision.

Since the TTT is only a handle made up by the target, when it sends R2T PDUs, it can be anything the target can fit in a 32-bit field. One of the things the target will probably do is allocate a buffer big enough to hold the data being requested (via the R2T) and then put the address of this buffer into the TTT. That address will then be used to place the returned data directly in the appropriate locations, which means that the storage controller does not need to do any additional data movement. The reason this is possible is that iSCSI requires the Data-Out PDUs to reflect back to the target the TTT that was used in the R2T. (See Figure 8–3.)

It is possible that the target buffers are not in a contiguous memory location. Perhaps they are "chained" together to satisfy the complete R2T request. In that case, the TTT value, instead of being a handle that contains a pointer to a buffer, may be an indirect pointer. As such it might point to a list of buffers that together satisfy the total R2T request. Whether the TTT value points directly to the final buffer or indirectly to a list of final buffers, the target storage controller will not have to perform extra data moves. The iSCSI HBA or chip, using the TTT, will be able to place the data directly in the storage controller's main memory.

The commentary just presented is demonstrated in Figure 8–3. We see that the initiator, via a write command (not shown), lets the target know the ITT and how much data the initiator needs to send to it. The ITT can be used as a relationship token to find information and state about the command. Along with related information, it can be used and queued on both

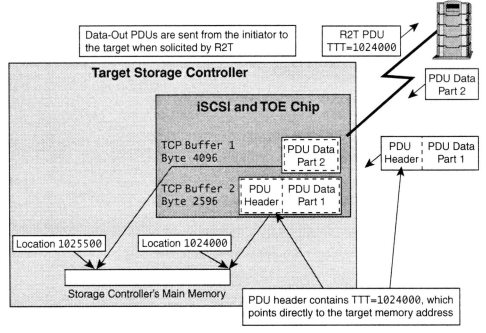

Figure 8–3  Direct target memory placement.

the initiator and the target. The target assigns a TTT when it solicits the needed data (via an R2T), and that TTT is reflected back to it when the initiator sends the data (via Data-Out PDUs). The target HBA can set the value of the TTT as a direct or indirect pointer to the storage controller's main memory. It places the data there directly without additional main memory moves. In this example, the TTT is assumed to be a direct pointer to the storage controller's main memory. This eliminates the extra data moves in the target, which are common with TCP/IP. Also in this example, as in Figure 8–2, the PDU with the data is shown split across different TCP segments, which arrive out of order. Thus, the second segment located in buffer 1 cannot be placed until the first segment located in buffer 2 arrives with the header and the TTT value.

## Data Placement (a Form of RDMA)

Because of the ITT, the iSCSI initiator can start putting the data directly in the host memory as soon as the HBA receives the TCP/IP segment containing the appropriate Data-In PDU header (with the ITT). This is true even if the subsequent TCP/IP packets arrive on the HBA out of order. What we have is a form of remote direct memory access (**RDMA**)* which I will call iSCSI RDMA.

The RDMA is not as useful as it would be if the TCP/IP packet itself contained the appropriate RDMA address. In that case you would never have to wait for the iSCSI Data-In PDU header to arrive if it is received out of order in the TCP/IP buffers. With or without TCP direct placement, data placement directly into the appropriate host buffers from the HBA is valuable for the following reasons:

- It reduces latency.

- It removes the need for the host to perform additional data movement and therefore reduces the impact on host CPU cycles.

- It greatly reduces the data-reassembly buffer memory on the HBA, or it turns these buffers into what is known as eddy buffers.

  ➢ Data reassembly buffers are used by TCP/IP to re-sort its segments into a byte-order stream.

  ➢ The eddy buffers are just holding areas, since as soon as the Data-In PDU header arrives the data can be placed in the final main memory location regardless of the order in which the Data-In TCP/IP packets were received.

There is current work going on within the IETF to create a TCP/IP feature for RDMA. However, iSCSI has direct data placement now, which works very effectively.

In order to permit the above direct data placement with the smallest possible amount of on-HBA memory (especially on the 10-Gb/s links), "markers and framing" may be useful. (See Chapter 13, Synchronization and Steering, for more information on markers and framing.)

## Chapter Summary

This chapter took the processes defined in Chapter 7 (Session Management) and extended them. Commands, command responses, and data flow were defined in much more detail, as were the specific commands that carry the needed flow control counters and expected counters, along with the process of dealing with them.

---

*Technically we are talking about direct data placement (DDP), which is a subset of RDMA.

The command sequence number (**CmdSN**) is set in all request PDUs sent from the initiator to the target, except the SNACK Request PDU. That means that the following PDUs contain the CmdSN:

- SCSI (command) Request

- Task Management Function Request

- Text Request

- Login Request

- Logout Request

- NOP-Out

The expected command sequence number (**ExpCmdSN**) value is returned on the following PDUs:

- SCSI (command) Response

- Data-In

- Request to Transfer (**R2T**)

- Asynchronous Message

- Text Response

- Login Response

- Logout Response

- Reject

- NOP-In

- Task Management Function Response

Thus, the two sides of the session can keep track of what each has received without extra interactions and acknowledgments.

The concept of "command windowing" and how it is used to control the use of memory in the iSCSI buffer pool was also explained. It was compared to the credit approach used with Fibre Channel, and it was explained when and why it is of value in the TCP/IP network.

The initiator task tag (**ITT**) was explained along with how it could be used to perform remote direct memory access (**RDMA**), that is, direct data placement (**DDP**) in the initiator's main memory without additional data movement.

Likewise, it was explained how the target transfer tag (**TTT**) performs RDMA, that is, direct data placement into the storage controller's main memory without the need for additional data movement.

The target receives data:

- In SCSI (command) Request PDUs that include immediate data.

- In unsolicited Data-Out PDUs.

- By explicitly requesting the data via R2T PDUs.

The chapter also explained the meaning and appropriate handling of the following key=value statements:

- DataSequenceInOrder: sends sets of Data-In or Data-Out sequences in memory order when set to Yes.

- DataPDUInOrder: sends Data-In or Data-Out PDUs, each in memory order, when set to Yes.

- MaxBurstLength: the maximum amount of data sent with any sequence of Data-In or Data-Out PDUs.

- MaxRecvDataSegmentLength: the maximum size of the data in a PDU, used mostly by HBAs to limit the arriving data to a size that will fit their memory buffers.

- FirstBurstLength: the maximum amount of data that can be received from the initiator without an R2T request; this is the maximum total amount of data sent in unsolicited Data-Out PDUs and data sent as immediate data in a SCSI (command) Request PDU for any specific command.

# 9

# Structure of iSCSI and Relationship to SCSI

## To the Reader

By necessity this chapter is a bit tedious; however, if you work through it, you will have a good understanding of iSCSI structures and iSCSI's relationship to SCSI concepts. Try to stay with the chapter as long as possible, then skip to the Chapter Summary. (*Note:* you will find more detail on the topics here in Appendix C.)

## iSCSI Structure and SCSI Relationship

SCSI was originally defined to be a single connection between a host and a set of storage devices (**SCSI devices**). This was extended to permit the host to connect to multiple sets of storage units (**multiple SCSI devices**), all with one or more logical units (LUs). iSCSI has stretched the normal SCSI definitions in order to cover its own operation and yet ensure that it adheres to SCSI semantics. The following sections discuss the makeup of the iSCSI architecture and its relationship to SCSI architecture.

Figure 9–1 shows the **iSCSI network client and server entities**. The iSCSI client is the OS that resides in a host computer; the iSCSI server is a storage controller of some type. Within the iSCSI client network entity is the **iSCSI initiator node**. In almost all configurations the iSCSI client network entity and the iSCSI initiator node have a one-to-one relationship, but this is not the case on the server side, where the iSCSI server network entity may often have more than one iSCSI target node (see Figures 9–2 and 9–3). It should be pointed out that the iSCSI target node has a one-to-one relationship to a SCSI device, which is usually made up of more than one LU. In Figure 9–1, the **iSCSI (SCSI) initiator port** has a one-to-one relationship with the iSCSI initiator node, although this is not always the case, as will be seen later.

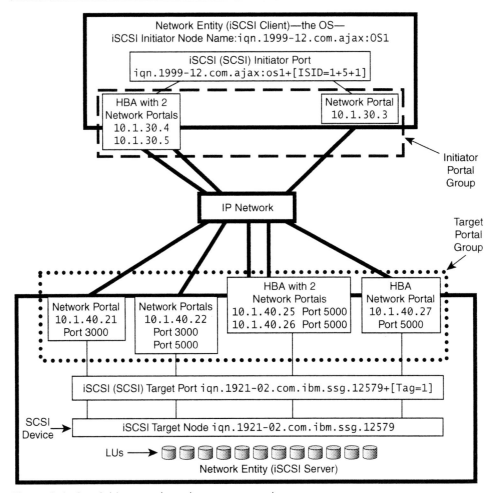

Figure 9–1  One initiator node and one target node.

As mentioned in Chapter 7, iSCSI has *not* defined anything known as an iSCSI initiator port or target port, but it has defined a SCSI initiator port and a SCSI target port (note the missing "i"). I find that somewhat restrictive, however, so in this book there will be a one-to-one relationship between an iSCSI initiator/target port and a SCSI initiator/target port. As I said previously, when I speak of them, I will often refer to them as "iSCSI (SCSI) ports" of type initiator or target. The word *port* has multiple meanings in combining SCSI and networking, so we need to watch carefully how it is used and in what context.

The IP network and connections will map to what SCSI calls its **Service Delivery Subsystem**. The network itself as well as the network interface cards (NICs), or HBAs, are part of that subsystem. The network interface has connections known by their **IP addresses and TCP ports.** *iSCSI calls such a connection point a portal.* The **iSCSI portal** connects to an **iSCSI (SCSI) port** (which is also what SCSI calls its service delivery port). The iSCSI (SCSI) port is where the various network portals come together and are treated as a single SCSI connection. This grouping of iSCSI portals is defined by iSCSI to be a portal group. A portal group can be located in either the iSCSI client network entity or the iSCSI server network entity. However, only the target portal groups are given a special identification, a target portal group tag (TPGT). This tag is a number between 1 and 64K that is unique to each iSCSI target node.

The **target SCSI port** delivers the commands to the LU in the order the **initiator SCSI port** sent them. In normal SCSI bus environments, this is straightforward. In iSCSI environments, however, it is more complicated. When the iSCSI (SCSI) initiator port sends its commands through multiple connections (often on different NICs), the commands may make their way through the network on independent paths and may arrive at the **iSCSI (SCSI) target port** in an order different from how they were sent. It is the job of the iSCSI delivery subsystem to ensure that the commands are delivered for SCSI processing as though they were sent on a single link. Therefore, the endpoints of the iSCSI delivery subsystem are considered to be the SCSI ports.

The **iSCSI target node** can be considered the SCSI device since both entities contain the LUs. As shown in Figure 9–1, the **iSCSI server network entity** contains only one iSCSI target node (or SCSI device); however, it may contain more than one, as we will see later.

Now let's go back and define how instances of each of the objects described above are given names.

In Chapter 4's Naming and Addressing section, we saw how to create a name for an iSCSI initiator or target node (via either the iqn or eui name). The iSCSI initiator node name almost always represents the total iSCSI client network entity (or OS), but, as will be seen later, there can be multiple iSCSI (SCSI) initiator ports, so it is important to create distinguishing names for them. Concatenating the iSCSI initiator node name with an additional identification of some type creates an iSCSI (SCSI) initiator port name. The additional identification is a value we call the ISID (initiator session ID), which is made up of a type flag followed by a vendor's coded ID and a qualifier. (Refer to Chapter 7 for details.) In this way, the various HBA vendors can manage the creation of their ISIDs independent of other vendors that might also have an adapter in the same initiator node. The iSCSI (SCSI) initiator port now has a complete name that is unique in the world, made up of the iSCSI initiator node name concatenated to a vendor-created ISID. In

Figure 9–1, the iSCSI initiator node name was `iqn.1999-12.com.ajax:os1`, concatenated with the ISID. The ISID was made up of a vendor ID type code of 1 plus the actual enterprise number of the vendor, which is 5 plus a qualifier of 1. Thus, the iSCSI (SCSI) initiator port name is `iqn.1999-12.com.ajax:os1+[1+5+1]`.

*Note:* The iSCSI (SCSI) initiator port name is actually made up of the iSCSI initiator node name concatenated with ",i," and the hexadecimal representation of the ISID. We will not show the ",i," or the hex in this chapter.

Figure 9–1 shows three initiator network interfaces, each with a TCP/IP address (`10.1.30.3`, `10.1.30.4`, or `10.1.30.5`). Notice that the **TCP/IP port** numbers are not shown, since the initiator does not listen for the establishment of a connection so there is no reason to advertise its port. SCSI requires that the initiator always be the entity that originates the contact to the target, so only the target's TCP/IP port needs to be identified and advertised.

In the figure we can also see five network interfaces on the target side with IP addresses of `10.1.40.21`, `10.1.40.22`, `10.1.40.25`, `10.1.40.26`, and `10.1.40.27`. Two different TCP/IP port numbers are specified as connection establishment IP network ports, on which the targets listen for a connection request. These are TCP/IP ports 3000 and 5000. The NIC that contains the IP address of `10.1.40.22` has both IP port numbers, meaning that it could have connections from initiators at either or both TCP/IP ports.

The iSCSI (SCSI) target port name can also be formed by beginning with the iSCSI target node name and concatenating the TPGT, making the iSCSI (SCSI) target port unique within the iSCSI server network entity (as well as within the world). In Figure 9–1 the iSCSI (SCSI) target port name has a TPGT of 1, so the resulting name is `iqn.1921-02.com.ibm.ssg.12579+[1]`.

*Note:* The iSCSI (SCSI) target port name is actually made up of the iSCSI target node name concatenated with the ",t," and the hexadecimal representation of the TPGT. We will not show the ",t," or the hex in this chapter.

Figure 9–2 is a bit more complicated. The iSCSI client network entity is the same as in Figure 9–1; however, the iSCSI server network entity is significantly changed. In this depiction, we see two iSCSI target nodes: `eui.02004567A425678A` (designated as node A) and `iqn.1921-02.com.ibm.ssg:12579` (designated as node B). It also depicts three iSCSI (SCSI) target ports and three target portal groups. They are designated as node A's portal groups 1 and 2 and node B's portal group 1.

Figure 9–2 also shows two NICs and two iSCSI HBAs. NIC 1 has one IP address and two TCP/IP ports (3000 and 5000); NIC 2 has only one TCP/IP port (3000) and one IP address.

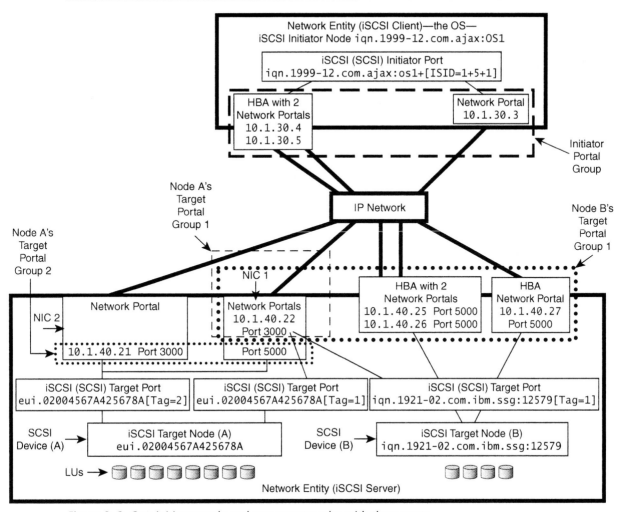

Figure 9–2  One initiator node and two target nodes with three ports.

NIC 1 TCP/IP port 3000 can access either node B, as part of B's portal group 1, or node A, as part of A's portal group 1. NIC 1 TCP/IP port 5000 can access node A, as part of A's portal group 2. This same group is shared by NIC 2.

In Figure 9–2, notice the one-to-one correspondence between iSCSI (SCSI) target ports and portal groups. That means that the port names can be made unique in the iSCSI server network entity (as well as within the world) by concatenating the iSCSI target node name with the TPGT (the same way it was done in Figure 9–1. Therefore, the names of the three iSCSI (SCSI) target ports are

- `eui.02004567A425678A+[1]`

- `eui.02004567A425678A+[2]`

- `iqn.1921-02.com.ibm.ssg:12579+[1]`

The iSCSI (SCSI) target port is the terminus for a session that starts in the iSCSI (SCSI) initiator port. The iSCSI target node (which is also known as a SCSI device) is the owner of the LUs; thus, the target port operates through the iSCSI target node to access the appropriate LUs.

Figure 9–2 depicts two HBAs, one with two portals (TCP/IP connections) and with only one. All three of these portals, along with the portal (TCP/IP port 5000) in NIC 1, make up B's target portal group 1.

Now let's move to Figure 9–3 where you should notice that the iSCSI server network entity remains as shown in Figure 9–2; however, the iSCSI client network entity is different. The iSCSI initiator node has two unique iSCSI (SCSI) initiator ports, labeled `iqn.1999-12.com.ajax:os1+[1+3+1]` and `iqn.1999-12.com.ajax:os1+[1+5+1]`. Either can contact the iSCSI target nodes via the appropriate portals.

The problems with this type of configuration are that both iSCSI (SCSI) initiator ports can address the same LUs, and the arrival of the application I/O (SCSI commands) needs to be coordinated in some manner, since command ordering is usually important to the various host applications. On the other hand, SCSI's persistent reserves can be used to prevent one iSCSI (SCSI) initiator port from accessing the LUs accessed by the other, but that too needs to be carefully coordinated.

To handle a problem like this in Fibre Channel, vendors often devised software known in the industry as a wedge driver. Usually wedge drivers were vendor specific, which could be problematic in a multiple target vendor environment. It should be noted that wedge drivers are *not* covered by any SCSI standard, and their function and capabilities are completely at their vendor's discretion. One of the reasons that the multiple connections per session (MC/S) function was put in the iSCSI specification was to prevent iSCSI from requiring wedge drivers.

Figure 9–3 shows the case where two different iSCSI (SCSI) initiator ports exist in one iSCSI initiator node, which points out that the target's "access controls" only have to be applied to the initiator node name and does not need to be applied to the individual port names. This capability saves a lot of administrative work when it comes to instructing the targets about which connections can be accepted. This is a significant reduction in administrative

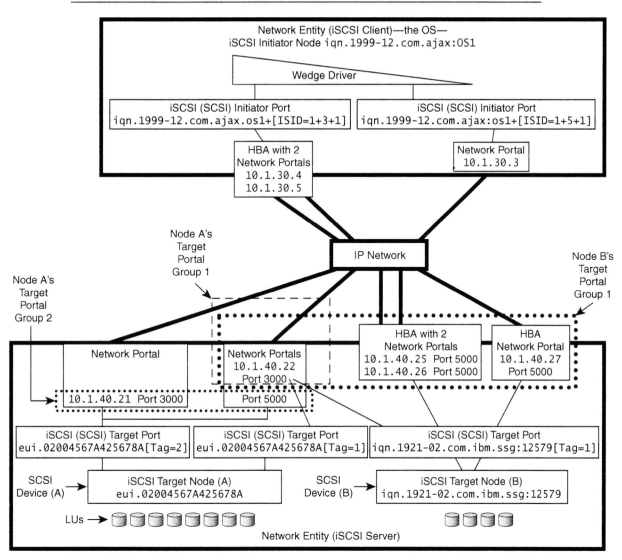

Figure 9–3 One initiator node with two ports and two target nodes with three ports.

effort from having to assign access rights to individual host adapters, as is the case with Fibre Channel.

If different users use the same host physical hardware and boot different operating systems, each OS image should have its own iSCSI initiator node name (perhaps concatenating the user ID to a generic iqn iSCSI initiator node name). Access controls should then be assigned to each resultant node name.

*Note:* Another consideration here is the access controls to hosts that operate multiple "virtual machines." Such systems should probably give a unique iSCSI initiator node name to each virtual machine, so that individual machines can have their own access controls.

In each of the three configurations (Figures 9–1, 9–2, and 9–3), the initiator should be able to establish a discovery session to any of the portals in the iSCSI server network entity and issue the `SendTargets` command. Table 9–1 lists the information to be returned in response to `SendTargets` for each of the configurations shown in the figures.

The `SendTargets` command will list all the iSCSI target node names that it knows about (or is authorized to show), as well as the portal addresses (TCP/IP[port]) that can be used to reach those nodes. (The TCP/IP port may not be shown if the default port* is used.) The TPGTs are included so that the initiator can tell what portals can be used as part of a multiple-connection session. Under any specific iSCSI target node name is a list of portal addresses that can be used to access the named node. If the initiator wants to start a multiple-connection session with that node, it uses the portal address with the same TPGT.

Notice that two different portal groups can connect to target node eui. 02004567A25678A (TPGT 1 and TPGT 2). Also notice that for Figures 9–2

---

**TABLE 9–1** SendTargets **RESPONSES FROM CONFIGURATIONS SHOWN IN FIGURES 9–1, 9–2, AND 9–3**

| **Figure 9–1** | **Figures 9–2 and 9–3** |
|---|---|
| **iqn.1921-02.com.ibm.ssg:12579** | **iqn.1921-02.com.ibm.ssg:12579** |
| 10.1.40.25[5000],1 | 10.1.40.25[5000],1 |
| 10.1.40.26[5000],1 | 10.1.40.26[5000],1 |
| 10.1.40.27[5000],1 | 10.1.40.27[5000],1 |
| 10.1.40.21[3000],1 | 10.1.40.22[3000],1 |
| 10.1.40.22[5000],1 | **eui.02004567A425678A** |
| 10.1.40.22[3000],1 | 10.1.40.21[3000],2 |
| | 10.1.40.22[5000],2 |
| | 10.1.40.22[3000],1 |

---

*iSCSI currently has a well-known port of 3260, but IANA will assign a "system" port number and that will be the default.

and 9–3 the `SendTargets` output shows the portal with the TCP/IP address of `10.1.40.22[3000]` can contact both target nodes A and B. These nodes happen to have the same TPGT, but that is a coincidence. The tag is only unique within the scope of an iSCSI target node.

## SCSI Nexus

An important thing to note when attempting to map SCSI concepts to an iSCSI environment is the concept of a SCSI nexus (relationship link). The key nexus we are talking about here is that between a SCSI initiator port and a SCSI target port (and sometimes an LU). This is called the **SCSI I-T nexus**; when an LU is involved, it is called the **SCSI I-T-L nexus**. The iSCSI I-T nexus is the same relationship link. Table 9–2 shows the SCSI I-T nexus involved in the configurations in Figures 9–1, 9–2, and 9–3.

The reason we bother with this is that SCSI defines the behavior within an I-T nexus but has no definition of behavior between I-T nexus. iSCSI takes this even further by defining two or more identical nexus to be an illegal configuration.

We may have MC/S between two iSCSI (SCSI) ports (initiator and target), but not two or more sessions between the same iSCSI (SCSI) port pairs.

The reason the configuration in Figure 9–3 is legal is that the initiator side is anchored in two *different* iSCSI (SCSI) initiator ports. Yes, they are both located in the same iSCSI client network entity and share the same iSCSI initiator node name, but they are *different* ends of SCSI I-T nexus. The operation of the wedge driver shown is not defined by SCSI, but most implementations attempt to make the different SCSI ports work in a coordinated manner. As one might imagine, this is a very tricky proposition.

SCSI defines the requirement that commands be delivered to the SCSI target port across an I-T nexus (i.e., an iSCSI session) in the same order in which they were given to the SCSI initiator port. However, the wedge driver is not defined to SCSI and it is not normal to have one on the target side, making the task of keeping things in order for delivery to the SCSI target port difficult.

However, the SCSI definitions are a bit vague on the in-order delivery statements, giving rise to the interpretation that they only apply to the I-T-L nexus. That interpretation gives the wedge drivers a method to ensure that the commands for a specific LU are outstanding only on a single I-T nexus (session) at a time. (This approach is much less efficient than iSCSI's MC/S, but for the most part it seems to work.)

If the wedge driver attempts any path balancing between the two sessions (I-T nexus) by placing LU traffic on the first available path, the design becomes

**TABLE 9–2  SCSI PERSISTENT RESERVE NEXUS FOR CONFIGURATIONS SHOWN IN FIGURES 9–1, 9–2, AND 9–3**

| Figure 9–1 | Figure 9–2 | Figure 9–3 |
| --- | --- | --- |
| iqn.1999-12.com.ajax: os1+[1+5+1] and iqn.1921-02.com.ibm. ssg.12579+[1] | iqn.1999-12.com.ajax: os1+[1+5+1] and iqn.1921-02.com.ibm. ssg.12579+[1] | iqn.1999-12.com.ajax: os1+[1+3+1] and iqn.1921-02.com.ibm. ssg.12579+[1] |
| | iqn.1999-12.com.ajax: os1+[1+5+1] and eui.02004567A425678A +[1] | iqn.1999-12.com.ajax: os1+[1+5+1] and iqn.1921-02.com.ibm. ssg.12579+[1] |
| | iqn.1999-12.com.ajax: os1+[1+5+1] and eui.02004567A425678A +[2] | iqn.1999-12.com.ajax: os1+[1+3+1] and eui.02004567A425678A +[1] |
| | | iqn.1999-12.com.ajax: os1+[1+5+1] and eui.02004567A425678A +[2] |
| | | iqn.1999-12.com.ajax: os1+[1+3+1] and eui.02004567A425678A +[2] |
| | | iqn.1999-12.com.ajax: os1+[1+5+1] and eui.02004567A425678A +[1] |

very sophisticated, especially when it is required that the wedge drivers also handle the SCSI concept of reserves (especially persistent reserves).

SCSI reserves permit access to a specific LU only via a specific I-T nexus. Persistent reserves permit reservations to last even across a restart of SCSI I-T nexus (such as a host reboot). That requires the wedge driver to know how to interpret SCSI reserves and then to ensure that the LU access is constrained to the appropriate session even across boots. This complexity is not a problem with iSCSI's MC/S since it has components in both the initiator and target that work together to permit multiple connections to operate as if they were one. Wedge drivers, on the other hand, operate with code that is only on the initiator side, thus making the job harder and less efficient. Though building a wedge driver is a sophisticated project and is usually vendor specific, this is the way multiple FC connections/sessions are handled.

You should understand by this point that the iSCSI capability of MC/S greatly simplifies multiple connection problems for the host (initiator) side of the connection.

 ## Chapter Summary

The configurations in Figures 9–1 through 9–3 show how the iSCSI naming conventions map to the various iSCSI entities and how those entities map to SCSI concepts and standards.

- Both the iSCSI client network entity and the iSCSI server network entity contain iSCSI nodes.

- The iSCSI nodes contain one or more iSCSI (SCSI) ports.

- The iSCSI (SCSI) ports connect to portal groups.

- The portal groups connect to the remote entity via the IP network.

- The iSCSI (SCSI) initiator port is identified by the iSCSI initiator node name concatenated with the ISID.

- The ISID is composed of the vendor code type, the vendor code, and a unique qualifier provided by the vendor's software or HBA.

- The iSCSI (SCSI) target port is identified by the iSCSI target node name concatenated with the appropriate target portal group tag (TPGT).

- Since the iSCSI initiator node name is usually common to all iSCSI (SCSI) initiators within an OS, it is appropriate to use the iSCSI initiator node name (`InitiatorName`) as the identifiable name in the access control process.

  ➢ This permits a significant reduction in administrative work by not requiring the access controls to be applied at anything lower than the iSCSI client network entity (i.e., the OS).

  ➢ If multiple OSs can be loaded (at different times) into the same physical machine, a user or application ID approach may be necessary. The user or application ID might be added to the end of the iqn initiator name.

➤ Virtual machine (**VM**) systems should probably give each VM its own iSCSI initiator node name (perhaps with a user or application ID concatinated to the base system name) so that they can each have their own access controls.

■ The constructs just given fit into the SCSI concept of a nexus:

➤ The I-T (initator-target) nexus

➤ The I-T-L (initator-target-LU) nexus

■ The iSCSI concept of MC/S is more efficient than the FC concept of a wedge driver.

■ MC/S tends to make the OS initiator-side software more straight-forward than is possible in Fibre Channel.

# 10 | Task Management

## To the Reader

This is another very technical chapter, so again, if you only want an overview, just skip to the Chapter Summary.

Task is another key concept within SCSI. A **task** is a command or set of commands that may or may not be linked via a "link" bit in the command description block (CDB).

## Tagged and Untagged Tasks

Each task is classified as "tagged" or "untagged." The SCSI initiator will allow only one untagged SCSI task to be outstanding/in process/in flight for any specific LU, but it will allow many tagged tasks to be outstanding/in process/ in flight. The individual tagged commands, or the first one in a linked chain of tagged commands, can have attributes that describe the type of queuing order they follow:

- Simple

- Ordered

- Head of queue

- Auto contingent allegiance (**ACA**)

Untagged tasks are always treated as requiring simple queuing.

A detailed explanation of the queuing order can be found in [SAM-2]. We will not discuss it here since it is a SCSI item that does not directly affect iSCSI processing; iSCSI is only required to carry the requested queuing attribute within its SCSI command PDU.

In iSCSI all commands have an initiator task tag (ITT), which can be used as the SCSI task tag, but in iSCSI even the so-called untagged tasks are given an ITT. Thus, the only way to understand what was intended to be an untagged task is through the iSCSI attribute field in the SCSI command PDU. If the PDU has none of the above attributes specified (a value of 0 in the attribute field), the task may be untagged, which simply means, on the SCSI target side, that it is treated with the simple queuing method. Other than that, there is no special treatment performed by the iSCSI target.

Note that the initiator is supposed to control the untagged tasks so that no more than one untagged task per LU is sent to the target at the same time. This requires that the untagged tasks be queued in the SCSI initiator. In contrast, tagged tasks are sent by the initiator as soon as it can do so. All execution queuing for tagged tasks is done at the target SCSI layer. In general, the iSCSI target is required to send tagged and untagged tasks to the target SCSI layer as soon as it can ensure in-order delivery. Some queuing in the iSCSI layer may occur, but that is the same for all nonimmediate commands. All this means is that, at the target, there is no iSCSI difference in the handling of tagged and untagged tasks. Nor does iSCSI do anything special based on the task attributes.

Linked commands are considered part of a single task, which is permitted to have only one command outstanding at a time. However, in this case the completion of any of the commands within the linked task with "good status" will have the status of "intermediate" or "intermediate condition met" returned by the target SCSI layer. When delivered by iSCSI to the initiator SCSI layer, that status triggers the next command in the linked task to be sent to the target by the initiator SCSI layer. This continues until the last command in the chain is completed or until a command in the chain returns "bad status."

Thus, the following points apply:

- Tasks are single or linked commands (linked flag in the CDB).

- SCSI initiator upper layer protocols (**ULPs**) control the submission of each of the linked commands for execution.

- The status of "intermediate" or "intermediate condition met" will be returned to the SCSI initiator; the ULP then issues the next command in the link chain.

- Tasks have a classification of "tagged" or "untagged."

- The SCSI initiator, *not* the SCSI target, is the primary controller of queuing for untagged tasks. *Note:* SCSI not iSCSI initiator controls the queuing of untagged tasks.

- The SCSI target controls the queuing of tagged tasks according to their attribute field (simple, ordered, head of queue, and ACA).

- The task attributes are carried by iSCSI in the SCSI command PDU, but they have no effect on iSCSI operation.

- The target SCSI layer applies the attribute field to the process of task queuing in the LU's task set.

- iSCSI initiators and targets treat tagged and untagged tasks the same.

- Only the SCSI layer treats tagged and untagged tasks differently.

Both iSCSI and SCSI have a set of task management functions, invoked via the iSCSI Task Management Request PDU. These functions provide the initiator with the ability to control the execution of one or more tasks (SCSI or iSCSI). Generally, "control" means the control to abort the action of specific tasks or groups of tasks. However, iSCSI has the capability to reestablish a task's connection allegiance to a different connection.

The Task Management Request PDU has a field called the referenced task tag (**RTT**). This is an ITT that can be used to identify the task to be affected by a task management function.

As you can probably understand, the iSCSI layer can identify a task by referencing the ITT of the subject command. What I have not stated, up to now, is that, when the iSCSI target layer hands off the command to the SCSI target layer, it also needs to pass a "task tag" identifier. This identifier can be anything, but the implementation is easier if it is the iSCSI ITT sent with the iSCSI command PDU. If the ITT is used, the iSCSI and SCSI task management service can easily identify the appropriate SCSI task and correctly apply the requested task management function.

It should also be noted that task management commands are often marked as "immediate" and so need to be immediately *considered* for execution as soon as the target receives them. (It is possible that the operations involved—all or part of them—may be postponed to allow the target to receive all relevant tasks.) Also, as with all commands marked as immediate, the CmdSN is *not* advanced.

The following paragraphs describe the functions that can be invoked by the task management PDU.

1. *Abort Task.* A specific task, identified by the reference task tag, needs to be aborted. When possible, SCSI actually aborts the task by stopping its execution. When not possible, the LU's normal processing returns the appropriate status to iSCSI. The previously established conditions, such as reservations and mode select parameters (parameters that apply to the operation of the specific LU; see [SPC-3] and [SAM-2]), are not changed.

   Both the iSCSI layer and the SCSI layer must work together to prevent any command covered by the abort but not yet executed from being executed. Any command to be aborted but not yet delivered to the SCSI target layer must be silently discarded and not executed by iSCSI. However, the task management response "function complete" does need to be sent to the iSCSI initiator. If the command to be aborted has already been delivered by iSCSI to the target SCSI layer, then this abort will just be passed to the target SCSI layer and SCSI will handle the abort. There will be a normal response to the command's execution with either good or bad error status, depending on whether the task completed or aborted in the SCSI layer.

   At the completion of the action, iSCSI will return the appropriate response to the iSCSI initiator via the Task Management Function Response PDU. Note that this is in addition to any SCSI (command) Response PDUs that might have been returned to the initiator. The initiator should continue to respond to all target R2Ts as normal, except that the Data-Out PDUs should be ended with the "final" flag set and without any data being sent.

2. *Abort Task Set.* This causes an Abort Task for every task associated with the session—on which this command is issued—for the LU that corresponds to the specified LUN. This is a multiple application of 1, Abort Task. No previously established conditions, such as reservation, will be changed by this action.

3. *Clear ACA.* This clears the auto contingent allegiance (**ACA**) condition for the LU specified by the LUN (not discussed in this book; see [SPC-3]).

4. *Clear Task Set.* This aborts all tasks from all initiators for the LU specified by the LUN. It performs like 2, Abort Task Set, but

additionally may throw an abort "over the fence" to the SCSI processes handling other sessions, causing the abort of every task in the LU's SCSI task set regardless of the session on which the tasks arrived. (The targets' mode page will determine the SCSI LU target reaction, which is not covered here.)

Even though the session on which this command is sent will silently discard all tasks in the iSCSI queue and subject to the clear, this is not the case for other sessions. The only effect on them is the abort of the tasks already in the SCSI task set (the queue of commands within SCSI but not yet executed). For these sessions, there will be no silent discard of commands that might still be in the iSCSI layer. In addition, all sessions, except the one on which the Clear Task Set management function PDU arrived, will have their aborted commands reflected back to their initiators with one or more unit attentions (see [SAM-2]). As stated regarding 1, Abort Task, the session on which the clear task set arrived will have its undelivered, aborted tasks silently discarded by iSCSI.

5. *Logical Unit Reset.* SCSI will abort all tasks in its task set, which means that a 4, Clear Task Set, will occur as explained above, that it will clear the ACA if it exists and reset all reserves established via the reserve/release method. However, persistent reservations are not affected. The LU operating mode is reset to its appropriate initial conditions, and the mode select parameters (parameters that apply to the operation of the specific LU; see [SPC-3]) will be reset either to their last saved values or to their default values. This may cause a unit attention condition to all other sessions using the LU (different from the one on which the Logical Unit Reset was issued). (The target SCSI action is defined by a mode page setting, which is not covered here.)

6. *Target Warm Reset.* This resets all LUs in the target device (iSCSI target node) and aborts all tasks in all task sets. In effect, it performs an LU reset (as explained in 5, Logical Unit Reset) for all LUs owned by the iSCSI target node.

7. *Target Cold Reset.* This performs all the functions of 6, Target Warm Reset, plus termination of all TCP/IP connections to all initiators. In other words, all sessions to the iSCSI target node are terminated and all connections are dropped.

8. *Task Reassign.* This reassigns connection allegiance for the task identified by the ITT field to this connection (the connection on

which the Task Reassign Task Management Request PDU arrived), thus resuming the iSCSI exchanges for the task. The target must receive the task reassign only after the connection used by the original task has been logged out.

Clearly the term "task management" has a positive sound; however, it is really a form of clearing up a disappointing situation. The Abort Task can be used to stop a specific task, but all of the other functions are a bit of a dull knife that will affect many I/O tasks beyond those of a simple application's failure. The higher the function number (up to and including 7), the more drastic the action and the more widespread the effect. Target vendors should consider an authorization permission list to ensure that none of those commands are issued by accident or by people who want to inflict damage.

## Chapter Summary

This chapter explained how a task is defined to SCSI and iSCSI and the appropriate queuing techniques for each task type. It also explained the various iSCSI or SCSI commands that need to be operated upon immediately. Some of the commands that need immediate operation status will reset or abort either iSCSI or SCSI status or actions.

Key commands that are part of task management include the following:

- Abort Task
- Abort Task Set
- Clear ACA
- Clear Task Set
- Logical Unit Reset
- Target Warm Reset
- Target Code Reset
- Task Reassign

These are powerful and very disruptive to iSCSI and SCSI processes. For that reason, they should not be used except in extreme emergencies.

# 11 Error Handling

ERROR HANDLING AND RECOVERY are two of the more difficult processes to understand. A quick overview follows.

## To the Reader

This chapter will now go into error recovery in some depth. If you do not need this much information, skip forward to the Chapter Summary, as usual.

There are three general classes of detected errors:

- *Protocol error.* As its name implies, this is generally a program error and requires restarting the session and error recovery by the SCSI layer.

- *CRC detected error.* This error could have been detected on the PDU header or data segment. It can be recovered by resending the data or response PDU or by reissuing the command PDU, depending on what was missing. Some implementations will not be able to recover from this error and will respond as for a protocol error.

- *TCP/IP or link failure.* This error can often be recovered by restarting another connection and shifting command and data allegiance to it from the failed connection. Some implementations will not be able to recover from such a failure and will respond as for a protocol error.

The session restart, which must be used on protocol errors, can be used on any of the other failures also. Because only session restart is mandatory, some implementations are likely to have only that technique. That is, all error recovery can use what is called technique 0.

## Error Recovery Levels

The three recovery techniques are classified into corresponding recovery levels by iSCSI:

- **ErrorRecoveryLevel=0**—Recovery only by session restart (also known as session failure recovery and sometimes just as session recovery)

- **ErrorRecoveryLevel=1**—Recovery by reissuing commands, data, or status (also known as CRC failure recovery)

  - ➤ Within connection recovery (commands and status resent)

  - ➤ Within command recovery (data and R2Ts resent)

- **ErrorRecoveryLevel=2**—Connection failure recovery

Implementing recovery from CRC-detected errors, though optional, prevents disruption to the application (especially if it is a tape application, which often has poor SCSI retry support.) However, this too can revert to session restart if the implementation does not want to perform the recovery effort and is content to leave it to the SCSI retry support.

The link failures, which are likely to be the most prevalent, have been addressed by iSCSI with an option to recover without SCSI or the application being aware that anything happened. This is also optional, however, and vendors can choose to revert to session recovery.

It is important to understand that iSCSI requires any implementation that supports an error recovery level greater than 0 to support the level below also. Therefore, implementations that support level 1 must be able to support level 0, and implementations that support level 2 must be able to support levels 1 and 0. This is required because the implementation at the other end of the connection may not be able to support the higher level of recovery. Following is a depiction of the error recovery level hierarchy.

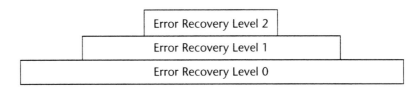

You should now be able to understand what the different recovery levels mean and their value to an installation. Therefore, if you are choosing an implementation and other features and performance are comparable, the supported recovery level may make the difference. An implementation that has an error recovery level of 2 can be expected to be the least disruptive to systems and applications. Since the error recovery level is negotiated between initiators and targets, the entire session is reduced to the level of the least-capable side.

Note that an implementation that negotiates to operate at 0 or 1 technically guarantees only that it will operate at least at that level. It is possible that for some errors the implementation might want to operate at a higher level. Here, in order to explain the processes, we will assume that the implementations operate only at whatever error level was negotiated. That said, since level 1 is intended for recovery from CRC digest errors, and since it is not always possible to find the next PDU (when a header error exists), the protocol is set up such that if error level 1 or 2 is negotiated, but a side cannot operate at that level of recovery, it is always valid to revert to a lower level of recovery, such as level 0 (session recovery).

## Error Recovery Level 0

This form of error recovery must be implemented, but hopefully will only be used when all other types fail or are inappropriate. There will be some simple iSCSI implementations that may have only this level of recovery. When an error of some sort is detected while operating at level 0, the implementation will end its processing of SCSI and iSCSI tasks. This means that all executing and queued tasks for the given initiator at the target will be aborted. This is true for the iSCSI tasks as well as the SCSI tasks. Simulated SCSI service responses also need to be returned by the initiator's iSCSI layer to its SCSI layer.

Also, all session TCP/IP connections are closed and then, once everything is cleaned up, the session may be reestablished by the initiator; and all of its connections need to log in as they did the first time.

On the target side the equivalent of the task management Abort Task function will be issued for each task known to iSCSI within the failed session (see Chapter 10). All iSCSI status is discarded, and all data for tasks in the session, whether coming or going, is discarded. For details about what SCSI-related status is reset, refer to the latest version of the [iSCSI] draft standard, the section Clearing Effects on SCSI Objects.

SCSI persistent reservations are an example of what is maintained throughout session closure and reestablishment. Only the appropriate persistent reserve commands will affect these reservations. Of course, this implies that the initiator node name, the ISID (initiator session ID), the target node name, and the TPGT (target portal group tag) remain the same across the session restart, because the persistent reserve is associated with the I-T-L nexus. The I-T part is described by the iSCSI (SCSI) initiator port (identified by the initiator node name plus ISID) at one end and the iSCSI (SCSI) target port (identified by the target node name plus TPGT) at the other.

As a rule, the initiator makes the determination that the session is to be torn down and rebuilt. It signals this with a logout PDU (in case of extreme confusion, the initiator may just drop the session). After the target receives the logout request PDU, all Task Aborts have been completed, and the cleanup is finished, the target will return a Logout Response PDU with a status of zero. Then it will drop all the TCP/IP connections that make up the session and clean up its state.

The initiator, after receiving the Logout Response PDU, will drop all its TCP/IP connections that make up the session and return pseudo task status to the SCSI layer for each outstanding task, indicating an appropriate error code. The iSCSI initiator will then perform task cleanup, disposing of all data and status regarding all tasks it may have had.

Upon the return of pseudo task status to the SCSI layer, the iSCSI initiator may start reestablishing the session, perhaps with all the same connections it had when it was first established. It may also start more connections or fewer.

If the initiator simply dropped the connection, without a logout, it should wait the default length of time specified by the **DefaultTime2Wait** (key-value pair), which permits the target to clean up its state and the initiator to return the pseudo task statuses to the initiator SCSI layer. After the DefaultTime2Wait, it may log back in and reestablish the session.

There is one other technique for terminating and reestablishing a session. This can be done with a new connection login that contains a zero TSIH and the ISID of the session to be restarted (and is from the same initiator node name and is to the same target node name and target portal group). In this case, all active tasks are terminated in the target and the initiator returns pseudo task status to the initiator SCSI layer for each outstanding task, indicating an appropriate error code.

## Error Recovery Level 1

Like level 0, this level of recovery can accomplish session recovery, but it can also recover from most CRC-detected errors. Error recovery level 1 is based on the following approaches:

- If a header digest error occurs, the PDU may be silently thrown away, and the "normal" (level-**1**) error recovery will realize that it is missing because of a "hole" in a sequence of one of the tracked sequence numbers.

- If a data digest error occurs, it can be handled at the point of detection by

  > The initiator responding with a SNACK (selective negative acknowledgment) PDU.

  > The target responding with a Reject PDU followed by an R2T (ready to transmit) PDU.

  > Either the target or the initiator silently throwing the PDU away and handling it later as if it had been a header digest error.

Two general principles should be understood as we go through the various error recovery processes for level **1** and above:

- Targets should not retransmit status or data except on a request made by the initiator via a **status SNACK** or a **data SNACK**.

- Targets can retransmit R2Ts when they think doing so is necessary. These are called recovery R2Ts.

  We will first look at techniques for recovering from header digest errors.

## Header Digest Recovery at the Initiator Side

A disclaimer is appropriate here. Unless the initiator and target are operating with some form of synchronization and steering, such as FIM (see Chapter 13), there is no absolute guarantee that in a header CRC error the boundaries of the PDU can be absolutely determined. You cannot always determine the length of the PDU because the CRC error could have been within the **Total-AHSLength** field. Therefore, it will be difficult to silently discard the PDU in all situations, and the implementation will have to restart either the session or the connection.

*Note:* This section should be read as if the initiator and the target have implemented the FIM support and agreed to use it. This means that they can absolutely identify some valid PDU boundaries. In real life, it is expected that many vendors will apply their own "secret sauce" (if FIM is not used) that usually permits them to find a valid PDU boundary even if the PDU header has a CRC error.

In error recovery level **1**, if the initiator is able to detect that one of its command/request PDUs is missing, it will attempt to recover it with the techniques described below. (These recoverable PDUs are all the nonimmediate PDUs that the initiator can send except Data-Out, NOP-Out, and SNACK.) The initiator detects missing PDUs by inspecting those returned from the target to see if the target's ExpCmdSN (expected command sequence number) is in sync with what the initiator sent. It can do this because each of the pertinent PDUs carries a CmdSN (command sequence number) and each side keeps a value of what it thinks the next CmdSN (the ExpCmdSN) should be. When the target sends back a value that the initiator thinks is too small, the initiator understands that the PDU—with the CmdSN equal to the returned ExpCmdSN value—may have been lost and therefore needs to be resent.

The initiator then attempts to correct the problem by resending the missing PDU. Because there may be a "race" condition in which the PDU arrives while the initiator is resending the replacement, the target is required to discard any duplicate PDUs that it receives. The key to this type of detection and recovery is that the initiator not be too quick to resend what it thinks is a missing command/request PDU. The full-duplex nature of a TCP/IP connection and the different paths a message can take through the network may make it look as though some commands are lost, when in fact their arrival has not been acknowledged yet. Given some time they may well be acknowledged. In any case the discard mentioned above will prevent any inappropriate action by the target.

Any missing Data-Out PDUs, though sent by the initiator, will be detected as missing by the target, which will determine either that the appropriate amount of data has not yet been received (and it thinks it should have) or that there is a missing DataSN (data sequence number) in a sequence of Data-Out PDUs. In either case, the target will issue an R2T PDU and explicitly request the missing data.

The initiator handles missing SNACK PDUs simply by waiting for a period of time to see if it receives the requested R2T, data, status, or other exception event (which, among other things, might cause the session or connection to terminate). If none of those responses occur within an implementation-determined time, the SNACK PDU can be reissued by the initiator.

The target may also complete the command and send final status while the initiator is waiting for a missing Data-In PDU. If this happens, the initiator will have received the final response PDU for the command. However, knowing it has not received the Data-In PDU, it should send the SNACK requesting it. The initiator should not advance its ExpStatSN (expected status sequence number) until all missing Data-In PDUs have been received. This is because the target, when it receives a PDU from the initiator with the ExpStatSN advanced, will interpret that as an acknowledgment that everything is okay and clear all information about the previous command, including the data.

On the other hand, the initiator may have a timeout in its ULP (upper-level protocol), deciding that enough is enough, and then retrying the command or just giving up.

*Note:* The initiator sets CmdSN on each PDU it sends, except for Data-Out and SNACK, but ExpStatSN is sent to the target on every PDU the initiator sends. iSCSI requires ExpCmdSN and StatSN on all the PDUs that flow from the target to the initiator.

The important thing the initiator does with the StatSN is to detect missing status which it will have resent by issuing a SNACK. It can also check the DataSN and ExpDataSN to see if there is a mismatch. If so it can retrieve the missing data via SNACK as specified above. The initiator must also reflect the value of StatSN back to the target (in the ExpStatSN) to show that the status has arrived at the initiator, all data has been received, and the target can free up its buffers and state for all commands with lower StatSN.

*Recap:*

- The initiator uses CmdSN and ExpCmdSN to detect that the command is lost and then resend the command.

- The initiator uses StatSN and ExpStatSN to detect that status is lost and then request the status be resent via SNACK.

- The initiator uses DataSN and ExpDataSN to detect missing data and then request the data be resent via a SNACK.

- The initiator reflects the ExpStatSN back to the target to inform the target that the status up to that point was received along with all appropriate data.

## Header Digest Recovery at the Target Side

The target can recover from almost all header digest errors just by silently discarding the PDU and allowing the initiator to notice a discontinuance in the ExpCmdSN (expected command sequence number) and thereby cause the initiator to resend the missing PDU.

When a SCSI command PDU is discarded, for example, the target will not be able to advance its ExpCmdSN value. In that situation, each PDU sent from the target to the initiator that contains the ExpCmdSN value will indicate to the initiator that the sequence was disrupted; the initiator will then resend the missing SCSI command PDU. The same thing will occur for Text Requests, Task Management Requests, and Logout Request PDUs.

When a Data-Out PDU is discarded, the target cannot advance its DataSN value. Thus, if it receives other Data-Out PDUs that show a discontinuance in the DataSN value, it can explicitly request that missing Data-Out PDU by sending the initiator an R2T PDU.

If the target sends an R2T PDU that the initiator discards because of a header digest error, unless it is the last R2T for the command it is expected that the initiator will subsequently detect that something is missing and request that the target resend it. It can identify the actual PDU in error when it does not receive the expected value for R2TSN. At that point it will issue a SNACK to request a resend of the missing PDU.

Note that discarded PDUs with DataSN, R2TSN, and StatSN are usually quickly detected, because they are all connection allegiant and TCP/IP does not permit them to be received out of order. Therefore, if one is missing, there must have been a CRC digest error that caused it to be discarded. However, if the R2T that is missing is the last R2T for the command, the initiator will not be able to detect that it is missing. Instead the target must take overt action whenever it does not receive the expected data within a reasonable time (on the last R2T of a command). Initiators are required to discard R2Ts with duplicate R2TSNs so no RACE condition will occur regardless of when the initiator or target time-out and take action.

If a lost SNACK was a positive acknowledgment requested by the target setting the A bit in a previous Data-In PDU (see SNACK Request PDU and SCSI Data-In PDUs in Appendix A), the initiator has no way of knowing that it is missing because the initiator does not expect anything in return. The target must therefore compensate for this on its own side. The target should ignore the fact that it did not get the positive SNACK and continue its operations. The target cannot free its buffers as it wished to do, however, and so must be capable of continuing without freeing its buffers. It can respond with another Data-In PDU with the A bit set, if resources are critical, but—unless more than a **MaxBurstLength** of data was sent between the end of data in the last Data-In PDU, with the A bit set, and the end-of-data in the current Data-In PDU—it can expect the initiator to ignore the A bit.

This is probably not a significant problem with a normal disk storage controller, because most implementations use a shared buffer pool with enough total memory to last through events such as a missing SNACK (and in fact probably do not even use the Data-In PDU with the A bit set). However, for memory-limited storage devices, such as a tape drive, a missing **DataACK SNACK** may be a problem. For that reason targets like these should be designed to keep at least two to three times the value of MaxBurstLength in old, sent buffers for each outstanding I/O they support, just in case the A bit PDU is lost or ignored by the initiator.

The only time that SNACK support is *not* required is when operating at error recovery level 0. In that case the initiator may still issue a SNACK for some PDU recovery capability. However, the target implementation may only know how to operate at level 0 and therefore silently discard the SNACK, respond with a Reject PDU, or request logout via the Asynchronous Message PDU. (Anything other than discarding the SNACK is not defined by the specification, so anything might happen.) Therefore, it is probably best to stick to level 0 recovery and restart the session.

### Data Digest Recovery

The significant thing about data digest recovery is that the error condition can be signaled to the opposite side and a requested recovery action thus can take place without delay. This is because the same recovery actions are possible when a data digest error is found directly, as when its discovery is delayed until the sequence values can determine what is missing.

In the case of a data digest error, the PDU header is considered valid. Therefore, it is possible to determine directly what the problem is and request a resend of the PDU. That is, if the initiator detects the error it can issue the SNACK, requesting the Data-In PDU again. If the target detects the data digest error, it is required to issue a Reject PDU with a reason code of "Data (payload) Digest Error" and to discard the in-error PDU. Then it should either request that the data be resent via an R2T PDU or terminate the task with SCSI Response PDU with the reason "Protocol Service CRC Error" and perform the appropriate cleanup. In the latter case, it is up to the initiator to retry the command or restart the session (as it would if the error recovery level were 0).

It is possible for all digest errors to be treated as header digest errors so that the PDUs can just be discarded. That will cause a postponement in the recovery until the sequence numbers can detect the problem. Of course, to be sure that the problem is detected before the SCSI layer times out and retries the command, we need to ensure that even an error at the end of a command or data burst is addressed without delay. This requires a rule that a NOP be added to the data flow whenever there is no data or command flowing on the link for a period of time. Such a rule permits any holes in the sequence numbers to be quickly detected, even at the end of the command or data burst.

## Error Recovery Level 2

Level-2 error recovery focuses on the recovery of the connection and the session along with the tasks therein, given that there has been some type of connection problem. The initiator may detect that a TCP connection has failed, or it may have received an Asynchronous Message PDU from the target stating that one or all the connections in a session will be dropped or requesting a connection logout. Any of these messages from the target, or any of its own information, can be enough for the initiator to attempt to recover the connection.

Targets and/or initiators can recognize a failing connection by detecting a transport (TCP/IP) failure or a gap in the command/response sequence that cannot be filled, or by detecting a failing iSCSI NOP (ping), among other conditions. If the TCP/IP connection failed, initiators that support error recovery level 2 will attempt to issue the Logout Request PDU for the failed connection from another connection active within the session (if there is one). This logout request should have a reason code that states that the connection should be "removed for recovery," meaning that the target must shut down the connection and prepare all its commands for a change in allegiance.

Once that is done, the initiator either logs in a new connection to re-cover the commands from the failed connection or uses an existing connection to recover the commands. To do this it sends the target, via one or more other connections, a series of Task Management Function Request PDUs, each of which tells the target to change the allegiance of a suspended task from the old connection to the connection on which the Task Management Function Request PDU is issued. These change-of-allegiance task management functions must be done task by task until all tasks that the initiator had pending on the old connection are changed to another connection. At the completion of this process, all the targeted tasks that were once on the old connection will continue as if they had originally been issued on the new connection. (Any immediate commands, however, are not recoverable.) If a new connection is not started, it might be advisable to reinstate the suspended tasks across a number of the other connections within the session, so as to balance the workload. Since the link failure could have occurred at any point in the command processing, when the new allegiance has been established, all unacknowledged status and data will be resent by the target. If no status or data exist, the initiator may need to retry the command.

Another version of connection recovery is the implicit logout of the failed connection and the re-login of a new one. The initiator issues a login to the same portal group as the original connection, with the same initiator node name, the same ISID and TSIH (target session identifier handle), and the same CID (connection ID) of the failed connection. In this case, as in the others, task allegiance must still be reassigned using a series of Task Management Function Request PDUs.

Even if the session is made up of only one connection, the logout of the single connection, by logging in a replacement (with the same initiator node name, ISID, TSIH, and CID), can be used to reestablish the single connection session on a new connection. This implies the opening of a second connection with the sole purpose of cleaning up the first. The allegiance of the commands on the old connection, even though it has the same CID, still needs to be transferred to the new connection as soon as it is instantiated into full-feature phase.

Two of the values that can be set at login time are **DefaultTime2Wait** and **DefaultTime2Retain**. These key=values, which each have a default of two and twenty seconds, respectively, if not changed by negotiation at login, are used as follows:

- If the connection goes away unexpectedly the initiator has until the DefaultTime2Wait (in seconds) before it can attempt to reconnect. This gives the target a chance to notice that the link is gone, do what ever cleanup is needed, and prepare for a reconnection.

- After this period, the initiator has additional DefaultTime2Retain (in seconds) to reestablish connections (if desired) and the allegiance of tasks suspended by the loss of the original connection. If not accomplished by this time, the target may abort and clean up all tasks and state (except persistent reserves).

If the target realizes that a connection is disrupted in some manner, it should do one of the following:

- Send an Asynchronous Message PDU to the initiator requesting a logout for the connection

- Send an Asynchronous Message PDU to the initiator stating that it will drop the connection and then

  - Specify that the target must wait a certain amount of time before reestablishing the connection

> ➤ Specify that after the wait time the initiator has an additional amount of time to reestablish the connection and the allegiance of suspended tasks. If this is not accomplished in that time, the target aborts and cleans up all tasks and state (except persistent reserves).

As a result, a failing connection may be reestablished and work continued without the SCSI layer or application being disrupted.

It is important to understand that some tape units need to have an error recovery capability of at least **1** and preferably **2**. This is because the SCSI level of error recovery for older tapes is generally very poor, which usually causes the application to abort. For that reason, everything that can be done to prevent the SCSI layer from seeing the iSCSI transport problems is worthwhile. Note that if a re-login of an existing connection is attempted and the error recovery level is less than **2**, a connection can still be reestablished but no task reassignment to another connection will be possible.

##  Chapter Summary

In this chapter we looked at the different levels of error recovery.

**Error recovery level 0** (also known as session recovery) recovers only by session restart according to the following:

- Whenever there is a problem with the connection, the session is torn down and reestablished.

- Whenever a header segment or data segment CRC error is detected, the session is terminated and the initiator internally returns failure codes to SCSI.

- The SCSI layer should be responsible for the recovery.

**Error recovery level 1** (also known as CRC failure recovery) is made up of within-connection recovery (commands and status resent) and within-command recovery (data and R2Ts resent). It recovers by reissuing commands, data, or status according to the following:

- Whenever required, it can revert to error recovery level **0**.

- When an initiator or target receives a header digest error, it is usually able to recover the failed PDU.

- The initiator can use SNACK to request missing status PDUs, Data-In PDUs, and R2T PDUs.

- The initiator can detect missing command/request PDUs and resend them.

- The target can detect missing Data-Out PDUs and issue R2Ts to recover them.

- The target must detect missing last R2T PDUs.

- The SCSI ULP (upper-level protocol) timeout will cause iSCSI to abort the task; but the ULP may or may not know about the best retry process to follow at that time. So, completion of iSCSI recovery should be attempted before SCSI times out.

**Error recovery level 2** (also known as connection failure recovery) recovers according to the following:

- The commands from a failed connection can have their allegiance transferred from a failing connection to a nonfailing connection.

- Allegiances must be transferred one task at a time.

- TCP/IP connection failures can be recovered by starting another connection and transferring allegiances from the old connection to it.

- An implicit logout and re-login can be done keeping the same connection ID; however, allegiances must still be transferred to the new connection.

- The session does not need to be failed or restarted, but can be continued by establishing another connection and using it to clean up and recover the allegiances of the first. In this way the session can continue (on a new TCP/IP connection) even if MC/S is not supported.

- On allegiance change the target must resend all unacknowledged data and status or the initiator may need to perform command retry.

- If needed, level 2 can revert to level 0; however, its purpose is to prevent such an action.

For foolproof operation at error recovery level 1 or 2, both the initiator and the target should operate with some form of synchronization and steering, such as iSCSI-defined FIMs (see Chapter 13).

# Companion Processes

**THE COMPANION PROCESSES THAT MAKE** up the iSCSI protocol suite are:

- Boot

- Discovery

- Security

- MIB and SNMP

We will cover these lightly in this book, but I encourage you to study the appropriate IETF drafts if you need additional information.

## To the Reader

This chapter is necessary for an understanding of the set of capabilities available to support a complete iSCSI environment. It is not overly technical, but if you become overwhelmed, as always, jump to the Chapter Summary for a general overview.

## Boot Process

The boot process exploits the features of the Dynamic Host Connection Protocol (**DHCP**), the Service Location Protocol (**SLP**), or the Internet Storage Name Service (**iSNS**). DHCP is used to obtain not only an IP address for the host (if needed) but also the address of either the boot device or the server that has its name and location. Once the name and location are obtained, an iSCSI session can be established with the boot device, and the boot process can continue normally. Note that, if the LUN is not included, the boot process will assume it to be LUN 0.

It is expected that the **BIOS** (Basic Input Output Service) that is built in to the booting system will incorporate the boot process. Alternatively, the iSCSI HBA will respond like a normal SCSI HBA to the unmodified system BIOS, and the extended BIOS on the HBA will permit the iSCSI HBA to have the boot procedures built in.

Another approach to booting is permitted, in which the HBA simply acts as a normal network interface card (NIC) with built-in remote boot support. In this mode the HBA will contact the DHCP to obtain a platform IP address, a boot server IP address, and a boot file name. Then, using the appropriate Preboot Execution Environment (**PXE**) processes, the NIC will load the specified boot image into memory and allow the host to execute the loaded code. The PXE process was defined years ago and is the traditional method for booting remote systems that do not have their own hard disk. (Some environments add Boot Integrity Services [**BIS**] to gain added security.) iSCSI architects include it as an option.

In general the host can employ one of the following:

■ The normal remote PXE process, supported by current NICs and DHCP (and optionally BIS)

■ The extended BIOS, to pose as a normal SCSI HBA, and then use an IP Address:Port (and LUN) as a boot target, as any SCSI HBA does except in this case using iSCSI.

■ A combination of PXE to load an iSCSI bootstrap and iSCSI boot to perform the actual boot.

The IP Address:Port (and LUN) can be obtained from any of the following:

■ DHCP

■ SLP

■ iSNS

■ Manual configuration of the HBA

## Discovery Process

The discovery process takes advantage of four ways to discover the appropriate target storage controllers by host systems.

*Note:* In all of the following cases the initiator and target node name may be set by an administrator, or default to factory settings.

## Discovery Using Administrative Specifications

First is an administrative technique for defining the targets to the host system. This process lets the administrator specify the target node name and IP Address:Port to the system or its HBA. All vendor iSCSI HBAs should allow an administrator to do this. This type of discovery is useful in small installations where more elaborate discovery is not needed. (See Figure 12–1.)

## Discovery Using SendTargets

Another approach permits the initiator to probe its environment (perhaps via broadcast and pings) and, when a possible iSCSI target is found, to start a **discovery session** with the entity by issuing a **SendTargets** command. (See Chapter 5, the section Discovery Session.) Any iSCSI device that contains targets must support a discovery session on all its IP addresses. These targets can reply to a SendTargets command by returning a list of all the iSCSI target nodes it knows about (which could be only itself) or the list it is authorized to send to the specific initiator. It includes in its reply any grouping of TCP/IP addresses (called a portal group) that can be used interchangeably to obtain single or multiple connections to the target node in any session.

The use of environment probes such as broadcasts and pings is not defined by the iSCSI protocol, and they are only useful on a small network or

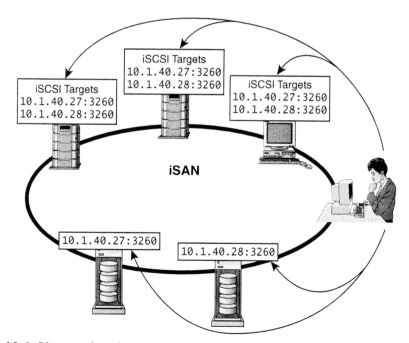

Figure 12–1 Discovery by administrator setting of IP addresses.

subnet. However, it is possible for an implementation to perform such functions in order to make the equipment acceptable in small environments.

It is also possible for the administrator to set the iSCSI addresses of all discovery targets in the initiator. Then the initiator can issue SendTargets to each of those addresses. Or the administrator can just enter a single IP address in the initiator and then set up one of the discovery targets, if permitted by the device, to contain all the other target devices' iSCSI addresses (including TPGTs [target portal group tags]). It is possible for this discovery port to contain the iSCSI addresses of targets not located within the same physical device as the discovery port.

IP storage area network (**IP SAN**) management software can support the SendTargets command while pretending to be an iSCSI discovery target. It responds with all the targets to which any specific initiator is permitted access. In this case the access control list (**ACL**) used with each real iSCSI target device should be set up to permit only the management node to establish a discovery session with it. This is an important reason why vendors should ensure that their storage controllers have ACL capability to permit (or not) the use of a discovery session by selected systems or software.

If an iSCSI storage controller is configured to permit only the storage management software to issue SendTargets, an initiator must go to the centralized IP SAN management software to get the addresses and names of all the iSCSI targets it is authorized to access. This means the initiator must establish discovery sessions with the management software and issue Send-Targets commands to get the IP addresses of all the iSCSI targets it is authorized to contact.

A management node should be able to issue a SendTargets command to all the real iSCSI targets (that it knows about) and obtain all available target names, addresses, and TPGTs. The management node may obtain the real addresses so that it can obtain all the real SendTargets information, portions of which it will selectivly give out to authorized initiators. It is expected that this management node will not report any targets as being available until the administrator assigns access rights to each initiator. Only then can the management node be used by the initiator HBAs to get their (real) target assignments.

SendTargets is a semi-automated discovery process that still requires the administrator to plug in a "discovery target" address for each storage controller, either in each initiator or in the management node. If a management node is available, the administrator may instead be required only to input into each initiator the IP address and iSCSI name of the management node. The management software can exist on any host, switch, or storage controller in the customers' IP SANs (iSAN). However, even though this approach is easier to administer than the previous techniques, it still has too much administrative work to be appropriate for larger networks.

Figure 12–2 shows the administrator setting the IP addresses in the storage controllers and the SendTargets address in the initiators. The various host systems discover the devices by logging into a discovery session on each controller and issuing a SendTargets command. Note that the iSCSI target network entities permit the login and the issuance of SendTargets only if the initiator is authorized via ACLs.

The above processes require various configurations to be created manually via administrative techniques. However, the management goal is to reduce as much as possible the manual configuration needed to control an IP SAN. Toward that end, the above suggested SendTarget, a management node (not shown in Figure 12–2) would be useful. Even then, it is still only a small improvement, and as iSCSI moves into larger networks we will need to reduce the administrative workload even more. Therefore, it would also be useful to eliminate the need for the administrator to enter any SendTargets address(es) of the discovery location(s). Likewise, it would be useful if the administrator no longer had to plug the target addresses and names into the management software. (Unfortunately, the access control list will still need administrative focus and attention.) It was to reduce the administrative work on larger networks further that the process of using SLP and iSNS discovery protocols were defined.

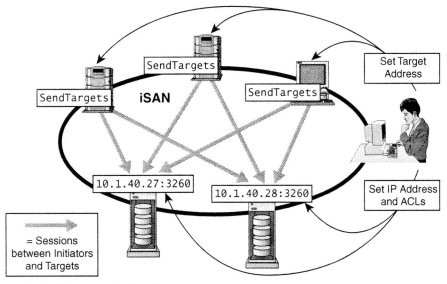

Figure 12–2 Discovery via SendTargets.

### Discovery Using the Service Location Protocol

The third discovery approach uses SLP (Service Location Protocol) to locate the iSCSI target devices. SLP operates with three elements: a user agent, a service agent, and a directory agent (see Figure 12–3).

The user agent (**UA**) works on behalf of the client (in this case the initiator) to help it establish contact with a service (in this case an iSCSI target). To do this, it retrieves service information from the service agents or directory agents.

The service agent (**SA**) works on behalf of one or more services (in this case iSCSI targets) to advertise their services and their capabilities. The directory agent (**DA**) collects service advertisements (in this case information for accessing an iSCSI target). iSCSI target advertisements are like register

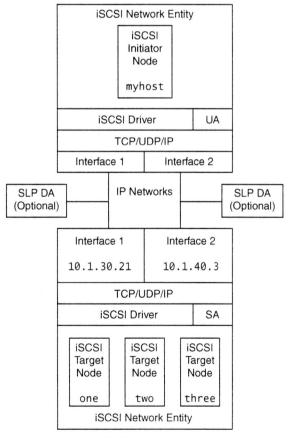

Figure 12–3  iSCSI initiator and target in SLP.

entries that are made up of the iSCSI target node name and all the URLs of the various paths to that node, along with the appropriate target portal group tag (TPGT).

The SA (iSCSI target) can either give the advertisements to the DA or keep them itself. If it keeps the advertisements, then when contacted by a UA (iSCSI initiator) it can let the UA see its advertisements directly.

If a DA is present, all the SAs will be able to give their advertisements to it. The DA can then answer the UA (iSCSI initiator) with all the installation's targets that the UA can access, and the initiator's query need go only to the single DA to get that information.

In SLP, the target SA advertises everything that is received by the initiator UA or the DA—its existence and features as well as its access list, which says which iSCSI initiator node names may access it. In that way the initiator UA can search for iSCSI targets and receive only those it is permitted to use.

This implies that there must be a method for the administrator to specify to the target which hosts can contact it. The target SA will then advertise the ACL to the DA, which will use that information in pruning the target list given to the initiator UA when it requests a list of appropriate targets.

It will also be possible for a storage management node to perform the duties of the DA and then apply direct administrator control over the configuration and access list from a central location. Or it could leave the DA intact but proxy information, such as access permissions. However, even if the storage management node proxies the permissions, it is still necessary for the iSCSI storage controller to receive that same ACL information. For this the storage management node will probably use a vendor-specific protocol or SNMP to set the ACLs. (See the section MIB and SNMP later in this chapter.)

The iSCSI target, or the storage management node, can also export the list of boot devices (IP Address:Port [and LUN]) it may contain. In this way, the boot process can be configured to use the SLP, and the administrator can assign any of the boot images to one or more initiators.

Figure 12–3 depicts the iSCSI initiator and target in an SLP environment. The iSCSI initiator node has a driver that includes the SLP UA. The iSCSI target node includes the SA.

Installations can configure the IP address of the DA in each initiator or target that supports the SLP discovery process. Or the UA can use Multicast to find the DA. If there is no DA, the UA must access each SA directly. Installations may use Multicast to do this, or if Multicast is not used (some networks do not support it), each target must have its address individually configured in each initiator. In that case, the customer might as well use SendTargets. Again, talking directly to the SAs (or targets) only makes sense for small networks. On larger networks a DA is very valuable in the reduction of administrative processes. To lower the administrative load, implementations should support the use of Multicast and/or DHCP to locate the DA.

If the network permits it, the UAs or SAs can Multicast to address **239.255.255.253** to see if any DA responds. In non-Multicasting networks, to provide a general method of support the SLP requires its agents to be able to get the DA's address from DHCP and then Unicast (or broadcast) their messages to that location (using TCP or UDP port **427**). This permits the customer to place the DA in the DHCP database (option fields **78** and **79**).

The DHCP can now be used by iSCSI for

- Obtaining a dynamically assigned IP address.

- Obtaining the location from which to boot.

- Obtaining the location of the SLP's DA (and iSNS; see the section Discovery Using iSNS).

With either Multicast or DHCP, a minimal amount of administrative effort is necessary to get the initiators and targets to contact the SAs directly or contact the DA, depending on the size of the network. Because medium-size IP networks normally contain a DHCP, and since the network administrator is often required to configure the DHCP's IP address in each IP device, there is very little additional administrative work needed to permit the installation to support SLP discovery via the DHCP.

The bottom line is this: The UAs and SAs need to implement both Unicast and Multicast, and must be able to accept the administrator configuring the IP address of the DA in each UA or SA. The UAs and SAs must also have the ability to request the DA's location from the DHCP. With this combination of support, the customer will be easily able to locate the iSCSI target nodes in any size network.

Figure 12–4 shows the administrative component and the other components in the discovery process. Once the SLP DA address is set in the DHCP (and the various IP addresses have been set), the storage controllers will be able to find the DA and advertise its existence and features. The host will be able to query the DA and receive information about the iSCSI storage device locations. From the DA the host can obtain all the information necessary to start a session with an iSCSI storage controller.

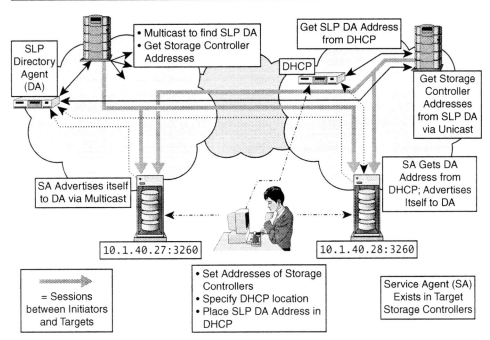

**Get SLP DA Address from DHCP**

**Multicast to find SLP DA**
**Get Storage Controller Addresses**

**SLP Directory Agent (DA)**

**DHCP**

**Get Storage Controller Addresses from SLP DA via Unicast**

**SA Advertises itself to DA via Multicast**

**SA Gets DA Address from DHCP; Advertises Itself to DA**

`10.1.40.27:3260`

`10.1.40.28:3260`

= Sessions between Initiators and Targets

- Set Addresses of Storage Controllers
- Specify DHCP location
- Place SLP DA Address in DHCP

Service Agent (SA) Exists in Target Storage Controllers

Figure 12–4 Discovery via SLP.

## Discovery Using iSNS

The fourth discovery approach uses a new protocol going through the IETF standards organization in parallel with iSCSI. This protocol is called Internet Storage Name Service (iSNS), and it will permit targets to register with the central control point and allow the administrator to set discovery domains (**DD**)—that is, zones of access—such that when the host queries the central control point for the locations of the iSCSI storage controllers, only the authorized controllers are reported. iSNS also has a "Notification" protocol that will permit the host to determine when a change in the DD occurs or when a new storage controller it is authorized to access comes online.

iSNS has a "heartbeat" service that tells clients where the current operational iSNS server is located. It also notifies a backup iSNS server that the primary iSNS server is down so that the backup can start servicing iSNS requests itself. Because of the new heartbeat, initiators and targets begin sending their messages to the backup instead of to the primary. In this way critical iSNS functions can continue.

iSNS supports its own special protocol as well as SLP. Therefore, except for the optional heartbeat and notification processes, iSCSI storage controllers and host systems need only implement the SLP protocol to be compatible with both SLP and iSNS discovery processes. Clearly things work better if the full iSNS protocol is utilized. However, a centralized iSNS discovery management system is good even when SLP support alone is implemented in a host or storage controller.

The iSNS server can be located by one of the following techniques:

- Multicasting to the iSNS server

- Setting the IP address in DHCP

- Setting the IP address in SLP

- The administrator setting the IP address in the iSCSI initiator or target

Figure 12–5 shows the administrator actions and the resulting host and the storage controller actions with the use of an iSNS server. After the iSNS server is set up and its address is placed in the DHCP, the storage controllers send all their discovery information to it. The hosts can then discover from it

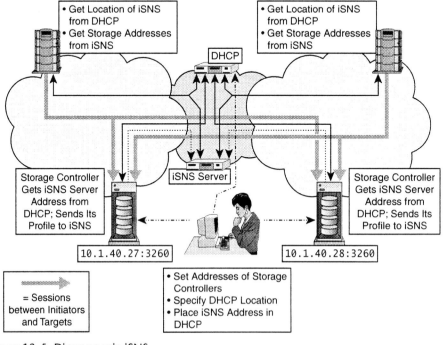

Figure 12–5  Discovery via iSNS.

the names of all the storage controllers they are permitted to see. The iSNS server may be configured further as to which host is allowed to access which storage controllers, and so forth.

The iSNS protocol permits the iSNS server functions to be implemented in a number of different devices: switches, switch routers, storage controllers, and even special host management nodes. An important capability of this protocol is that the customer can designate a primary iSNS server; the other iSNS servers will delegate responsibilities to it.

When an installation uses SLP or iSNS, the iSCSI storage controllers' discovery sessions should be set up to permit no access by any requester. In this way any initiator making such a request will be denied and have to go through the SLP or iSNS servers.

iSNS also permits the registration of iSCSI devices as well as Fibre Channel (FC) devices. (See Figure 12–6.) It supports both the FC **SNS** (Storage Name

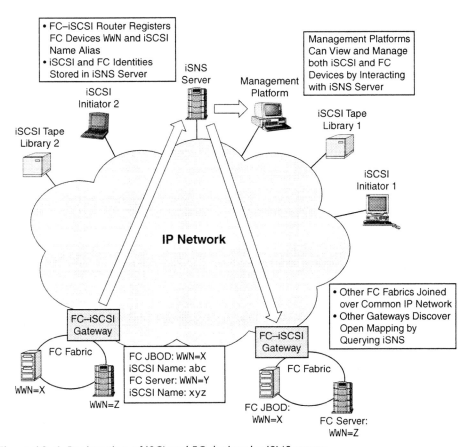

Figure 12–6 Registration of iSCI and FC devices by iSNS server.

Server) protocols and the iSNS iSCSI protocols. When the installation is using an iSNS server, the FC devices can still invoke their SNS protocol and receive their normal FC worldwide names (**WWN**s), and the like. However, when the network has an FC–iSCSI router, the SNS request can also receive an FC compatible name, which represents the iSCSI device. In addition, iSNS will not only operate in the normal iSCSI manner described above but, when queried, returns to an iSCSI initiator an iSCSI-compatible node name (pseudo name) and address for an FC device (as long as a router path exists between the iSCSI entities and the FC units). This should be of significant help with the high-end integration of iSCSI and FC devices. Finally, iSNS can be used to house public key certificates that may be used in iSCSI security.

Nishan Systems has made its implementation of iSNS open source and thus available to any vendor. This includes both server and client code. Its client protocols, which hosts and storage controllers use, are very lightweight and can be easily included in all iSCSI implementations.

## Security Process

iSCSI must operate in hostile environments like the Internet. In order to do so, it has defined a set of security processes and protocols, which according to the standard, are "must" implement and "may" implement. Every iSCSI device that meets the protocol specification enables must-implement security process and protocols.

The basic must-implement protocols are IP Security (IPsec) and Internet Key Exchange (IKE). When used together, they identify legitimate endpoints and permit the encryption of the connection that binds them. IKE authenticates the endpoints (and creates an encryption key) using either certificates or preshared keys. A preshared key is a string of bits given to the various iSCSI endpoints, probably via a manual process, so that they can be used in the establishment of a secure connection.

With IPsec (along with IKE) the endpoints can be secured from a number of threats, one being the "man in the middle" attack where a system changes the packets as it pretends to each side to be the endpoint. The authentication and integrity features of IPsec (with IKE) ensure that the endpoint is authorized. IPsec can also ensure that each packet received is from that endpoint and contains exactly what the other endpoint sent (leaving no chance for a "man in the middle" attack to change the packet or pretend to be the endpoint). Another threat is replay. This is where recording a session and playing it later may seem to a target to be valid, but the replaying of a previous session may be destructive to values set in intervening sessions. IPsec's Anti-replay feature can protect from this damage.

An installation may also require a security feature for privacy. Privacy (i.e., confidentiality) is the encryption of the session so that no one except the endpoints can understand the message. These IPsec features are options that an installation can attach to its iSCSI connections. Figure 12–7 depicts the IKE and IPsec processes.

It should be noted that, even though the endpoints have the right certificates or preshared keys, nothing is said about the endpoints' iSCSI rights. TCP/IP and IKE with IPsec may secure the connection, but that layer is underneath the iSCSI layer and does not have an understanding of the iSCSI layer's needs. For example, remote systems (initiator systems) can be given the option to submit a "self-signed" certificate. Also, one preshared key might be given to all authorized remote systems (initiator systems), or sets of preshared keys might be given to groups of remote systems. In any of these

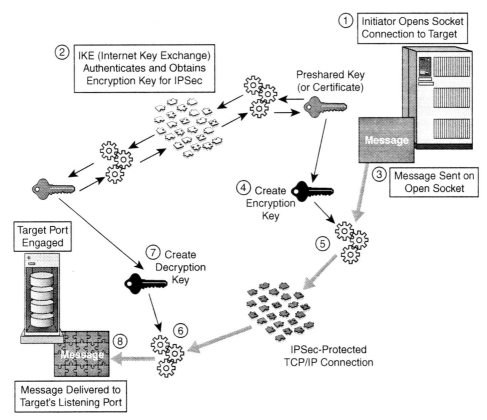

Figure 12–7 iSCSI with IPsec.

cases, it is impossible to clearly know who the endpoint is; however, it can be determined that it *might* be an appropriate system.

In actuality, with self-signed certificates or group preshared keys, all that can be accomplished is that the remote systems can validate the target as a valid target. However, the target cannot determine that the initiator is a valid iSCSI initiator. The endpoints can have a secure connection established, with integrity and even privacy (as specified above); it is just impossible to know that the initiator side is trustworthy.

Trustworthiness is optionally provided by the iSCSI layer. Once the basic connection has been established, an iSCSI authentication process begins that ensures that the endpoints, which established the secure IPsec connection, are actually the iSCSI nodes they claim to be, and that the iSCSI initiator is authorized to access the iSCSI target.

iSCSI not only exploits the IPsec and IKE protocols to secure the links, but also authenticates the endpoints via the security processes and protocols that computing centers use to authenticate their other users. These processes and protocols can be Kerberos (v5), SRP, CHAP (which uses **RADIUS** servers), **SPKM-1**, or **SPKM-2**. (For additional information, see Introduction to the Login Process in Chapter 5.)

It should also be noted that all the various security processes and features are optional to use, but some (e.g., CHAP and IPsec) are required to implement. Therefore, the customer may choose, for example, not to turn on any security (which is probably okay for small isolated networks), not to use IPsec authentication and integrity, or not to use IPsec encryption. It is also possible that the customer may not want to turn on iSCSI authentication, whether or not IPsec is used. In other words, the customers can select only the security features that they want.

## To the Reader

You may not be interested in the level of detail to come; if so, you can skip to the section Access Control Lists with little loss in overall understanding. The information that follows can serve as a base for further investigation.

### IPsec Features

IPsec has a set of features that vendors must, should, or may implement. I will not go into them in any depth here except to mention them so that you may do further research as appropriate.

- IPsec provides two main security services:

  - ➤ Authentication (origin assurance), integrity (a cryptographic digest), and anti-reply protection

  - ➤ Confidentiality (i.e., privacy) via encryption

- IPsec's Encapsulating Security Payload (**ESP**) protocol provides

  - ➤ A header structure to incorporate security services.

  - ➤ A place for authentication and integrity headers.*

  - ➤ A place for encryption headers.

- ESP permits a number of security algorithms that fill in the ESP headers:

  - ➤ Encryption algorithms

  - ➤ Authentication and integrity algorithms

- The following encryption algorithms are considered part of iSCSI/IPsec:

  - ➤ **Null encryption,** which *must* be implemented

  - ➤ **3DES in CBC mode** (Triple Data Encryption Standard in cipher block chaining mode), which *must* be implemented

  - ➤ **AES in counter mode** (Advanced Encryption Standard in counter mode), which *should* be implemented*

- The following authentication and integrity algorithms are considered part of iSCSI/IPsec:

  - ➤ **HMAC-SHA1** (Hashed Message Authentication—Secure Hash Algorithm version 1), which *must* be implemented

  - ➤ **AES in CBC MAC mode with XCBC extensions** (Advanced Encryption Standard in cipher block chaining message authentication code mode with extended CBC extensions), which *should* be implemented

- ESP *must* be supported in **tunnel mode** and *may* be supported in **transport mode.**

---

*At the time of writing, AES in counter mode was still subject to IETF IPsec workgroup's standardization plans.

- AES in counter mode was designated as should-implement instead of must-implement (as was 3DES) because, though it supports high-speed links better then 3DES, 3DES is in wider use. However, AES use is preferred over 3DES.

- AES in CBC MAC mode with XCBC extensions was designated as should-implement because of the code savings if AES is supported for encryption

- The ESP Anti-replay service *must* be implemented.

IKE (Internet Key Exchange) must be used for peer authentication, negotiation of security associations, and key management. It has the following implementation details:

- **Manual keying** cannot be used because it does not provide the necessary re-keying support.

- **Peer-to-peer authentication using digital signatures** *must* be implemented.

- **Certificate-based peer authentication using digital signatures** *may* be implemented.

- Peer authentication using public key encryption methods *should not* be supported.

- **IKE Main Mode** *must* be implemented.

- **IKE Aggressive Mode** *should* be implemented.

- When preshared keys are used for authentication and dynamically assigned IP addresses are used, IKE Main Mode *should not* be used. Therefore, IKE Aggressive Mode must be used for authentication. If IKE Aggressive Mode is not implemented or used, preshared keys should not be permitted.

- Authentication of digital signatures can be done with IKE Main Mode or IKE Aggressive Mode.

It is important to understand that, even though CHAP is included as an iSCSI layer authentication protocol, it must only be used without restrictions (see further discussion below) if the CHAP secret is made up of at least 96 random bits (there must be support for up to 128 bits). iSCSI is required to generate these conforming CHAP secrets as well as accept them when they are created in other ways.

If the customer just wants a human-understandable CHAP password, the implementation must ensure that the login phase of the connection is covered by IPsec encryption. (This applies to any secret that is less then 96 random bits.) In this case the IPsec-protected connection must *not* have been established with group preshared keys. Thus, the customer who wants to work with IPsec but use group preshared keys should either choose a vendor that has implemented SRP or use the 96-bit secret for CHAP.

### Access Control Lists

The various security functions and features just discussed are not the only ones needed. Other functions actually authorize access to both the storage controllers and the LUs within them. Although not part of the iSCSI protocol, it is expected that the various implementations will take advantage of iSCSI's authentication capability to provide the appropriate authorization facilities. Most vendors, or at least the successful ones, will add access control lists (**ACLs**) to their storage controllers, and perhaps to the iSNS server, so that only authorized host systems can access them. Those vendors will also offer ACLs that specify which LUs can be accessed by which hosts/users. Some vendors will even place these LU ACLs in switches and virtualizers.

The point is that, with the appropriate LU ACLs, the iSAN can be used without worry that hosts will interfere with each other's LUs. It is strongly suggested that each iSCSI storage controller implement ACLs for accessing the storage controller and for accessing the various LUs within it. In this way the storage controller will fit easily into both high-end and low-end environments, even if full-feature storage SAN management software is not installed on the various hosts. More important, the storage controller needs the full set of ACL functions, because iSCSI may be connected via any network, including campus intranet and the Internet.

## MIB and SNMP

The Management Information Base (**MIB**) and the Simple Network Management Protocol (**SNMP**) processes permit an iSCSI device to be managed like other IP network devices. The iSCSI MIB has been defined to reflect the basic structures of iSCSI initiators and targets so that the standard IP network rendering routines can draw a network with iSCSI devices just as they would draw a network without them. Each iSCSI device will permit access to its MIB via SNMP. The MIB will have an appropriate header that allows a normal SNMP inquiry to receive enough information to choose the appropriate icon for the network rendering, without having to know anything about the actual iSCSI network entity. This should not require any change of code in the IP network manager. Likewise, SNMP alerts will be issued at the appropriate times to let the network manager know when something has gone astray. It is expected that the vendor and/or installation will have appropriate SNMP agents to process the alerts and take appropriate action, which will probably include informing the network or the storage administrators.

iSCSI has defined both read and write fields within the MIB that can be used to manage the entity from afar. Therefore, version 2 or 3 of SNMP (SNMPv2 or SNMPv3) should be used with iSCSI because both versions have the security functions needed to permit the management node to both read and write MIB fields. There has been notable security exposure even with SNMP, however, and so the installation may need to use IPsec for any session that could change the MIB. The implementation should thus support IPsec on the SNMP connection.

One of the traditional uses of MIBs and SNMP has been the recording and extraction of information on the performance or health of the object containing a MIB. The iSCSI MIB is no different in that it has a number of defined entries that hold statistics, which can be queried and used in management reports. Figure 12–8 depicts the use of MIBs and SNMP in an iSCSI environment.

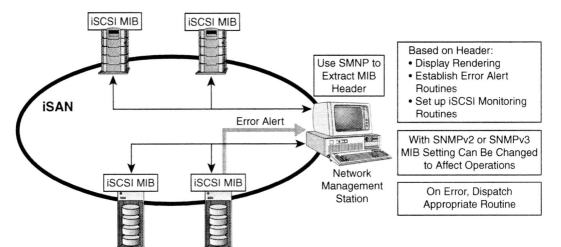

Figure 12–8  MIB and the SNMP protocol.

# Chapter Summary

This chapter covered many of the companion processes that go into creating a complete iSCSI environment. For example, any transport protocol that supports SCSI should support the boot process. In this way the host can use that protocol not only to access the application production data but also to perform the operating boot so that some other type of hard disk drive is not required.

- The boot process was missing from FC implementations for some time; this was a setback for full FC utilization.

- The iSCSI framers and architects defined the boot process to accomplish this needed function.

Another companion process is discovery. Its highlights are the following:

- When storage devices are connected via a network (IP or FC), the initiators (hosts) can only be permitted to access the storage controllers they are meant to contact.

- Limiting which hosts can see which storage controllers is both a security feature and an error avoidance feature.

- If done right, discovery can reduce the administrative effort needed to maintain appropriate configuration control.

- Four approaches can be used as part of the iSCSI discovery process:

  ➣ Manual

  ➣ iSCSI discovery session

  ➣ Service Location Protocol (**SLP**)

  ➣ Internet Storage Name Service (**iSNS**)

This chapter also covered the security protocols that can be used with iSCSI.

- IPsec (with IKE), which operates transparently to iSCSI and protects the links from being compromised.

- IPsec support for authentication and integrity assurance, along with anti-replay protection.

- A number of security processes that work in IPsec for iSCSI to provide the authentication and integrity checks:

  ➤ HMAC-SHA1 (must implement)

  ➤ AES in CBC MAC mode with XCBC extensions (should implement)

- IPsec optional protection of data privacy by encrypting the headers and data flowing on the link.

- A number of encryption processes that work with IPsec:

  ➤ Null encryption (must implement)

  ➤ 3DES in CBC mode (must implement)

  ➤ AES in counter mode (should implement)

- IPsec provides an Encapsulating Security Payload (**ESP**) that contains the header structure to support IPsec authentication, integrity, and encryption.

- ESP *must* operate in tunnel mode and *may* operate in transport mode.

- **IKE** (Internet Key Exchange) *must* be used for peer authentication, negotiation of security associations, and key management for IPsec:

  ➤ IKE Main Mode (must implement)

  ➤ IKE Aggressive Mode (should implement)

  ➤ Manual keying (must not implement)

In addition to IPsec are companion authentication protocols that iSCSI can employ to ensure that the system or user at the other end of the link is the system or user it claims to be and that the system or user attempting to connect has the right to hold an iSCSI conversation with the target storage controller. These additional companion protocols are

- SRP (may implement).

- CHAP (must implement).

- Kerberos (may implement).

- SPKM-1 (may implement).

- SPKM-2 (may implement).

Successful iSCSI storage controller vendors will offer access control list (**ACL**) management for both storage controllers and LUs. In so doing they can sell to installations of any size (especially smaller ones) while protecting the customer's data from unauthorized users.

Another key companion process is the Simple Network Management Protocol (**SNMP**), which can be used to manage the iSCSI network entity. This protocol uses a Management Information Base (**MIB**), which permits a normal SNMP session to extract general as well as operational information about the entity. Various types of IP network management software will be able to use SNMP to extract the header from the MIB and render a network depiction that shows the iSCSI entity. A standard part of SNMP processing is the sending of "alerts" to a central management process that records the problem and triggers appropriate correction routines. Also, an iSCSI-aware SNMP application can extract counts, measurement, and status, collecting and displaying it as needed.

In some cases SNMP may even set values and fields, thereby providing completely remote management of the iSCSI network entity. Because this is a companion standard protocol and because the layout of the MIB is being standardized for iSCSI in general, the same management program should be able to manage many different vendors' iSCSI storage controllers.

# 13

# Synchronization and Steering

**AS I BEGAN WRITING THIS BOOK,** there were two techniques before the IETF dealing with the synchronization and steering of iSCSI data. One is included in the base iSCSI document since it only applies to iSCSI. Called fixed interval marking (FIM), it involves placing markers directly in the TCP/IP stream that will identify the start of iSCSI PDU headers. The other technique, a framing proposal, is called TCP upper-level-protocol framing (**TUF**). Since TUF is also applicable to non-iSCSI upper-level protocols (ULPs), it has another path through the IETF standards group and will be only lightly covered here. As I complete this book, another proposal has been developed. I call this TUF/FIM, as it is based on both TUF and FIM.

## To the Reader

This chapter is mildly technical and perhaps will be interesting even to non-technical readers. I suggest that you attempt to work through it, but if you get bogged down, then skip ahead to the Chapter Summary.

FIM adds things to the TCP/IP byte stream before TCP/IP sees it. Therefore, it causes no modification to the TCP/IP stack for sending or receiving the markers. In contrast, TUF requires changes to the base TCP/IP stack and can only be used with TCP/IP implementations that have been upgraded to perform TUF operations. Since it cannot be required that all TCP/IP implementations change their TCP/IP stacks, iSCSI cannot carry TUF as a must-implement. Also, because of TUF's lack of determinism (that is, it cannot always be known where the TUF frame starts), it cannot become a part of the iSCSI protocol, even as a may-implement—at least not until it has shown its usefulness as an experimental IETF protocol. TUF is covered here for completeness, but it is not part of the iSCSI standard and may or may not continue to a standard on its own. Moreover, the TUF proposal is considered experimental at this time.

## Main Memory Placement

The important thing to understand is that an iSCSI function integrated with a TCP/IP offload engine (TOE) can inspect and retrieve segments directly from the Ethernet/IP frame buffers. Once it does that, it can start placing commands and/or data directly in the main memory of the host or storage controller even before the other parts of the PDU have arrived. (Recall in Chapter 8, the section Data Placement.)

Direct memory placement can begin as soon as the appropriate iSCSI PDU header arrives in a TCP/IP buffer. When a basic header segment (BHS) is found in the buffers, it can be used by the iSCSI function to place, or "steer," that BHS and the rest of its PDU directly into the final main memory locations. In this way the host or storage controller needn't expend the extra CPU cycles and put up with the bus interference that occurs when extra data moves are required. These extra moves normally occur when the main processor moves the data from "anonymous" main memory "staging buffers" into final main memory. The speedy and direct placement of data from the HBA into final main memory also permits the HBA to keep its "on-board" RAM to a minimum.

### Errors and Congestion

There is one situation that prevents the HBA from using a small on-board RAM, and that has to do with TCP segments that get dropped because of errors detected by TCP or the link layer or because of congestion somewhere along the transmission path. These include errors detected on the HBA.

The longer the transmission distances and the higher the bandwidth, the more on-board memory is needed for the reassembly buffers or eddy buffers. If a TCP segment is missing from the TCP buffers—because of errors or network congestion—a relatively long time may pass before the segment is retransmitted and received at the HBA. However, if that TCP segment does not contain an iSCSI BHS (basic header segment), there is not much of a problem. The rest of the data can be placed in main memory and will not cause a significant back-up in the HBA's buffers. However, if the missing segment contains a BHS, the eddy buffer needs to be large enough to hold the stream of TCP/IP bytes as they come down the line, until it receives the missing segment and can then begin placing the data in main memory. Depending on line speed and distance, the size requirements for the eddy buffer may become quite large.

When the BHS is missing, the iSCSI HBA or chip cannot tell where the data should be placed and, even more important, cannot tell where the next PDU begins. When this happens, the iSCSI session connection is stalled until either the missing segment arrives or TCP's error recovery process causes the TCP segment to be resent and finally received without error. This is where marking and framing come into the picture.

### Missing TCP Segments and Marking

Markers assist the HBA by identifying subsequent BHSs and thereby relieve the pressure on the eddy buffers. This is possible because subsequent BHSs (those beyond the missing one) can be used to place themselves and their data directly in main memory. Yes, the TCP/IP sections of the PDU with the missing BHS still need to be queued until that missing BHS arrives. However, that is a relatively small amount of buffer space, limited in size by the value of the iSCSI variable called **MaxRecvDataSegmentLength** (plus the maximum size of the PDU header). Even so, it should be noted that this might occur concurrently on many of the connections in the HBA. In fact, with server network congestion problems, many if not most of the connections may have missing TCP segments, several of which may include BHSs. The actual amount of needed eddy buffer in any specific HBA will be determined on the basis of the vendor's probabilistic calculations.

A major error event, such as an Ethernet link or switch problem, can cause missing TCP segments on most of the connections to an HBA. However, if the event is quickly resolved, the HBA can continue to receive the subsequent segments. Since most, if not all, connections will be queuing TCP segments waiting for the resend, the probabilistic total eddy buffer size may then be in jeopardy of overrunning. In this case, TCP generally reduces its window and starts throwing TCP segments away so that the needed missing segments can arrive and enable the normal flow of TCP traffic. Still, it is possible that the discarded segments may also contain a BHS and, if discarded, could prevent a quick return to normalcy. Because markers are able to point to the BHSs, the iSCSI-integrated function can help TCP determine what segments not to discard. That is, iSCSI should be able to identify segments with a BHS and hopefully prevent them from being discarded.

## Fixed-Interval Markers

The FIM techniques require something to be added to the TCP/IP byte stream that permits the receiving process to recognize a subsequent BHS, even in the presence of missing ones. For example, FIM inserts pointers into the data stream, each of which points to the location of the next PDU. A FIM can be readily inserted into the TCP/IP stream by iSCSI software implementations without any changes in the operating system's TCP/IP stack. This makes markers useful in environments where desktop and laptop systems are connected to an iSCSI storage controller that has iSCSI HBAs or chips.

There is one problem with direct placement in memory without using eddy (or reassembly) buffers. That is the issue of validating the CRC (cyclical redundancy check) digest. Many vendors believe that it is necessary for the complete PDU to be available before the CRC digest can be computed. Therefore, when operating with CRC digests these vendors will require a larger eddy buffer size than when not in CRC mode. Some other vendors have determined that they can perform incremental CRC digest computation, and for them the full value of markers is available without reduction, whether using CRC digests or not.

### FIM Pointers

FIMs place two one-word pointers in the outgoing TCP/IP stream at fixed intervals that point to the next PDU in the stream. This permits the receiving side to determine where the next PDU is located or, if that segment is missing, where the next marker is located. It is possible that the next marker's segment may also be missing, but subsequent marker positions can be computed, and when those segments arrive one will again have a pointer to a subsequent PDU.

The two one-word pointers are required because the partitioning of data into TCP/IP segments may occur at any point within a TCP/IP byte stream. This implies that the segmentation can occur within the marker itself, thereby making the single pointer unusable. To avoid this problem, the pointer is doubled to guarantee that a whole pointer will be located within a segment.

If the receiving entity is a software receiver, there is normally little purpose in receiving markers. Software TCP/IP implementations do not permit the user to peek into their buffers, and even if they did the data would already be in main memory. This is why markers are negotiable. Sending them is a simple task for both hardware and software. Thus, if a software initiator or target is working with a hardware target or initiator, the software should normally negotiate to send markers but not receive them. Hardware vendors, on the other hand, should permit the negotiations for both sending and receiving. (I said "normally" here; I will explain soon why it can be useful to receive markers even in software implementations.)

## Marker Implementation

The iSCSI specification states that vendors *may* implement the sending of markers and *may* implement their receipt. Clearly, if the vendor does not implement sending markers, the customer cannot turn them on, and the receiving side won't be able to receive them. Likewise, if the receiver does not implement receiving markers, it does little good to send them.

This "may-implement" wordage is generally considered a problem, since few vendors would go to the expense of implementing markers in silicon unless they knew that they could inter-operate with other vendors' HBAs. Most of the major iSCSI HW vendors are implementing markers, as it turns out, so there seems to be the necessary critical mass to permit vendors to exploit them and reap the benefits.

All this is necessary because TCP/IP delivers just a string of bytes and there is no method of ensuring that the PDU header is always at a known displacement within a segment.

There is one other reason to implement markers, and that is to help ErrorRecoveryLevel>0 implementations find the subsequent PDU boundaries after determining that a header CRC error has occurred. This means that markers are useful to HBA vendors in saving on-board RAM and to both hardware and software vendors in achieving determinist recovery following a header digest error.

## FIM Synchronization Scheme

FIM presents a simple scheme for synchronization that places a marker with synchronization information at fixed intervals in the TCP stream. A marker is shown in Figure 13–1 and consists of two pointers indicating the offset to the next iSCSI PDU header. It is 8 bytes in length and contains two 32-bit offset fields that indicate how many bytes to skip in the stream in order to find the next header location. The offset is counted from the marker's end to the beginning of the next header. The marker uses two copies of the pointer; thus, a marker spanning a TCP segment boundary would leave at least one valid copy in one segment.

| Byte | 0 | 1 | 2 | 3 |
|------|---|---|---|---|
| Bit | 0 1 2 3 4 5 6 7 | 0 1 2 3 4 5 6 7 | 0 1 2 3 4 5 6 7 | 0 1 2 3 4 5 6 7 |
| 0 to 3 | Next-iSCSI-PDU-Start Pointer—Copy #1 | | | |
| 4 to 7 | Next-iSCSI-PDU-Start Pointer—Copy #2 | | | |

Figure 13–1  Fixed-interval marker.

The offset to the next iSCSI PDU header is counted in terms of the TCP stream data. Anything inserted by iSCSI into the TCP stream is counted for the offset—specifically, any bytes "inserted" in the TCP stream but excluding any "downstream" markers inserted between the one being examined and the next PDU header. The marker interval can be small enough so that several markers are placed between the one currently being examined and the next PDU. However, the value placed in the current marker should be the same as the value that would have been placed there if the interval were larger, with no intermediate markers.

As specified previously, the use of markers is negotiable. During login the initiator and target may separately indicate their readiness to receive and/or send them for each connection. (The default is no.) In certain environments a sender may not be willing to supply markers to a receiver willing to accept them, and therefore the connection may suffer from considerable performance degradation.

Markers are placed at fixed intervals in the TCP byte stream. Each end of the iSCSI session specifies during login the interval at which it is willing to receive the marker, or it disables the marker altogether. If during negotiation a receiver indicates that it desires a marker, the sender should agree (if it implements markers) and provide the marker at the desired intervals.

In iSCSI terms, markers must indicate the offset to the next PDU and must be a 4-byte word boundary in the stream. The last 2 bits of each marker word are reserved and are considered zero for offset computation.

To enable the connection setup, including the login phase negotiation, marking (if any) is started only at the first marker interval after the end of the login phase. However, the marker interval is computed as if markers had been used during the login phase. Figure 13–2 depicts a TCP/IP stream with PDUs and markers.

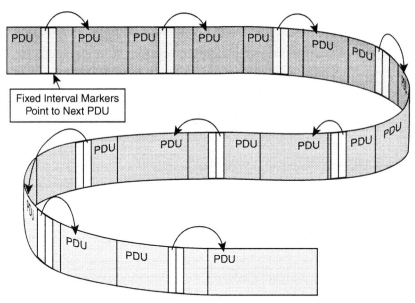

Figure 13–2 iSCSI PDUs with FIMs.

## TCP Upper-Level-Protocol Framing (TUF)

A related technique for managing data backup on HBAs is the **TUF** proposal, which is moving through the IETF on a separate track. If it moves from experimental status into "Last Call" and beyond, a future iSCSI specification may be updated to reference TUF and recommend it as a "should" or "may" implement. However, the IETF has other interrelated efforts in flight to develop new protocols, called DDP (Direct Data Placement) and RDMA (Remote Direct Memory Access), and these protocols may choose instead a related technique which I call TUF/FIM (covered later).

## The TUF Scheme

TUF can be used as a way to package iSCSI PDUs so that they fit into a TCP segment. It ensures that the PDU starts at the beginning of a TCP segment. The application, in this case iSCSI, needs to ensure that it makes the PDU no bigger than the TUF frame. The maximum size PDU an application such as iSCSI can give TUF is specified by a yet-to-be-defined TUF API. TUF sets its frame size by determining the effective maximum segment size (**EMSS**) of the network and subtracting 8 bytes for a header of its own. It is possible to place more than one iSCSI PDU within a TUF frame; however, no PDU can span multiple frames. Therefore, every TCP segment that arrives at the iSCSI HBA or chip can be placed directly in main memory since it always has a BHS at its beginning and it might have more than one within the segment. In any case, the BHS can always be located, and based on the information it holds, it and the data within the PDU can be placed directly in main memory. Moreover, if more than one PDU is present in the segment, all of them can be placed directly in main memory.

The important thing about TUF is that there is no requirement for an eddy buffer within the HBA/chip; hence, the cost of the HBA can be greatly reduced and the latency caused by reassembly buffers can be eliminated.

### The TUF Header

That last statement is not completely true. One minor condition demands that TUF still have a small eddy buffer. To understand it we need to look at the TUF header. TUF needs its header to determine if its frame has been segmented while traveling through the network. The header, currently made up of a 2-byte frame length and a 6-byte randomly chosen key, is used in an important, though rare, situation: when the EMSS dynamically changes as TCP segments travel through the network. In any case either the TCP segment contains a complete TUF frame or TUF needs to detect, via the header, that a segmentation occurred and then gather up smaller TCP segments and present them to iSCSI. This is a type of eddy buffer, but it is generally less than two times the size of a TUF frame and it is only used on a highly exceptional basis. In fact, its use should be so rare that the probability of an error condition at the same time is small enough to treat the segment recovery in a normal TCP/IP manner. Even then it would only have a very small total memory set aside for use in this rare case. (The total buffer is probably small enough to be maintained directly on an iSCSI chip.)

### Advantages and Disadvantages

One of the key advantages of TUF, in addition to direct placement of data in main memory, is that it works well with the CRC digest calculation because the CRC digest does not apply across TCP/IP segments. Figure 13–3 shows how multiple iSCSI PDUs can be placed in a single TUF frame.

The disadvantage of TUF is that it requires changes to the current TCP/IP stack. This is generally not a problem for HBA vendors since they have their own TOEs and hence their own TCP/IP stacks, which they can change to suit their needs. However, it is a problem for iSCSI software vendors that want

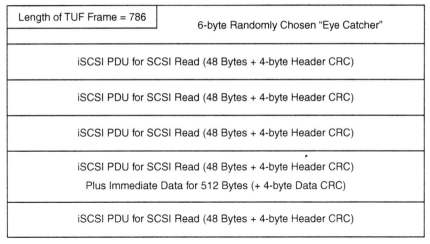

| Length of TUF Frame = 786 | 6-byte Randomly Chosen "Eye Catcher" |

| iSCSI PDU for SCSI Read (48 Bytes + 4-byte Header CRC) |

| iSCSI PDU for SCSI Read (48 Bytes + 4-byte Header CRC) |

| iSCSI PDU for SCSI Read (48 Bytes + 4-byte Header CRC) |

| iSCSI PDU for SCSI Read (48 Bytes + 4-byte Header CRC)<br>Plus Immediate Data for 512 Bytes (+ 4-byte Data CRC) |

| iSCSI PDU for SCSI Read (48 Bytes + 4-byte Header CRC) |

Figure13–3  Multiple PDUs in a single TUF frame.

their software to inter-operate with the new iSCSI hardware but have to use the TCP/IP stacks in their customers' host systems. It is this, and the small but finite probability that it will not be able to detect a re-segmentation, that may cause iSCSI not to require TUF even if it obtains a standards RFC number.

## TUF/FIM

A combination protocol is being considered for use with RDMA/DDP. This protocol, TUF/FIM, combines features of TUF and FIM. It has a framing technique similar to TUF plus fixed interval markers. The frame starts at the beginning of the TCP segment with the length of the UPL's PDU(s) that are included in the frame. That is followed by the UPL's PDU(s) plus padding of 0 to 3 bytes. The padding ensures that the UPL's PDU(s) always begin and end on a 4-byte boundary. The frame may also contain a CRC-32c digest. The digest may be redundant with the iSCSI digests if iSCSI were to use both TUF/FIM and header/data digests.

The fixed interval markers for TUF/FIM are placed every 512 bytes and they point to the beginning of the frame. This means that instead of pointing forward to the next PDU, the marker points backward by carrying the number of bytes between the beginning of the frame and the start of the marker. A special case exists if a frame begins in the first byte following the marker; in that case the marker and is considered to be part of the frame and has a value of 0. (See Figure 13–4.)

Using this approach, the marker is not doubled (as in FIM, described previously). If synchronization to the frame is ever lost, the receiver may

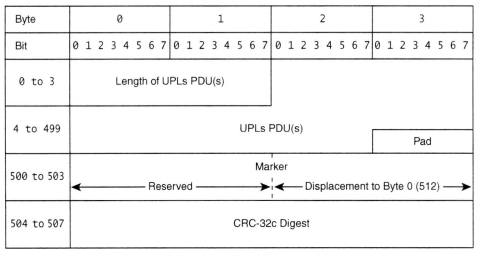

| Byte | 0 | 1 | 2 | 3 |
|---|---|---|---|---|
| Bit | 0 1 2 3 4 5 6 7 | 0 1 2 3 4 5 6 7 | 0 1 2 3 4 5 6 7 | 0 1 2 3 4 5 6 7 |
| 0 to 3 | Length of UPLs PDU(s) | | | |
| 4 to 499 | UPLs PDU(s) | | | Pad |
| 500 to 503 | Marker — Reserved ←——→ ←—— Displacement to Byte 0 (512) ——→ | | | |
| 504 to 507 | CRC-32c Digest | | | |

Figure 13–4 Example of TUF/FIM frame. Please note that in this example the previous marker was 12 bytes before this frame.

compute the location of the next marker and use it to reestablish the frame's beginning. Like TUF explained above, it is assumed that the frame can be made to start on a segment boundary; however, if not, the TUF/FIM will still operate.

## Chapter Summary

In this chapter we covered the advantages of integrating the TOE function with the iSCSI on the same HBA or chip.

- This integration permits the iSCSI process to pull TCP/IP segments directly from the TCP/IP buffers and place them in their final main memory positions.

- Three proposals were covered: FIM, currently part of the iSCSI standard; TUF, which is only in an experimental state; and TUF/FIM, which is being proposed as part of a possible RDMA/DDP standard.

- The FIM specification requires insertion of two 4-byte pointers into the TCP/IP byte stream.

- Each FIM marker points to the next PDU in the stream.

- The interval between markers is negotiated at connection login.

- The first marker is not inserted until after the login is complete, at the first marker interval in full-feature phase.

- The markers are placed at a position that would have been correct if the marker had been inserted during login.

- Markers are "*may* implement," but if implemented should be sent if requested by the receiver.

- The TUF protocol is not currently part of iSCSI and is on the IETF's experimental track.

- TUF places PDUs in segments so that the segments always start with PDUs.

- TUF detects when networks re-segment the TCP/IP segment and adjusts accordingly.

- The TUF/FIM protocol may be developed as part of a possible RDMA/DDP standard.

- TUF/FIM is a combination of the TUF framing and fixed interval markers.

- The fixed interval markers in TUF/FIM are backward pointers that are placed every 512 bytes and point backward to the beginning of the frame.

# 14
# iSCSI Summary and Conclusions

## To the Reader

The first part of this chapter is a summary of previous chapters. Following that are my conclusions as well as my expectations for iSCSI and how it may be deployed. I also discuss how iSCSI may evolve in the future. All readers should be able to follow this information.

## Summary

iSCSI is a transport for the SCSI protocol, carrying commands and data from the host processor to the storage controller and carrying data and status from the storage controller to the host processor. The host processor is considered the initiator system; the storage controller, the target device.

iSCSI has chosen to base its protocol on TCP/IP because TCP/IP is the most prevalent and robust networking technology available today. Customers are familiar with TCP/IP and currently depend on it for their "bet-your-business" applications.

Because it uses TCP/IP, iSCSI's protocol data units (PDUs) are wrapped in TCP segments, which have IP routing protocol headers. Thus, iSCSI flows on top of many different link protocols such as Ethernet, SONET, and ATM. Therefore, iSCSI protocols can cross almost any physical network on their way from the initiator system to the target storage controller.

The advantage of network storage is, of course, the distance between the initiator and the target. More than that it is the flexibility obtained by having storage externally connected and the interconnect shared with several different systems and storage controllers. This permits the storage to have more than one system connected to it, which means that the installation can balance its total resources among all its connected systems. Instead of one system having unused storage and another one being storage constrained, the total storage resource can be balanced across the systems without either overcommitting the resource or underutilizing it. Also, pooled storage is generally less expensive per megabyte.

The value of pooling can best be seen in its use with a tape library. Clearly it is not practical for every server or desktop system to have its own tape library, especially if we are talking about the enterprise type. With a network connect and the right software, however, the library can be shared by all systems. The story is less obvious with disk storage, but as customers begin to pool their storage, they will see the economies of scale in both the total price and the robustness of the resultant storage controller.

Fibre Channel (FC) offers a network solution that permits pooling. However, Fibre Channel, though robust, is generally more expensive than what a midrange to low-end system can afford. In fact, the cost of Fibre Channel may reduce or eliminate any savings that would otherwise have accrued from pooling.

iSCSI, on the other hand, is being priced low enough by its vendors to be readily accepted by midrange and small office servers, and it is as robust as Fibre Channel on the high end. Further, it can be used with desktop and laptop systems that have software iSCSI device drivers.

This book explained the range and flexibility of iSCSI by describing the environments in which it can operate. These environments are

- SoHo home office

  - One or more desktops/laptops

  - Peer-to-peer serial file sharing

  - Computer-store software

  - iSCSI storage devices connected on small LANs

  - iSCSI software device drivers in desktops or laptops

  - iSCSI storage devices with software interconnects

- SoHo small office

  - One or more small servers

  - Desktops and/or laptops

  - Computer-store software

- ➤ Specialty software

- ➤ File and database applications

- ➤ E-mail serial file sharing

- ➤ Peer-to-peer serial file sharing

- ➤ Sometimes a file server or NAS

- ➤ iSCSI storage devices connected via office LAN for use by servers and desktops/laptops

- ➤ Servers and desktop/laptop software device drivers

- ➤ iSCSI storage devices made up of software or iSCSI HBA/chip interconnects

- ➤ Optionally a dual-dialect device that replaces both the NAS and the iSCSI storage controllers

- ■ Midrange office environment

  - ➤ Multiple servers

  - ➤ Desktops and laptops

  - ➤ Standard software, specialty software, self-created software

  - ➤ File and database applications

  - ➤ Some installations with FC connections to storage devices for servers

  - ➤ iSCSI storage controllers

  - ➤ Servers accessing iSCSI devices on special iSANs

  - ➤ iSCSI HBAs in servers

  - ➤ iSCSI HBAs and chips in storage controllers

  - ➤ Desktops and laptops accessing iSCSI devices via LAN

  - ➤ iSCSI software device drivers in desktops and laptops

  - ➤ Sometimes FC SAN and iSAN interconnect routers and gateways

  - ➤ Optionally a dual-dialect device that replaces both the NAS and the iSCSI storage controllers

- High-end environment—campus area (departmental)

  - One or more local servers

  - Peer-to-peer serial file sharing

  - Computer-store software

  - Software approved by central office

  - File and database applications

  - Local servers accessing iSCSI devices on iSANs

  - Local servers with software device drivers or iSCSI HBAs

  - Local iSCSI storage devices with HBAs or chips for interconnect

  - NAS file-sharing servers for general file sharing

  - Backups via iSCSI to tapes in central office

  - Optionally a dual-dialect device that replaces both the NAS and the iSCSI storage controllers

- High-end environment—general campus

  - Desktops and laptops

  - E-mail serial file sharing

  - Desktops and laptops accessing department and central storage via LANs

  - Desktops and laptops using software device drivers

  - NAS devices used to share files across the campus

- High-end environment—satellite office

  - One or more small servers

  - Desktops and laptops

  - E-mail serial file sharing

  - Peer-to-peer serial file sharing

  - Sometimes a file server or NAS

  - Software approved by central office

- ➤ Some computer-store software

- ➤ File and database applications

- ➤ iSCSI storage devices connected via office LANs for use by both servers and desktops/laptops

- ➤ Servers and desktop/laptop software device drivers

- ➤ Servers with iSCSI HBA/chips

- ➤ iSCSI storage devices made up of software or iSCSI HBA/chip interconnects

- ➤ Connection to central office via leased lines or VPNs across the Internet

- ➤ Optionally a dual-dialect device replacing both the NAS and the iSCSI storage controller

- ■ High-end at-distance environment

  - ➤ Tape backup devices located remotely

  - ➤ Disk storage located remotely—connected via proprietary protocols or via iSCSI and other IP standard protocol devices

- ■ High-end central environment

  - ➤ Multiple high-end servers

  - ➤ Multiple high-end storage devices

  - ➤ FC network

  - ➤ iSCSI-to-FC routers and gateways

  - ➤ File and database applications (some created by central office)

  - ➤ Connections to the at-distance environment

  - ➤ Connections to the iSCSI satellite office

  - ➤ Connections across the campus via iSCSI links

  - ➤ iSCSI HBAs or chips used by all iSCSI connections

  - ➤ iSCSI campus connections to iSCSI storage and FC storage via routers and gateways

As you can see, iSCSI has a position in almost every environment. However, Fibre Channel has not gone away and will probably be ingrained in the high-end environment, especially in the central location, far into the future. This will ensure a strong business for FC to/from iSCSI bridges, routers, and gateways for a very long time. That said, it is important to know that many pundits predict that iSCSI will surpass Fibre Channel. I believe that the crossover point will be in 2006–2007.

## iSCSI Development History

iSCSI was initially developed at IBM Research. A collaboration between IBM and Cisco brought it to the IETF, and since then many people have worked on it. Other Ethernet and IP storage efforts were ongoing at the time, at Adaptec and Nishan. However, these one-time competitors have been won over to iSCSI and are now vital players in the iSCSI industry.

When iSCSI was created, its designers hoped to solve the problem of remote interconnect via intranets and the Internet and they wanted to solve it in a way that avoided some of the problems they had encountered in Fibre Channel. One of those problems was how to handle multiple connections without resorting to wedge drivers and having to deal with the incompatibility they caused. Their solution was multiple connections per session (MC/S), which permits the in-order delivery of commands across multiple connections within a session.

As they worked on the protocol, the designers began to see how hardware HBAs and chips could be created to make the protocol work not just on low-end software implementations but on high-end performance-critical systems. At the core of this hardware approach was the TCP/IP offload engine (TOE). As development progressed it became obvious how an iSCSI engine could be used with the HBA/chip to also offload most of the iSCSI processing from the host.

The designers also realized that when iSCSI and TOE were combined, the iSCSI processor could see into the TCP/IP buffers and place the data directly into the final main memory locations. This saved even more processor overhead and meant that the resultant host CPU cycles would be as low as those of SCSI or Fibre Channel.

The iSCSI designers knew that they had to make some resource-heavy features optional, so they created a key=value negotiation process for the initiator and target to agree on items that could support different vendor solutions and customer needs. In order not to put the customers' data at risk, they added additional CRC digests to ensure that no data error would go undetected.

To make the administrative process easier and to solve some of the problems encountered with Fibre Channel, the iSCSI designers created worldwide unique names that applied to the initiator node (the whole OS) and target node. In this way, customers could apply the same access control to any iSCSI session from the same OS.

The designers also decided to define both a boot and a discovery protocol as part of the family of iSCSI-related standards. This included definitions of the iSCSI MIB and how it would be used with SNMP and the normal IP network management functions. Boot and discovery capabilities came very late to Fibre Channel, and the FC MIB is just now arriving. In contrast, these items were defined from the very beginning of the iSCSI standardization effort.

iSCSI's designers realized that discovery needs were dependent on host and storage network size. Thus, simple administrator settings were all that was needed for home office environments, and iSCSI discovery sessions were all that was needed for small office configurations. The Service Location Protocol (SLP) was appropriate for the midrange networks. It was also determined that the iSNS protocol was appropriate for enterprise configurations, especially since iSNS could work for the various installations across a campus (including the departmental systems) and work remotely for satellite locations. The designers worried about tape operation at-distance, and so ensured that the protocol had the necessary capabilities to permit continuous streaming of data.

The IETF would not accept iSCSI unless it had strong security that included privacy (encryption). In today's world the solution is known as IPsec. As things stand now, the iSCSI standard implements IPsec with a selection of pertinent features and functions.

By the time the iSCSI Protocol Standards Draft document was written, the designers were sure that iSCSI could be successful in environments of all types and sizes. It would perform well, it could be implemented in both hardware and software, and it would come with a complete suite of support protocols—all of which would make it robust, secure, and reliable.

## Conclusions

The completion of the IETF process permits iSCSI to become a well-understood protocol. However, the protocol definition process never fully ends; as soon as level 1 of the protocol is complete, there will probably be follow-on improvements. In fact the more successful the protocol, the more interest there will be in improving it.

When IETF assigns an RFC number to the iSCSI protocol, iSCSI will be applied to the various topologies described above. This will entail heavy education and marketing to the storage industry. Expect the SNIA (Storage Networking Industry Association) to take the lead in this via the SNIA IP Storage Forum. It will explain what iSCSI will do for the customer without reference to any specific product. This will be done to build general demand for the various iSCSI products. The various vendors will then be able to tell customers about their own specific products, without having to build and organize demand by themselves.

### iSCSI Network Management

Probably the most important factor in iSCSI's market success will be storage network management. There will be a demand for storage network management similar to Fibre Channel, but integrated with IP network management. Customers will expect to have a rendering of both nonstorage network entities and iSCSI entities. They will also expect the management software to help the administrator monitor storage usage, as well as assign and authorize the use of the various storage target devices by the appropriate host systems. Customers will also expect LUN management and allocation to be part of the total storage management package.

Storage management software should be appropriate for small, midrange, and very large networks. In addition, it will need to manage FC SANs (if any) along with the iSCSI SANs. This will be especially true in the central computing center, because that is where the bridges and gateways permit iSCSI hosts to reach FC targets and FC hosts to reach iSCSI targets. Therefore, we should expect that the more full-function iSCSI SAN management software is delivered to the market, the more successful the iSCSI protocol will be.

### Ease of Administration

Customers will expect the iSCSI network to be easy to use as well as manage. Storage controller setup needs to be straightforward. For example, a customer should feel that it is as easy to add a logical LU to, say, "Frank's" system as it is to add Frank to a NAS file system. If that happens, then iSCSI will be assured of success.

With Fibre Channel there was never a requirement to manage hundreds to thousands of processing "end nodes," so there was never an overriding need to make it as simple as NAS to capture the desktop market. iSCSI storage controllers should take ease of administration seriously so that they can sell in the mid- to low-end market. The same ease of use should then flow into the mid to high end, thus reducing TCO across the board.

Because it is possible to assign human-readable names to iSCSI initiators, the administrator can assign permissions for a user (say "Frank") to a storage controller and assign a logical LU of appropriate size via the same simple interface. This should permit automatic setting of access controls in the storage controller so that only "Frank" can get at the newly created LU. It may be possible to accomplish this by entering the user's name along with the LU size needed. Then the system can allocate the needed space, build a logical LU, and assign permissions to it for Frank's desktop. Frank should be sent a message that tells him the storage LU was created and that provides the password (shared secret) to use during future iSCSI logins. The subsequent discovery process ought to permit Frank's system to see the storage controller and the assigned LUN within it.

### Backup and Disaster Preparation

Expect heavy use of iSCSI as part of remote backup and disaster recovery. Remote backup has always been considered the "killer app" for iSCSI, because users want the backup location for their data to be somewhere their primary system is not, and iSCSI clearly facilitates that. However, since the 9/11 disaster, there has been much additional interest in disaster recovery. This includes remote site recovery—and not just a single remote site but perhaps an extra backup site located at a "significant distance" to protect it should a disaster spread from the local site to the near-remote site.

In the aftermath of 9/11, many businesses found, not only that their primary site was taken out, but also that they could not get into the backup site because access in the general area was restricted. Others had only limited contracts with their backup site provider and within a few weeks needed yet another backup site but did not have one.

A new focus of "disaster recovery backup" thus permits key applications to be quickly started at a remote location. This is called "active remote backup." Today, the most prevalent active remote backup configuration uses a set of "edge connect" boxes (one local and one remote) that convert the I/O protocols into a form that permits operation across various WANs (wide area networks). The techniques and equipment used, along with the amount of bandwidth to the remote storage devices, determine the amount of data that can be sent to a remote location, with as little data loss in a disaster as is consistent with a company's business impact tolerance. Some companies find a data loss of more than a few minutes intolerable, and others are willing to lose hours. iSCSI will not directly affect the amount of data loss or the bandwidth needed to minimize that loss. However it may have an indirect effect given that it doesn't need the special "edge connect" protocol converters and so is cheaper to implement. This permits the purchase of additional (IP tone) bandwidth from various common carriers.

Edge connect devices are not needed because iSCSI can directly address the remote storage unit across the WAN, and can write anything directly to the storage controller regardless of its location. With the carrier delivering an "IP tone" to the host and the storage devices, a virtual private network (VPN) can be established that allows iSCSI to send data directly from hosts to remote recovery centers. As a rule, common carriers that provide the "IP tone" charge much less than they do for dedicated lines or "dark fiber," again providing more bandwidth at lower cost. With more and cheaper bandwidth made available, budget-conscious iSCSI solutions can be put together that permit less data loss than with non-iSCSI solutions.

Snapshotting and mirroring software (or microcode) is usually part of active remote backup disaster management. This software permits "partnered" storage devices to be brought in sync and kept that way because all writes normally sent to a specific LU are now sent to another LU usually located in a different storage controller. In some situations the secondary device can be located at a remote location that will need to utilize some of the bandwidth and connections mentioned above.

iSCSI permits mirroring operations to proceed as normal, but just happens to have its "mirror to" device connected on a longer (TCP/IP) connection than the connection for a local FC "mirror to" device. The key thing is that only the writes are duplicated to the remote device. As a rule, the number of writes is a third of the total number of I/Os, so the remote links have to carry only a fraction of the I/Os sent to the primary devices.

Even if the host is using an FC network as its primary storage path, mirroring software can write directly to the remote storage unit just as easily as it can mirror the writes to a local FC storage controller.

Sometimes disaster recovery involves a technique known in IBM as Flash Copy and in EMC Symmetrix as Time Finder. This technique spins off a "snapshot" copy to another LU. Sometimes the spinoff is then sent to the remote location to be restored. In the future, we may see processes like this being done via iSCSI connections between storage controllers of all sizes.

To sum up, with the sudden revived interest in disaster preparation and recovery, we can look at iSCSI as a JIT (just in time) technology.

## Performance

At first, one of the key worries about iSCSI was whether it would perform as well as Fibre Channel. However, HBA and chip vendors are now reporting that their products do perform as well. This brings us to two additional ways to gauge iSCSI performance:

- iSCSI's "at-distance" interconnect, covered in this book, should clearly permit solutions that are faster than the various techniques currently used to extend Fibre Channel into remote environments. This is because iSCSI was designed from scratch to operate well at long distances.

- Multiple connections can be joined in a single session from a given initiator to a given target. Therefore, even though Fibre Channel can transmit on 2–4Gb (or more in the future) connections from an initiator to a target, iSCSI permits 4Gb, 8Gb, and higher connections, all of which can be treated as if they were a single session. Thus, it is possible to match or exceed the bandwidth of an FC connection.

We will see many different methods for supporting 10Gb/s interconnections. Some vendors will directly offer 10Gb link support; others will offer up to ten 1Gb links within their chips and therefore within their HBAs, or "blades." Based on the current high price and high power needs of 10Gb optics, the use of lower-bandwidth link clusters to meet the higher bandwidth demand may be very useful in a number implementations.

Since Ethernet is now taking the lead in defining the optical link characteristics of 10Gb (and above) links, we should see the jump from 10Gb to 40Gb links in Ethernet before Fibre Channel. However, there is even more potential with iSCSI. Since you will be able to use MC/S with any speed connection, it will be possible to create a single session made up of multiple 10Gb links and, beyond that, multiple 40Gb links.

You can expect iSCSI technology—like all important technologies—to be extended and enhanced. iSCSI was designed to operate not only over many different link level protocols but also over higher-level protocols such as **SCTP/IP** (stream control transmission protocol) and InfiniBand. The key thing to remember is that these additional transmission protocols will bring iSCSI into even wider use. All new implementations will be required to support back level versions, so customers should feel comfortable investing in iSCSI version 1.

Remote direct memory access (RDMA) with direct data placement (DDP) is a new protocol you will see coming to market in the next few years. It will permit the RDMA protocols developed for InfiniBand to be used on TCP/IP (known as iWARP) and maybe SCTP/IP. You can expect current iSCSI vendors to support this RDMA protocol on their HBAs and chip sets while also supporting iSCSI. You should also expect an extension of iSCSI to operate with the RDMA transmission protocols; this extension is called iSER (iSCSI Extension for RDMA). However, these vendors will also support iSCSI version 1, and therefore the movement of the industry into iSER should be gradual.

## The Future

iSCSI is a reality today. How successful it will become will depend not just on its compelling possibilities, but also on how well IP network management software can integrate with storage networking software to make the environment easy to use and administer. Part of this will also depend on how well the iSAN will integrate and be managed with upgraded versions of existing SAN management software.

SAN/iSAN coexistence needs will last a long time. Thus, the key to quick and long-lasting deployments will be how soon, and how well, they can inter-operate and be managed together (in bet-your-business configurations).

It is temping for iSCSI bigots to speculate on how long Fibre Channel will last once iSCSI hits its stride. In fact, it will last for as long as it provides a solution to customer needs that are not acceptably addressed by other technologies. iSCSI is one of those technologies; its only important difference is that it can play in areas where Fibre Channel cannot play, as well as in the same central computing facilities in which Fibre Channel currently dominates. Whether this is reason enough to drop Fibre Channel and move to iSCSI is not clear.

In any event, expect both Fibre Channel and iSCSI to be around for the foreseeable future, and for iSCSI to continue to evolve and be supported by several additional transmission technologies that will permit it to extend into even wider use. Even the InfiniBand technology will embrace iSCSI (in the form of iSER).

## Summary of Conclusions

- The availability of iSAN storage network management software is the key to success for iSCSI deployments.

- The storage network's management software must be able to inter-operate with FC SAN management software.

- SAN/iSAN management software must be able to manage the interconnect of FC devices and iSCSI devices and networks.

- Since most FC SAN management also administers LUs, iSCSI-connected LUs should be administered in the same or a similar manner.

- An important consideration in iSCSI success will be how easy it is to administer.

- iSCSI networks will contain more initiators than Fibre Channel has, so its ease of administration is critical.

- iSCSI implementations should be as easily configured, administered, and used as NAS deployments are.

- It should be as easy to assign an iSCSI LU to a user as it is to assign that user to a NAS file system.

- Ease of use is as important in the upper end of the market as it is in the low end of the market.

- Backup is the "killer app" for iSCSI, because iSCSI was made for "at-distance" I/O.

- In disaster recovery backup, the data must be kept at a remote location in a form that is or can be made ready to use there, often at a moment's notice.

- Active remote backup, which includes mirroring, Flashcopy, Timefinder, and so forth, is often deployed to permit quick restart of the application at the remote site.

- iSCSI can be deployed across VPNs as part of mirroring.

- iSCSI will be part of active remote backup, either in the host system or in the storage controller.

- Vendors are deploying chips and HBAs whose performance is comparable to Fibre Channel's.

- iSCSI will perform well "at distance," since that was a key part of the design of the iSCSI protocol.

- iSCSI's ability to utilize multiple connections per session, including multiple physical connections on a chip or HBA, will permit an iSCSI session to match or exceed the performance of an FC connection.

- Ethernet should continue to set the pace on optical fiber bandwidth.

- iSCSI will be successful if it can deploy appropriate network and storage management software.

- iSCSI will be successful if it can attach an LU to a user's system as easily as a user can be joined to a NAS file system.

- iSCSI will be extended to utilize additional transmission technology, such as RDMA/DDP, but all implementations will be required to support previous versions, thus permitting a gradual and continuous refresh of the technology.

- iSCSI and Fibre Channel will coexist for a long time.

- InfiniBand will adopt a variant of iSCSI called iSER.

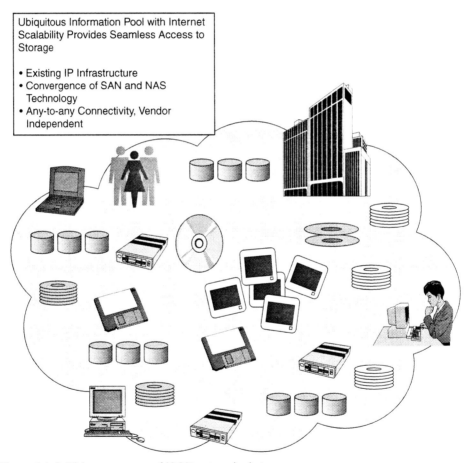

Figure 14–1  Vision summary of iSCSI networked storage.

# Appendix A
# iSCSI Function PDUs

Below are descriptions of the iSCSI PDUs. Unlike the iSCSI IETF specification, all these PDUs are arranged in alphabetical order. Though much of this information has been taken directly from the IETF iSCSI standard track drafts, it includes additional information that might be useful for implementations or that might help the reader better understand the various functions, values, or settings. But unlike the iSCSI IETF specification, all the fields in the PDUs that are shown here, are also described

In the descriptions, as in all things in this book, the official IETF iSCSI drafts are the last word on any differences between it and what is written here.

## Serial Number Arithmetic

The 32-bit serial number fields in the PDUs are treated as 32-bit serial arithmetic numbers. Serial number arithmetic is fully defined in [RFC1982] and will be lightly covered here.

- If the absolute difference between two serial numbers being examined is less than or equal to 2,147,483,647 ($2^{32}-1$), the operation of comparison is defined. (This is called the max difference.)

- Think of this type of arithmetic as a flexible/rubbery sliding window, the top of which wraps around to zero when the unsigned absolute value of the serial number attempts to exceed 4,292,967,295 ($2^{32}-1$). When wrapped, the top of the window can have a lower absolute value than the bottom in a signed arithmetic sense. However, in serial number arithmetic the bottom of the window is always considered to have a lower value than the top, even when numerically higher. This works as long as the absolute difference between the top and the bottom is less than or equal to max difference.

- Only the operations of addition and comparison are defined in serial number arithmetic.

## Asynchronous Message PDU

An asynchronous message may be sent from the target to the initiator without corresponding to a particular command. The target specifies the reason for the event and sense data. Some asynchronous messages are strictly related to iSCSI whereas others are related to SCSI. (See [SAM2] for more information on SCSI messages.)

| Byte | 0 | 1 | 2 | 3 |
|---|---|---|---|---|
| Bit | 0 1 2 3 4 5 6 7 | 0 1 2 3 4 5 6 7 | 0 1 2 3 4 5 6 7 | 0 1 2 3 4 5 6 7 |
| 0 to 3 | .\|.\|1 1 0 0 1 0 | 1\| | Reserved | |
| 4 to 7 | 0 | DataSegmentLength | | |
| 8 to 15 | LUN or Reserved | | | |
| 16 to 19 | Reserved—hex FFFFFFFF | | | |
| 20 to 23 | Reserved | | | |
| 24 to 27 | StatSN | | | |
| 28 to 31 | ExpCmdSN | | | |
| 32 to 35 | MaxCmdSN | | | |
| 36 to 39 | AsyncEvent | AsyncVCode | Parameter1 or Reserved | |
| 40 to 43 | Parameter2 or Reserved | | Parameter3 or Reserved | |
| 44 to 47 | Reserved | | | |
| 48 to 51 | Header Digest (if any) | | | |
| 52 (or 48) to *n* | DataSegment (Sense Data or iSCSI Event Data) | | | |
| *n*+1 to *n*+4 | Data Digest (if any) | | | |

**DataSegmentLength** is the data payload length of the asynchronous message. DataSegment contains an asynchronous message that should be filled with any number of message bytes, from 1 to $2^{24}-1$. However, the length must be less than or equal to the variable known as MaxRecvDataSegmentLength.

**LUN (logical unit number)** is the number of the SCSI logical unit to which the message applies. This field must be valid if AsyncEvent is 0. Otherwise this field is reserved.

**StatSN (status sequence number)** is a number that the target iSCSI layer generates per connection that enables the initiator to acknowledge reception of status. Asynchronous messages are considered acknowledgeable events, which means that the StatSN local variable is incremented.

**ExpCmdSN (next expected command sequence number)** is a sequence number that the target iSCSI layer returns to the initiator to acknowledge command reception. It is used to update a local register with the same name. An ExpCmdSN equal to MaxCmdSN+1 indicates that the target cannot accept new commands.

**MaxCmdSN (maximum CmdSN)** is a sequence number that the target iSCSI layer returns to the initiator to indicate the maximum CmdSN that the initiator can send. It is used to update a local register with the same name. A MaxCmdSN+1 equal to ExpCmdSN indicates to the initiator that the target cannot receive any additional commands.

**AsyncEvent** is an asynchronous event code. The following table lists the codes used for iSCSI asynchronous messages (events). All other event codes are reserved.

**AsyncVCode** is a vendor-specific detail code valid only if the AsyncEvent field indicates a vendor-specific event (255). Otherwise, it is reserved.

**Parameter1,** when present, is the CID of the connection to be dropped (otherwise reserved with 0).

**Parameter2** is the time to wait (Time2Wait). See the description in the table.

**Parameter3** is the time to retain (Time2Retain). See the description in the table.

## ASYNC EVENT CODE TABLE

**0**    A SCSI asynchronous event is reported in the sense data. Sense data
         that accompanies the report in the data segment identifies the condition.
         If the target supports SCSI asynchronous event reporting (see [SAM2])
         as indicated in the standard INQUIRY data (see [SPC3]), its use may be
         enabled by parameters in the SCSI control mode page (see [SPC3]).

**1**    Target requests logout. This message must be sent on the same
         connection as the one requested to be logged out. The initiator must
         honor this request by issuing a logout as early as possible, but no later
         than Parameter3 seconds. The initiator must also send a logout with a
         reason code of "Close the connection" (if not the only connection) to
         cleanly shut down the connection or with a reason code of "Close the
         session" to completely close the session, thus closing all connections.
         Once this message is received, the initiator should not issue new iSCSI
         commands on this connection. The target may reject any new I/O requests
         on this connection that it receives after this message with the reason code
         "Waiting for Logout." If the initiator does not log out in Parameter3 seconds,
         the target should send an async PDU with the iSCSI event code "Dropped
         the connection" if possible, or simply terminate the transport connection.
         Parameter1 and Parameter2 are reserved.

**2**    Target indicates that it will drop the connection.

         ■ The Parameter1 field indicates on what CID the connection will
           dropped.

         ■ The Parameter2 (also known as Time2Wait) field indicates, in seconds,
           the minimum time to wait before attempting to reconnect and/or
           reassign task allegiance.

         ■ The Parameter3 (also known as Time2Retain) field indicates the
           maximum time to reconnect and/or reassign commands (say, after a
           reconnection) after the initial wait (Parameter2).

         If the initiator does not attempt to reconnect and/or reassign the outstand-
         ing commands within the time specified by Parameter3, or if Parameter3 is
         0, the target will terminate all outstanding commands on the connection.
         No other responses should be expected from the target for the outstand-
         ing commands on this connection.

             A value of 0 for Parameter2 indicates that reconnect can be attempted
         immediately.

**3** Target indicates it will drop *all* connections of this session.

- The Parameter1 field is reserved.

- The Parameter2 (also known as Time2Wait) field indicates, in seconds, the minimum time to wait before attempting to reconnect and/or reassign commands.

- The Parameter3 (also known as Time2Retain) field indicates the maximum time to reconnect and/or reassign commands after the initial wait (Parameter2).

If the initiator does not attempt to reconnect and/or or reassign the outstanding commands within the time specified by Parameter3, or if Parameter3 is 0, the session is terminated.

In this case, the target will terminate all outstanding commands in this session; no other responses should be expected from the target for those commands.

A value of 0 for Parameter2 indicates that reconnect can be attempted immediately.

**4** Target requests parameter negotiation on this connection.

The initiator *must* honor this request by issuing a text request (that can be empty) on the same connection as early as possible but no later than Parameter3 seconds, unless a text request is already pending on the connection or the initiator issues a logout request.

If the initiator does not issue a text request, the target may reissue the asynchronous message requesting parameter negotiation.

**255** Vendor-specific iSCSI event. The AsyncVCode details the vendor code and vendor-specific data that may be included in the DataSegment.

### DataSegment (sense data or iSCSI event data)

- For a SCSI event, sense data further identifies the condition.

- For an iSCSI event, additional vendor-unique data (response data) may accompany the async event. While processing the rest of the PDU, initiators may ignore the data when they don't understand it.

- If DataSegmentLength is not 0, the format of DataSegment is as shown in the data segment diagram of the SCSI (command) Response PDU (p. 266).

## Login Request PDU

After establishing a TCP connection between an initiator and a target, the initiator must start a login phase to gain further access to the target's resources. The login phase (discussed in Chapter 5, Session Establishment) consists of a sequence of login requests and responses that carry the same initiator task tag (ITT). Login requests are always considered immediate requests.

*Note:* This PDU does not support digests, since such checking cannot occur until after the session goes into full-feature phase (which, by definition, is after the login is complete).

| Byte | 0 | 1 | 2 | 3 |
|---|---|---|---|---|
| Bit | 0 1 2 3 4 5 6 7 | 0 1 2 3 4 5 6 7 | 0 1 2 3 4 5 6 7 | 0 1 2 3 4 5 6 7 |
| 0 to 3 | .\|.\|0 0 0 0 1 1 | T\|C\|0 0\|CSG\|NSG | Version-Max | Version-Min |
| 4 to 7 | 0 | DataSegmentLength | | |
| 8 to 15 | ISID | | TSIH | |
| 16 to 19 | ITT | | | |
| 20 to 23 | CID | | Reserved | |
| 24 to 27 | CmdSN | | | |
| 28 to 31 | ExpStatSN or Reserved | | | |
| 32 to 47 | Reserved | | | |
| 48 to $n$ | DataSegment (Text-Login Parameters) | | | |

There are three stages/phases through which the login process must transit; they are listed and numbered as follows:

0—Security negotiation phase

1—Login operational negotiation phase

2—(not used)

3—Full-feature phase

These phases are recorded in the current stage (CSG) and next stage (NSG) fields described below.

**T (transit bit),** when set to **1,** indicates that the initiator is ready to transit to next stage/phase. If the NSG is set to the value of full-feature phase, the initiator is ready for the final login response PDU. The target may answer with the T bit set to **1** in a login response PDU only if the bit was set to **1** in the previous login request PDU.

**C (continue bit),** when set to **1,** indicates that the text (i.e., the set of key=value pairs) in this login request PDU is not complete (it will be continued on a subsequent login request PDU); otherwise, it indicates that this login request PDU ends a set of key=value pairs. If the C bit is set to **1,** the F bit must be set to 0.

**CSG and NSG** are fields that associate the login negotiation commands and responses with a specific stage/phase in the session (security negotiation, login operational negotiation, and full-feature) and may indicate the next stage/phase to which the initiator or target wants to move. (See Chapter 5, the section Introduction to the Login Process.) The next-stage value is valid only when the T bit is set to **1** and is reserved otherwise.

**Version-Max** is the maximum version supported. It must be the same for all login requests within the login process. The target must use the value presented with the first login request.

**Version-Min** is the minimum version supported. It must be the same for all login requests within the login process. The target must use the value presented with the first login request.

**DataSegmentLength** is the data payload length of the login request PDU. Data segment (the login-parameter text) should be filled with any number of text bytes, from 1 to $2^{24}-1$; however, the total size of this PDU data segment must be less than or equal to the variable known as MaxRecv-DataSegmentLength.

**ISID (initiator session ID)** is an initiator-defined component of the session identifier (SSID), structured as shown in the following diagram. (For more information, refer to [iSCSI], the section Conservative Reuse of ISIDs).

| Byte | 0 | 1 | 2 | 3 |
|---|---|---|---|---|
| Bit | 0 1 2 3 4 5 6 7 | 0 1 2 3 4 5 6 7 | 0 1 2 3 4 5 6 7 | 0 1 2 3 4 5 6 7 |
| 8 to 11 | T    A | B | | C |
| 12 to 13 | D | | | |

The type (T) field identifies the format of the naming authority field and the qualifier field. There are three defined type values and formats and a reserved value. The possible values and formats are listed in the table.

| Type (T) | Naming Authority and Qualifier Format |
|---|---|
| **00b** | Lower 22 bits of IEEE OUI across fields A and B (the bits known as I/G and U/L are omitted); qualifier is in fields C and D. |
| **01b** | IANA enterprise number (EN) across fields B and C; qualifier is in field D (field A is reserved). |
| **10b** | "Random" number across fields B and C; qualifier is in field D (field A is reserved). |
| **11b** | A reserved value. |

The naming authority field identifies the vendor or organization whose component (software or hardware) is generating this ISID. A vendor or organization with one or more OUIs and/or one or more enterprise numbers must use at least one of these numbers and select the appropriate value for the type field when its components generate ISIDs. An OUI or EN must be set in the naming authority field in network byte order (big-endian).

If the value in the type field is **2** (**10b**), the naming authority field should be set to a random or pseudo-random 24-bit unsigned integer value in network byte order (big-endian). The random value only needs to be unique within the specific host initiator node. It is intended to be used by universities and by individuals who do not have an OUI or an EN.

The qualifier field is a 16- to 24-bit unsigned integer value that provides a range of possible values for the ISID within the type and naming authority namespace. It may be set to any value within the constraints specified in the iSCSI protocol.

The same ISID should be used by an initiator iSCSI (SCSI) port in all its sessions to all its targets. This is considered conservative reuse (see [iSCSI]). If the ISID is derived from something assigned by a vendor to a hardware adapter or interface as a preset default value, it must be configurable by an administrator or management software to a new default value. The ISID value must be configurable so that a chosen ISID may be applied to a portal group containing more than one interface. In addition, any preset default value should be automatically adjusted to a common ISID when placed in a network entity as part of a portal group. Any configured ISID must also be persistent (e.g., across power cycles, reboots, and hot swaps). (See [iSCSI] for name and ISID/TSIH use.)

**TSIH (target assigned session identifying handle)** must be set in the first login request. The reserved value, zero, must be used on the first connection for a new session. Otherwise, it must send the TSIH that was returned by the target at the conclusion of successful login of the first connection for this session. The TSIH, when nonzero, identifies to the target the associated existing session for this new connection. It must be the same for all login requests within a login process.

The target must respond with login response PDUs that contain the value presented with the first login request of the series. All subsequent login responses in the same series must also carry this value, except the last if the TSIH has a value of zero. The last login response of the login phase must replace a zero TSIH value, if set, with a nonzero unique tag value that the target creates.

The TSIH is the target-assigned tag for a session with a specific named initiator. The target generates the TSIH during session establishment, and its internal format and content are not defined except that it must not be zero. Zero is reserved and used by the initiator on the first connection for a new session to indicate that a new session is wanted. The TSIH is returned to the target during additional connection establishment for the same session.

A nonzero TSIH normally indicates a request to add a connection to an existing session. However, if the ISID and the CID match an existing connection from the same initiator node, the connection will be reestablished. (See CID.) If the ISID is in use to the same initiator node and the TSIH is zero, *the session will be reinstated without any of the current tasks,* which will be internally terminated.

ITT **(initiator task tag)** is the initiator-assigned identifier for this login request PDU. If the command is sent as part of a sequence of login requests and responses, the ITT must be the same for all requests within the sequence.

CID **(connection ID)** is a unique ID for this connection within the session. It must be the same for all login requests within a login series. The target must use the value presented with the first login request of the connection.

If the TSIH is not zero, and if the CID value is not in use within the session, a new connection within the session is started. However, if the CID is currently in use, that will cause the corresponding connection to be terminated and a new connection started with the same CID. *If the error recovery level is* **2,** *any active tasks will be suspended and made ready for their allegiance to be reassigned* (one at a time in response to individual task management requests for task reassign). This reassignment will be to this new connection or to some other connection within the same session. If the error recovery level is less than **2,** the tasks that were active within the old CID are internally terminated.

CmdSN **(command sequence number)** is the initial command sequence number of a session, the "initial leading" login, or (for additional connections) the next command sequence number in the command stream. Since the login is considered an immediate command, the CmdSN is not incremented throughout the initial login process for a session. On the first login request of a session (the leading login), the implementation can specify any CmdSN it wishes. (The use of zero is discouraged.) If a leading login in the first connection carries a CmdSN of **123,** all other login requests in that interchange also carry a CmdSN of **123** and the next command in the session, whether sent on the same connection or not, also carries that CmdSN.

During secondary connection logins, commands may continue to flow from the initiator to the target on any connection that is in full-feature phase. These commands continue on other connections, as they would if the login process were not currently active. The CmdSN used by the logging-in secondary connection is also used for the very next command flowing to the target within the session. This is because the login command is treated as an immediate command and, as such, does not advance the CmdSN or the ExpCmdSN. Therefore, the very next command sent within the session will also use the same CmdSN.

On subsequent logins on different connections within the same session, the value used for each Login PDU in a sequence is always the next CmdSN, which can be used by any command on any connection of the session. Therefore, the CmdSN may change with each login PDU in the login sequence, depending on the activity on other active full-feature connections.

**ExpStatSN (expected status sequence number)** is the expected status sequence number for the old connection that has been restarted; otherwise, it is reserved. This field must contain a valid value only if the login request restarts a connection (i.e., the ISID exists, the TSIH exists, and the CID exists). On subsequent login requests within the sequence, this field holds the expected increasing StatSN values and is thereby used to acknowledge the login responses.

This ExpStatSN value is used by tasks that have their allegiance reassigned. They use it to automatically send unacknowledged status and data to the initiator.

**DataSegment (text-login parameters)** The initiator may provide some basic parameters in order to enable the target to determine if the initiator may use the target's resources, the initial text parameters for the security exchange, and the general operating values and settings. All the rules dealing with text requests/responses hold for login requests/responses. Chapter 6 discussed the rules dealing with text keys and their negotiation. Keys and their explanations are listed in Appendix B.

## ISID, TSIH, and CID Values

The following table lists the values of ISID, TSIH, and CID and the actions to be taken when the indicated values are set.

| ISID | TSIH | CID | Target Action |
| --- | --- | --- | --- |
| New | Nonzero | Any | Fail the login. |
| New | Zero | Any | Create a new session. |
| Existing | Zero | Any | **Session reinstatement** (all tasks are terminated). |
| Existing | Existing | New | Add a new connection to the session. |
| Existing | Existing | Existing | **Connection reinstatement**. If error recovery level is less than **2**, tasks are not recoverable. If error recovery level is **2**, task allegiance may be reassigned; that is, the connection can be recovered. |
| Existing | Not existing | Any | Fail the login. |

## Login Response PDU

The login response PDU indicates the progress of and/or the end of the login process.

| Byte | 0 | 1 | 2 | 3 |
|------|---|---|---|---|
| Bit | 0 1 2 3 4 5 6 7 | 0 1 2 3 4 5 6 7 | 0 1 2 3 4 5 6 7 | 0 1 2 3 4 5 6 7 |
| 0 to 3 | .\|.\|1 0 0 0 1 1 | T\|C\|0 0\|CSG\|NSG | Version-Max | Version-Act |
| 4 to 7 | 0 | DataSegmentLength | | |
| 8 to 15 | ISID / TSIH | | | |
| 16 to 19 | ITT | | | |
| 20 to 23 | Reserved | | | |
| 24 to 27 | StatSN | | | |
| 28 to 31 | ExpCmdSN | | | |
| 32 to 35 | MaxCmdSN | | | |
| 36 to 39 | Status-Class | Status-Detail | Reserved | |
| 40 to 47 | Reserved | | | |
| 48 to *n* | DataSegment (Text-Login Parameters) | | | |

*Note:* this PDU does not support digests, since such checking cannot occur until after the connection goes into full-feature phase (which by definition is after the login is complete).

The three stages/phases through which the login process must transit (with their values) are

0—Security negotiation phase

1—Login operational negotiation phase

2—(not used)

3—Full-feature phase

These stages/phases are recorded in the CSG and NSG fields described below:

**T** (**transit bit**), when set to **1**, indicates that the target is ready to transit to the next stage/phase. When it is set to **1** and the NSG field is set to the value of the full-feature phase (**3**), the target is sending the final login response. When set to 0, it is a "partial" response, which means "more negotiation is needed."

If the status-class is zero, the target can respond with the T bit set to **1** only if that setting was in the previous Login Request PDU. A login response with a T bit set to **1** must not contain key=value pairs that may require additional answers from the initiator within the same stage/phase.

**C** (**continue bit**), when set to **1**, indicates that the text (a set of key=value pairs) in this login response PDU is not complete (it will be continued on a subsequent login response PDU); otherwise, it indicates that this PDU ends a set of key=value pairs. A PDU with the C bit set to **1** must have the F bit set to 0.

**CSG and NSG** are fields that associate the login negotiation commands and responses with a specific stage/phase in the session (security negotiation, login operational negotiation, and full-feature) and may indicate the next stage to which the initiator or target wants to move (refer to stage/phase values above). The next-stage value is valid only when the T bit is set to 1; it is reserved otherwise.

**Version-Max** is the highest version number supported by the target. It must be the same for all login responses within the login phase. The initiator must use the value presented as the response to the first login request.

**Version-Active** is the highest version supported by the target and initiator. If the target does not support a version within the range specified by the initiator, it rejects the login by setting the Status-Class and the Status-Detail to indicate that the initiator specified an unsupported version. Then Version-Active is set to indicate the lowest version supported by the target.

All login responses within the login phase must carry the same `Version-Active`. The initiator must use the value presented as a response to the first login request.

**DataSegmentLength** is the data payload length of the login response PDU. Data segment (the login response parameters text) should be filled with any number of text bytes, from 1 to $2^{24}-1$; however, the total length must be less than or equal to the variable MaxRecvDataSegmentLength.

**ISID (initiator session ID)** is the same value specified in the corresponding login request PDU, which the target must copy into this PDU.

**TSIH (target-assigned session identifying handle)** is the tag for use with a specific named initiator. It must be unique within the target node for each session with the same named initiator. The target generates the TSIH during session establishment, and its internal format and content are not defined except that it must not be zero, which is reserved and used by the initiator to indicate a new session. The TSIH value is generated by the target and returned to the initiator on the last login response from the target on the leading login. In all other cases the field should be set to the TSIH provided by the initiator in the first login request of the series.

**ITT (initiator task tag)** matches the tag used in the initial login request PDU. The target must copy the ITT from that PDU into the corresponding login response PDU.

**StatSN (status sequence number)** for the first login response PDU (the response to the first login request PDU) is the starting status sequence number for the connection, which can be set to any "in-range" value. The next response of any kind, including the next login response if any in the same login phase, will carry this number plus 1. This field is valid only if the Status-Class is 0.

**ExpCmdSN (expected CmdSN)** is the reflection of the current value of the local register with the same name. On nonleading logins, ExpCmdSN can change throughout the exchange of parameters. This is because each login response PDU for a secondary connection may have different values, which reflect the current values of the local register with the same name.

The target iSCSI returns ExpCmdSN to the initiator to acknowledge command reception. It is used to keep the local registers of the same name and within the initiator and target in sync. An ExpCmdSN equal to MaxCmdSN+1 indicates that the target cannot accept new commands.

**MaxCmdSN (maximum CmdSN)** is returned by the target iSCSI to the initiator and is used to keep local registers of the same name within both the target and the initiator in sync. If MaxCmdSN+1 equals ExpCmdSN, that indicates to the initiator that the target cannot receive any additional commands.

**Status-Class and Status-Detail** the status returned in a Login Response PDU indicates the execution status of the login phase. A zero Status-Class indicates success. A nonzero Status-Class indicates exception. In this case, Status-Class alone is sufficient for a simple initiator to use when handling exceptions, without having to look at the Status-Detail. Status-Detail allows finer-grained exception handling for more sophisticated initiators, as well as better information for logging.

The status classes are described as follows:

- 0 (success)—The iSCSI target successfully received, understood, and accepted the request. The numbering fields (StatSN, ExpCmdSN, and MaxCmdSN are valid only if Status-Class is 0).

- 1 (redirection)—Further action must be taken by the initiator to complete the request, usually because the target has moved to a different address. All of the redirection status-class responses must return, in DataSegment, one or more text key parameters of type TargetAddress, which indicates the target's new address. The redirection may be issued by the target before or after completion of the security negotiation.

- 2 (initiator error, not a format error)—The initiator likely caused the error, maybe because of a request for a resource for which the initiator does not have permission. The request should not be tried again.

- 3 (target error)—The target found no errors in the initiator's login request, but is currently incapable of fulfilling the request. The client may retry the request later.

| Status | Status-Class | Status-Detail | Description |
|---|---|---|---|
| Success | 00 | 00 | Login is proceeding okay.* |
| Target Moved Temporarily | 01 | 01 | Requested ITN has moved temporarily to the address provided. |
| Target Moved Permanently | 01 | 02 | Requested ITN has moved permanently to the address provided. |
| Initiator Error | 02 | 00 | Miscellaneous iSCSI initiator errors. |
| Authentication Failure | 02 | 01 | Initiator could not be successfully authenticated, or authentication not supported |
| Authorization Failure | 02 | 02 | Initiator is not allowed access to the given target. |
| Not Found | 02 | 03 | Requested ITN does not exist at this address. |
| Target Removed | 02 | 04 | Requested ITN has been removed and no forwarding address is provided. |
| Unsupported Version | 02 | 05 | Requested iSCSI version range is not supported by the target. |
| Too Many Connections | 02 | 06 | No more connections can be accepted on this Session ID (SSID). |
| Missing Parameter | 02 | 07 | Missing parameters (e.g., iSCSI initiator and/or target name). |
| Can't Include in Session | 02 | 08 | Target does not support session spanning to this connection (address). |
| Session Type Not Supported | 02 | 09 | Target does not support this type of session or not from this initiator. |
| Session Does Not Exist | 02 | 0a | Attempt to add a connection to a nonexistent session. |

(continued)

| Status | Status-Class | Status-Detail | Description |
|--------|--------------|---------------|-------------|
| Invalid during Login | **02** | **0b** | Invalid request type during login. |
| Target Error | **03** | **00** | Target hardware or software error. |
| Service Unavailable | **03** | **01** | iSCSI service or target is not currently operational. |
| Out of Resources | **03** | **02** | Target has insufficient session, connection, or other resources. |

*If the response T bit is set to **1** (in both the request and the response) and the NSG is in full-feature phase (in both the request and the response), the login phase is finished and the initiator may issue SCSI commands.

The following table lists all of the currently allocated status codes, shown in hexadecimal. ("ITN" stands for iSCSI target node.)

If the Status Class is not 0, the initiator and target must close the TCP connection. If the target rejects the login request for more than one reason, it should return the primary reason to the initiator.

**DataSegment (text-login parameters)**—The target may provide or respond with some basic parameters in order to enable the initiator to determine if it may use the target's resources. The target must provide some basic parameters in order to enable the target to determine if it is connected to the correct port as well as the text parameters for the security exchange, and general operating values and settings.

All rules dealing with text requests/responses hold for login requests/responses. Chapter 6 discussed the rules dealing with text keys and their negotiation. Keys and their explanations are listed in Appendix B.

## Logout Request PDU

The logout request is used by the initiator to perform a controlled closing of a connection. An initiator may use a logout command to remove a connection from a session or to close the session entirely.

| Byte | 0 | 1 | 2 | 3 |
|---|---|---|---|---|
| Bit | 0 1 2 3 4 5 6 7 | 0 1 2 3 4 5 6 7 | 0 1 2 3 4 5 6 7 | 0 1 2 3 4 5 6 7 |
| 0 to 3 | .\|I\|0 0 0 1 1 0 | 1\| Reason Code | Reserved | |
| 4 to 7 | 0 | 0 | | |
| 8 to 15 | Reserved | | | |
| 16 to 19 | ITT | | | |
| 20 to 23 | CID or Reserved | | Reserved | |
| 24 to 27 | CmdSN | | | |
| 28 to 31 | ExpStatSN | | | |
| 32 to 47 | Reserved | | | |
| 48 to 51 | Header Digest (if any) | | | |

**I (immediate bit)** is used to ensure that the command is handled without delay.

**Reason code** indicates the reason for logout as one of the following:

- 0—Close the session (the session is to be closed). All commands associated with the session (if any) are to be terminated.

- 1—Close the connection (the connection is to be closed). All commands associated with the connection (if any) are to be terminated.

- **2**—Remove the connection for recovery (connection is to be closed). All commands associated with it (if any) are to be prepared for a new allegiance.

All other values are reserved.

**ITT (initiator task tag)** is the initiator-assigned identifier for this Logout Request PDU.

**CID (connection ID)** is the ID of the connection to be closed (including the TCP stream). This field is valid only if the reason code is not "close the session."

**CmdSN (command sequencing number)** enables in-order delivery of commands to the iSCSI layer. If the I flag is set to **1**, CmdSN is not advanced.

**ExpStatSN (expected status sequence number)** is the last ExpStatSN value for the connection to be closed.

### Notes on the Logout Request PDU

After sending the Logout Request PDU, an initiator must not send any new iSCSI commands on the closing connection. Moreover, if the logout is intended to close the session, no new iSCSI commands can be sent on *any* of the connections participating in the session.

When receiving a logout request with a reason code of "close the connection" or "close the session," the target must terminate all pending commands, whether acknowledged via ExpCmdSN or not, on that connection or session, respectively. When receiving a logout request with the reason code "Remove connection for recovery":

- The target discards all requests not yet acknowledged via ExpCmdSN that were issued on the specified connection.

- The target suspends all data/status/R2T transfers on behalf of pending commands on the specified connection.

- The target then issues the logout response and half-closes the TCP connection (sends FIN).

- After receiving the logout response and attempting to receive the FIN (if still possible), the initiator completely closes the logging-out connection.

- For aborted commands, no additional responses are expected.

A logout for a CID may be performed on a different transport connection if the TCP connection for the CID has already been terminated. In such a case, only a logical "closing" of the iSCSI connection for the CID is implied with a logout. All commands not terminated or not completed (with status) and acknowledged when the connection is completely closed can be reassigned to a new connection if the target supports connection recovery.

If an initiator intends to start recovery for a failing connection, it must use either of the following:

- The logout request to clean up the target end of a failing connection and enable recovery to start

- The login request with a nonzero TSIH and the same CID on a new connection.

*In sessions with a single connection, the connection can be closed and a new one opened; and a reinstatement login can be used for recovery.*

Successful completion of a logout request with the reason code "close the connection" or "remove the connection for recovery" results in some unacknowledged commands received on this connection being discarded at the target. (An example is tasks waiting in the command-reordering queue, which are allegiant to the connection being logged out for one or more commands with smaller CmdSN.) These "holes" in command sequence numbers have to be handled by appropriate recovery unless the session is also closed. (See Chapter 11, Error Handling, the section Error Recovery Level 1.)

The entire logout discussion in this section is applicable to an implicit logout by way of a connection reinstatement or session reinstatement. (See the Login Request PDU.)

*Note:*

- When a Login Request PDU causes a session reinstatement, an implicit logout with reason code 0 is performed.

- When a Login Request PDU causes a connection reinstatement and the error level is less than 2, an implicit logout with reason code 1 is performed.

- When a Login Request PDU causes a "remove connection for recovery" (just like connection reinstatement, but with error recovery level equal to 2), an implicit logout with reason code 2 is performed.

## Implicit Termination of Tasks

A target implicitly terminates the active tasks for four reasons having to do with the iSCSI protocol:

- When a connection is implicitly or explicitly logged out with the reason code of "close the connection" and there are active tasks allegiant to that connection

- When a connection fails and the connection state eventually times out and there are active tasks allegiant to that connection

- When a successful recovery logout is performed while there are active tasks allegiant to that connection, and those tasks eventually time out after the Time2Wait and Time2Retain periods without allegiance reassignment

- When a connection is implicitly logged out with the reason code of "close the session" and there are active tasks in that session

If the tasks terminated in any of the above cases are SCSI tasks, they must be internally terminated as if with CHECK CONDITION status. This status is meaningful only for appropriate handling of the internal SCSI state and SCSI side effects with respect to ordering (such as queued commands) because this status is never communicated back as a terminating status to the initiator. However, additional actions may have to be taken at the SCSI level depending on the SCSI context as defined by the SCSI standards (e.g., queued commands and ACA, UA for the next command on the I_T nexus in the first three cases above, etc.—see [SAM] and [SPC3]).

## Logout Response PDU

The logout response is used by the target to indicate that the cleanup operation for the connection has completed. After logout, the TCP connection referred by the CID must be closed at both ends. If the Logout Request PDU reason code was for session close, all connections in the session must be logged out and the respective TCP connections closed at both ends.

| Byte | 0 | 1 | 2 | 3 |
|------|---|---|---|---|
| Bit | 0 1 2 3 4 5 6 7 | 0 1 2 3 4 5 6 7 | 0 1 2 3 4 5 6 7 | 0 1 2 3 4 5 6 7 |
| 0 to 3 | .\|.\|1 0 0 1 1 0\|1\| | Reserved | Response | Reserved |
| 4 to 7 | 0 | 0 | | |
| 8 to 15 | Reserved | | | |
| 16 to 19 | ITT | | | |
| 20 to 23 | Reserved | | | |
| 24 to 27 | StatSN | | | |
| 28 to 31 | ExpCmdSN | | | |
| 32 to 35 | MaxCmdSN | | | |
| 36 to 39 | Reserved | | | |
| 40 to 43 | Time2Wait | | Time2Retain | |
| 44 to 47 | Reserved | | | |
| 48 to 51 | Header Digest (if any) | | | |

**Response** can have the following defined values:

    0—Connection or session closed successfully

    1—CID not found

2—Connection recovery not supported (if logout reason code was "remove connection for recovery" and target does not support it—as indicated by the error recovery level being less than 2)

3—Cleanup failed for various reasons

4—255 Reserved

**Initiator task tag (ITT)** matches the tag used in the Logout Request PDU. The target must copy it from there into the corresponding Logout Response PDU.

**StatSN (status sequence number)** is a sequence number that the target iSCSI layer generates per connection and that in turn enables the initiator to acknowledge status reception. It is incremented by 1 for every response/ status sent on a connection. In this Logout Response PDU, StatSN must be present and valid but is only of value when logging out for connection recovery.

**ExpCmdSN (next expected CmdSN)** is a sequence number that the target returns to the initiator to acknowledge command reception. It is used to update a local register with the same name. An ExpCmdSN equal to MaxCmdSN+1 indicates that the target cannot accept new commands. ExpCmdSN must be present and valid but is only of value if the corresponding Logout Request PDU did not specify the logout of a session.

**MaxCmdSN (maximum CmdSN)** is a sequence number that the target iSCSI returns to the initiator to indicate the maximum CmdSN the initiator can send. It is used to update a local register with the same name. If Max- CmdSN+1 is equal to ExpCmdSN, the initiator will understand that the target can't receive any additional commands. MaxCmdSN must be present and valid, but it is only of value if the Logout Request PDU did not specify the logout of a session.

**Time2Wait** is the minimum time, in seconds, to wait before attempting task reassignment when the logout response code is 0 and error recovery level is 2. If the logout response code is 0 and the error recovery level is less than 2, this field should be ignored. It is also not valid if the logout response code is 1.

If the logout response code is 2 or 3, this field specifies the minimum time to wait before attempting a new implicit or explicit logout. If Time2Wait is 0, the reassignment or a new logout may be attempted immediately.

**Time2Retain** is the maximum time after the initial wait of Time2Wait that the target waits for the allegiance reinstatement for any active task, after which the task state is discarded. If the error recovery level is less than 2 and the logout response code is 0, this field should be ignored. It is also not valid if the logout response code is 1.

If the logout response code is 2 or 3, this field specifies the maximum time, in seconds, after Time2Wait that the target waits for a new implicit or explicit logout. If this is the last connection of a session, the entire session state is discarded, after the Time2Retain is passed. If the Time2Retain is 0, the target has already discarded the connection (and possibly the session) state along with the task states. No reassignment of tasks or logout is required or possible in this case.

## NOP-In PDU

NOP-In is sent by a target as a response to a NOP-Out, as a "ping" response to an initiator, or as a means to carry a changed ExpCmdSN and/or Max-CmdSN if there has been no other PDU to carry them for a long time.

Either the initiator or the target may originate a NOP-type PDU. However, the target cannot send data with a NOP-In that it originates.

| Byte | 0 | 1 | 2 | 3 |
|---|---|---|---|---|
| Bit | 0 1 2 3 4 5 6 7 | 0 1 2 3 4 5 6 7 | 0 1 2 3 4 5 6 7 | 0 1 2 3 4 5 6 7 |
| 0 to 3 | .\|.\|1 0 0 0 0 0 | 1\| | Reserved | |
| 4 to 7 | 0 | DataSegmentLength | | |
| 8 to 15 | LUN or Reserved | | | |
| 16 to 19 | ITT or hex FFFFFFFF | | | |
| 20 to 23 | TTT or hex FFFFFFFF | | | |
| 24 to 27 | StatSN | | | |
| 28 to 31 | ExpCmdSN | | | |
| 32 to 35 | MaxCmdSN | | | |
| 36 to 47 | Reserved | | | |
| 48 to 51 | Header Digest (if any) | | | |
| 52 (or 48) to *n* | DataSegment (Returned Ping Data) | | | |
| *n*+1 to *n*+4 | Data Digest (if any) | | | |

**DataSegmentLength** is the length of the DataSegment with the returned ping data that the target is reflecting back to the initiator, or zero. MaxRecv DataSegmentLength (a directional declared value) limits the size of this data segment.

Zero is a valid value for the DataSegmentLength and indicates the absence of ping data. An unsolicited ping request from the target will always have this field set to zero, since the target cannot originate ping data.

**LUN (logical unit number)** is the logical unit number that accompanies a ping from the target to the initiator. The initiator must return it along with the TTT whenever the TTT is not set to hex FFFFFFFF.

The LUN is included here because a hang-up may often be seen as relating to a specific LUN, or an implementation that is queuing based on a LUN might detect at that point that something is amiss. This permits the target to force a round-trip of the PDU, which causes the hardware and software path to be completely exercised. Clearly if this is not a LUN-related issue, the target might place any valid value here, such as zero.

This must be set to a valid number whenever the TTT is not set to the reserved value of hex FFFFFFFF.

**ITT (initiator task tag)** is an initiator-assigned identifier for the operation. It is reflected back to the initiator along with ping data whenever it is set to a value other than hex FFFFFFFF. If the target wishes to send the NOP-In independently of any previous NOP-Out sent by the initiator, this field must be set to the reserved value of hex FFFFFFFF (the DataSegment Length will be zero).

**TTT (target transfer tag)** is a target-assigned identifier for the operation. If the target is responding to a NOP-Out, this field is set to the reserved value hex FFFFFFFF. The same is true if the target is initiating a NOP-In without wanting to receive a corresponding NOP-Out. If the target is sending a NOP-In as a ping request (intending to receive a corresponding NOP-Out), this field is set to a valid value (not hex FFFFFFFF).

**StatSN (status sequence number)** is a sequence number generated by the target iSCSI layer per connection which enables the initiator to acknowledge reception. iSCSI defines it as containing the response number. This number can be checked by the initiator to ensure that the initiator has received all the responses sent by the target.

The StatSN field always contains the next StatSN. However, when the ITT is set to hex FFFFFFFF, the StatSN for the connection is not advanced.

**ExpCmdSN (next expected CmdSN)** is a sequence number that the target iSCSI returns to the initiator to acknowledge command reception. It is used to update the initiator's local register of the same name with the value of the target's local ExpCmdSN register.

**MaxCmdSN (maximum CmdSN)** is a sequence number returned by the target iSCSI to the initiator to indicate the maximum CmdSN the initiator can send.

**DataSegment (ping data)** contains the ping data to being reflected back to the initiator that the initiator requested from the target. This data must be reflected by this NOP-In PDU. No data can be included when the target is originating the NOP-In PDU (ping). Also, the ITT must be set to the value of hex FFFFFFFF.

## NOP-Out PDU

A NOP-Out may be used by an initiator as a ping request, to verify that a connection/session is still active and that all its components are operational. It is expected that the target will return a NOP-In that echos whatever this NOP-Out sends in its DataSegment. A NOP-Out may also be used to confirm a changed ExpStatSN if there has been no other PDU to carry it for a long time.

| Byte | 0 | 1 | 2 | 3 |
|---|---|---|---|---|
| Bit | 0 1 2 3 4 5 6 7 | 0 1 2 3 4 5 6 7 | 0 1 2 3 4 5 6 7 | 0 1 2 3 4 5 6 7 |
| 0 to 3 | .\|I\|0 0 0 0 0 0\|1\| | Reserved | | |
| 4 to 7 | 0 | DataSegmentLength | | |
| 8 to 15 | LUN or Reserved | | | |
| 16 to 19 | ITT or hex FFFFFFFF | | | |
| 20 to 23 | TTT or hex FFFFFFFF | | | |
| 24 to 27 | CmdSN | | | |
| 28 to 31 | ExpStatSN | | | |
| 32 to 47 | Reserved | | | |
| 48 to 51 | Header Digest (if any) | | | |
| 52 (or 48) to *n* | DataSegment—Ping Data (optional) | | | |
| *n*+1 to *n*+4 | Data Digest (if any) | | | |

**I** (**immediate bit**) is set to 1 when the initiator just wants to send the target the latest value of ExpStatSN. It is useful when there has been no other PDU carrying the ExpStatSN in a long time. When this flag is set, the CmdSN is not advanced and the ITT is set to hex FFFFFFFF.

**DataSegmentLength** is the length of the DataSegment with its ping data. This is the data the initiator wants the target to reflect back to it. MaxRecv DataSegmentLength (a directional declared value) limits the DataSegment size. Zero is a valid value for the DataSegmentLength and indicates the absence of ping data.

**LUN** (**logical unit number**) is the number that may accompany a ping from the initiator to the target. The target must return it with the ITT and the ping data whenever the ITT is not set to hex FFFFFFFF.

The LUN is included here because a hang-up is often seen as relating to a specific LUN, or an implementation that is queuing based on the LUN might detect at that point that something is wrong. This permits the initiator to force a round-trip of data, which causes the hardware and software path to be completely exercised. Clearly if this is not a LUN-related issue, the initiator might place any valid value here, such as zero.

**ITT** (**initiator task tag**) is an initiator-assigned identifier for the operation. The NOP-Out must have it set to a valid value only if a NOP-In response is requested; otherwise, the ITT is set to the reserved value of hex FFFFFFFF. If the ITT contains hex FFFFFFFF, the CmdSN field contains as usual the next CmdSN, but the CmdSN is not advanced after this PDU is sent and the I bit must be set to 1.

**TTT** (**target transfer tag**) is a target-assigned identifier for the operation. The NOP-Out must have it set only if it is issued in response to a NOP-In with a valid TTT. In that case the initiator copies the TTT from the NOP-In PDU; otherwise, the TTT is set to the reserved value of hex FFFFFFFF.

When the TTT is set to a value other than hex FFFFFFFF, the LUN must also be copied from the NOP-In PDU. When the NOP-Out being sent by the initiator is not a response to a ping by the target, this TTT is set to hex FFFFFFFF.

**CmdSN** (**command sequence number**) is set whenever the initiator sends the NOP-Out to the target. However, if the initiator is just updating the target's value for ExpStatSN, the CmdSN is not incremented, but the I bit is set and the ITT contains hex FFFFFFFF.

**ExpStatSN (expected status sequence number)** is the initiator's next expected value for StatSN. It is always sent by the initiator whenever the NOP-Out is sent. It is the value of the local register of the same name that is to be coordinated with the target. In this way the target can tell which numbered responses the initiator has seen.

**DataSegment (ping data)** is the ping data that the initiator wants the target to send back to it via a NOP-In PDU.

## Ready To Transfer (R2T) PDU

When the initiator submits a SCSI command that requires it to send data to the target, such as in a write, the target may need to ask for that data explicitly using an R2T PDU. The target may specify which blocks of data it is ready to receive, and it may request, via the R2T, that the data blocks be delivered in an order convenient for the target at that particular instant. These instructions are all sent to the initiator from the target in this R2T PDU.

| Byte | 0 | 1 | 2 | 3 |
|---|---|---|---|---|
| Bit | 0 1 2 3 4 5 6 7 | 0 1 2 3 4 5 6 7 | 0 1 2 3 4 5 6 7 | 0 1 2 3 4 5 6 7 |
| 0 to 3 | .\|.\|1 1 0 0 0 1 | 1\| | Reserved | |
| 4 to 7 | 0 | 0 | | |
| 8 to 15 | LUN | | | |
| 16 to 19 | ITT | | | |
| 20 to 23 | TTT | | | |
| 24 to 27 | StatSN | | | |
| 28 to 31 | ExpCmdSN | | | |
| 32 to 35 | MaxCmdSN | | | |
| 36 to 39 | R2TSN | | | |
| 40 to 43 | Buffer Offset | | | |
| 44 to 47 | Desired Data Transfer Length | | | |
| 48 to 51 | Header Digest (if any) | | | |

As explained in Chapter 8, the section Data Ordering, R2T PDUs are used when the immediate or unsolicited data PDUs have handled all the data permitted to them and additional data remains to be transferred.

After receiving an R2T, the initiator may respond with one or more SCSI Data-Out PDUs with a matching TTT.

The target may send several R2T PDUs (up to a negotiated **MaxOut-standingR2T** value) and thus have a number of data transfers pending. Within a connection, outstanding R2Ts need to be fulfilled by the initiator in the order in which the initiator received the corresponding R2Ts. (To allow write operations without an explicit initial R2T, the initiator and target must have negotiated the key **InitialR2T** to **No** during login.)

**Lun (Logical Unit Number)** is the number of the SCSI Logical Unit for which data is to be transferred.

**ITT (initiator task tag)** is the unique value that the initiator gave to each task to identify the commands (as explained in Chapter 8). It is returned with this PDU. In this case it serves as an identifier to enable the initiator to find the corresponding output (e.g., write) command that has more data to send and is waiting for this (R2T) request before sending the additional data.

**TTT (target transfer tag)** is the value the target assigns to each R2T request it sends to the initiator. The target can easily use it to identify the data it receives. The TTT and LUN are copied into the outgoing data PDUs by the initiator and used by the target only. The TTT cannot be set to hex FFFFFFFF, but any other value is valid.

**StatSN (status sequence number)** contains the next StatSN, but when this number is assigned the target's local StatSN for this connection will not be advanced after this PDU is sent.

**ExpCmdSN (expected CmdSN)** is a sequence number that the target iSCSI returns to the initiator to acknowledge command reception. It is used to update a local register with the same name. An ExpCmdSN equal to MaxCmdSN+1 indicates that the target cannot accept new commands.

**MaxCmdSN (maximum CmdSN)** is a sequence number returned by the target to the initiator to indicate the maximum CmdSN the initiator can send. It is used to update a local register with the same name. If MaxCmdSN+1 equals ExpCmdSN, the initiator knows that the target cannot receive any additional commands.

**R2TSN (R2T sequence number)** is the number of this R2T PDU. Its values start at 0 and are incremented by 1 each time an R2T PDU for a specific command is created. The maximum value is $2^{32}-1$ (hex FFFFFFFF). The ITT identifies the corresponding command. R2T and Data-In PDUs used with bidirectional commands must share the numbering sequence (assign numbers from a common sequencer).

**Buffer offset**—The target can request that the order of data sent to it from the initiator in response to this R2T PDU be something other than the actual data byte order. The buffer offset field specifies a displacement (offset) into the total buffer where the data transfer should begin.

The R2T can be used to request the data to arrive in a number of separate bursts and in a specific order.

**Desired data transfer length** is the amount of data (in bytes) that should be transferred by the initiator in response to this R2T PDU. It will begin at the point in the buffer specified by the buffer offset and extend to the length specified here. The value should be greater than zero and less than or equal to MaxBurstLength.

### Notes on the R2T PDU

The target may request the data from the initiator in several chunks, not necessarily in the data's original order. Order is actually determined by the setting of **DataSequenceInOrder**—if set to **Yes**, consecutive R2Ts should refer to continuous nonoverlapping ranges; if set to **No**, the ranges can be requested in any order.

**DataPDUInOrder** governs the buffer offset ordering in consecutive R2Ts. If it is set to **Yes**, the buffer offsets and lengths for consecutive PDUs must form a continuous nonoverlapping range and the PDUs must be sent in increasing offset order. If an R2T is answered with a single Data-Out PDU, the buffer offset in that PDU must be the same as the one specified by the R2T and its data length must be the same as that specified in the R2T. If the R2T is answered with a sequence of Data PDUs, the buffer offset and length must be within the range of those specified by R2T and the last PDU must have the F bit set to **1**. If the last PDU (marked with the F bit) is received before the desired data transfer length is transmitted, a target may choose to reject that PDU with a "Protocol error" reason code.

R2T PDUs *may* also be used to recover Data-Out PDUs. Such an R2T (**Recovery-R2T**) is generated by a target upon the detection of the loss of one or more Data-Out PDUs due to a header digest error, a sequence error, or a sequence timeout.

A Recovery-R2T carries the next unused R2TSN, but requests part or all of the entire data burst that an earlier R2T (with a lower R2TSN) had already requested.

DataSequenceInOrder governs the buffer offset ordering in consecutive R2Ts. If DataSequenceInOrder is **Yes**, then consecutive R2Ts *must* refer to continuous nonoverlapping ranges except for Recovery-R2Ts.

# Reject PDU

Reject is used to indicate that a target has detected an iSCSI error condition (protocol, unsupported option, etc.).

| Byte | 0 | 1 | 2 | 3 |
|------|---|---|---|---|
| Bit | 0 1 2 3 4 5 6 7 | 0 1 2 3 4 5 6 7 | 0 1 2 3 4 5 6 7 | 0 1 2 3 4 5 6 7 |
| 0 to 3 | .\|.\|1 1 1 1 1 1 | 1\| Reserved | Reason | Reserved |
| 4 to 7 | 0 | DataSegmentLength | | |
| 8 to 15 | Reserved | | | |
| 16 to 19 | Reserved—hex FFFFFFFF | | | |
| 20 to 23 | Reserved | | | |
| 24 to 27 | StatSN | | | |
| 28 to 31 | ExpCmdSN | | | |
| 32 to 35 | MaxCmdSN | | | |
| 36 to 39 | DataSN/R2TSN or Reserved | | | |
| 40 to 43 | Reserved | | | |
| 44 to 47 | Reserved | | | |
| 48 to 51 | Header Digest (if any) | | | |
| 52 (or 48) to *n* | (DataSegment) Complete Header of Bad PDU and/or Vendor-Specific Data | | | |
| *n*+1 to *n*+4 | Data Digest (if any) | | | |

**Reason** is the reason for the reject. The codes are shown in this table. All other values are reserved.

| Code (hex) | Explanation | Can Original PDU Be Resent? |
|---|---|---|
| 01 | Reserved | No |
| 02 | Data (payload) digest error | Yes* |
| 03 | SNACK reject | Yes |
| 04 | Protocol error (e.g., SNACK request for a status that was already acknowledged) | No |
| 05 | Command not supported | No |
| 06 | Immediate command reject—too many immediate commands | Yes |
| 07 | Task in progress | No |
| 08 | Invalid data acknowledgment | No |
| 09 | Invalid PDU field | No** |
| 0A | Long operation reject—can't generate target transfer tag—out of resources | Yes |
| 0B | Negotiation reset | No |
| 0C | Waiting for logout | No |

*For an iSCSI Data-Out PDU, retransmission is done only if the target requests it with a recovery R2T. However, if this is the data digest error on immediate data, the initiator chooses how to retransmit the whole PDU, including the immediate data. It may decide to send the PDU again (including the immediate data) or resend the command without the data. If the command is sent without the data, the data can be sent as unsolicited or the initiator can wait for an R2T from the target.

**A target should use this reason code for all invalid values of PDU fields that are meant to describe a task, a response, or a data transfer. Some examples are invalid TTT/ITT, buffer offset, LUN qualifying a TTT, or an invalid sequence number in a SNACK.

**DataSegmentLength** is the length of the DataSegment, which contains the complete header of the bad PDU and perhaps vendor-specific data, if any. MaxRecvDataSegmentLength (a negotiated value) limits the data segment size.

**StatSN (status sequence number)** is a sequence number the target iSCSI layer generates per connection to enable the initiator to acknowledge reception. Reject PDUs are considered acknowledgeable events, which means that the StatSN local variable is incremented and presented in this field. (This field is not related to the rejected command.)

**ExpCmdSN (next expected CmdSN)** is a sequence number that the target returns to the initiator to acknowledge command reception. This field updates the initiator's local register of the same name with the value of the target's local ExpCmdSN register. (This field is not related to the rejected command.)

**MaxCmdSN (maximum CmdSN)** is a sequence number that the target returns to the initiator to indicate the maximum CmdSN the initiator can send. (This field is not related to the rejected command.)

**DataSN/R2TSN** is a valid field only if the rejected PDU is a Data/R2TSNACK and the reason code is "Protocol error." The DataSN/R2TSN is the last valid sequence number the target sent for the task.

**DataSegment** is the complete header of the bad PDU and vendor-specific data. The target returns the header (not including the digest) of the PDU in error as the data of the response.

### Notes on the Reject PDU

In all the cases in which a preinstantiated SCSI task is terminated because of the reject, the target must, in addition, issue a proper SCSI command response with CHECK CONDITION (see the section SCSI [Command] Response PDU). In cases in which a status for the SCSI task was already sent before the reject, no additional status is required. The error may be detected while data from the initiator is still expected (the command PDU did not contain all the data, and the target has not received a Data-Out PDU with the final bit set to **1**). If so, the target must wait until it receives the Data-Out PDU with the F bit set before sending the response PDU, because the command PDU may not have contained all the data and the target may not have received a Data-Out PDU with the final bit set.

Targets must not implicitly terminate an active task just by sending a reject PDU for any PDU exchanged during the task's life. If the target decides to terminate, it must return a response PDU (SCSI, text, task, etc.). If the task was not active before the reject (i.e., the reject is on the command PDU), the target should send no further responses since the command itself is being discarded.

This means that the initiator can eventually expect a response even on rejects if the reject is not for the command itself. The noncommand rejects have only diagnostic value in logging the errors but they may be used by the initiators for retransmission decisions as well. The CmdSN of the rejected PDU (if it carried one) must not be considered received by the target (i.e., a command sequence gap must be assumed). This is true even when the CmdSN can be reliably ascertained, as in the case of a data digest error on immediate data.

However, when the DataSN of a rejected data PDU can be ascertained, a target must advance ExpDataSN for the current burst if a recovery R2T is being generated. The target may also advance its ExpDataSN if it does not attempt to recover the lost data PDU.

## SCSI (Command) Request PDU

| Byte | 0 | 1 | 2 | 3 |
|---|---|---|---|---|
| Bit | 0 1 2 3 4 5 6 7 | 0 1 2 3 4 5 6 7 | 0 1 2 3 4 5 6 7 | 0 1 2 3 4 5 6 7 |
| 0 to 3 | . \|I\|0 0 0 0 0 1 | F\|R\|W\|0 0\| ATTR | Reserved | |
| 4 to 7 | TotalAHSLength | DataSegmentLength | | |
| 8 to 15 | LUN | | | |
| 16 to 19 | ITT | | | |
| 20 to 23 | Expected Data Transfer Length | | | |
| 24 to 27 | CmdSN | | | |
| 28 to 31 | ExpStatSN | | | |
| 32 to 47 | SCSI CDB | | | |
| 48 to 51–x | Header Digest (if any) or AHS (if any) plus Header Digest (if any) | | | |
| 52 (or 48) or x+1 to n | DataSegment—Command Data (optional) | | | |
| n+1 to n+4 | Data Digest (if any) | | | |

The SCSI command PDU flags are as follows:

- **I** (**immediate flag**) causes the command to be considered for immediate delivery to the target SCSI layer as soon as it arrives.

- **F** (**final bit**) is set to **1** when no unsolicited SCSI Data-Out PDUs follow this one. When F=1 for a write, and the expected data transfer is larger than DataSegmentLength, the target may solicit additional data through R2T.

- **R (read bit)** is set to **1** when the command is expected to input data.

- **W (write bit)** is set to **1** when the command is expected to output data.

  Having both the W bit and the F bit set to 0 is an error.

  For bidirectional operations, either or both the R bit and the W bit may be **1** when the corresponding expected data transfer lengths are 0, but they cannot both be 0 when the corresponding expected data transfer length and the bidirectional read expected data transfer length are not 0.

**ATTR (task attributes)** have one of the following integer values (see [SAM2]):

  0—Untagged

  1—Simple

  2—Ordered

  3—Head of queue

  4—ACA

  5–7—Reserved

**TotalAHSLength** is the total length (in 4-byte words) of the additional header segments (if any). This value will include any padding.

**DataSegmentLength** is the length of the DataSegment (in bytes), if any. A nonzero value means that immediate data is present in DataSegment. It is valid only when the W bit is set. MaxRecvDataSegmentLength (a directional declared value) limits the size of DataSegment.

**LUN (logical unit number)** is the number of the SCSI logical unit to which the command applies.

**ITT (initiator task tag)** is the unique value given to each task, used to identify the commands (as explained in Chapter 8, Command and Data Ordering and Flow).

**Expected Data Transfer Length**, for unidirectional operations, contains the number of bytes of data involved in this SCSI operation. For a unidirectional write operation (the W flag is set to 1 and the **R** flag is set to 0), the initiator uses this field to specify the number of bytes of data it expects to transfer for this operation. For a unidirectional read operation (the W flag is set to 0 and the **R** flag set to 1), the initiator uses this field to specify the number of bytes of data it expects the target to transfer to the initiator.

For bidirectional operations (both R and W flags are set to 1), this field contains the number of data bytes involved in the write transfer. An additional header segment (AHS) must be present in the PDU that indicates the bidirectional read expected data transfer length.

If the expected data transfer length for a write and the length of the immediate data part that follows the command (if any) are the same, no more data PDUs are expected to follow. In this case, the F bit must be set to 1. If the expected data transfer length is higher than the FirstBurstLength (the negotiated maximum length of unsolicited data the target will accept), the initiator must send the maximum length of unsolicited data *or only* the immediate data, if any.

Upon completion of a data transfer, the target informs the initiator (through residual counts) of the number of bytes actually processed (sent and/or received) by the target.

**CmdSN (command sequence number)** enables in-order delivery of commands to the target SCSI layer (as explained in Chapter 8).

**ExpStatSN (expected status sequence number)** acknowledges status responses that have been received on the connection (as explained in Chapter 7, Session Management).

**CDB (command descriptor block)** contains 16 bytes to accommodate the commonly used SCSI CDBs. Whenever a CDB is larger than 16 bytes, an extended CDB AHS is used to hold the spillover. These "spillover CDBs" are used for the extended copy functions (also known as third-party copy commands), which may have bidirectional data flow.

**AHS (additional header segment)** has the general format shown on the next page. It contains the fields described in the following paragraphs.

**AHSLength** contains the effective length in bytes of the AHS, excluding **AHSType** and AHSLength (not including padding). The AHS is padded to the smallest integer number of 4-byte words (i.e., from 0 up to 3 padding bytes).

| Byte | 0 | 1 | 2 | 3 |
|---|---|---|---|---|
| Bit | 0 1 2 3 4 5 6 7 | 0 1 2 3 4 5 6 7 | 0 1 2 3 4 5 6 7 | 0 1 2 3 4 5 6 7 |
| 0 to 3 | AHSLength | | AHSType | |
| 4 to *x* | AHS-Specific | | | |

AHSType is coded as follows:

Bits 0–1—Reserved

Bits 2–7—AHS code

0—Reserved

1—Extended CDB

2—Expected bidirectional read data length

3–59—Reserved

60–63—Non-iSCSI extensions

**Extended CDB** has the format shown in the figure below. This type of AHS must not be used if the total CDB length is less than 17. Note that the CDB Length –15 is used (instead of 16) to account for one reserved byte. (The reserved byte is counted in AHSLength.) The rest of the CDB is contained in the 16-byte CDB field in the BHS. The padding is not included in AHSLength.

| Byte | 0 | 1 | 2 | 3 |
|---|---|---|---|---|
| Bit | 0 1 2 3 4 5 6 7 | 0 1 2 3 4 5 6 7 | 0 1 2 3 4 5 6 7 | 0 1 2 3 4 5 6 7 |
| 0 to 3 | AHSLength (Total CDB Length minus 15) | | 0\|0\|0\|0\|0\|0\|0\|1 | Reserved |
| 4 to *x* | Extended CDB . . . plus Padding to 4-Byte Boundary | | | |

**Bidirectional Expected Read-Data Length AHS** has the format shown in this figure.

| Byte | 0 | 1 | 2 | 3 |
|------|---|---|---|---|
| Bit | 0 1 2 3 4 5 6 7 | 0 1 2 3 4 5 6 7 | 0 1 2 3 4 5 6 7 | 0 1 2 3 4 5 6 7 |
| 0 to 3 | AHSLength (=5) | | 0\|0\|0\|0\|0\|0\|1\|0 | Reserved |
| 4 to *x* | Expected Read-Data Length | | | |

**Data segment (command data)** may contain user data (as from a write operation). Alternatively, some SCSI commands require additional parameter data to accompany the SCSI command, and this data may be placed in the same location in the PDU (both cases are referred to as immediate data).

## SCSI (Command) Response PDU

The SCSI Response PDU is sent from the target to the initiator to signal the completion of a SCSI command and carries information about the command, such as whether it completed successfully or not, residual data counts, ending status, and in some cases sense data.

| Byte | 0 | 1 | 2 | 3 |
|---|---|---|---|---|
| Bit | 0 1 2 3 4 5 6 7 | 0 1 2 3 4 5 6 7 | 0 1 2 3 4 5 6 7 | 0 1 2 3 4 5 6 7 |
| 0 to 3 | .\|.\|1 0 0 0 0 1 | 1\|. .\|o\|u\|O\|U\|. | Response | Status |
| 4 to 7 | 0 | DataSegmentLength | | |
| 8 to 15 | Reserved | | | |
| 16 to 19 | ITT | | | |
| 20 to 23 | SNACKTAG or Reserved | | | |
| 24 to 27 | StatSN | | | |
| 28 to 31 | ExpCmdSN | | | |
| 32 to 35 | MaxCmdSN | | | |
| 36 to 39 | ExpDataSN or Reserved | | | |
| 40 to 43 | Bidirectional Read Residual Count or Reserved | | | |
| 44 to 47 | Residual Count or Reserved | | | |
| 48 to 51 | Header Digest (if any) | | | |
| 52 (or 48) to *n* | DataSegment—Command Data (optional) | | | |
| *n*+1 to *n*+4 | Data Digest (if any) | | | |

*Note:* if a SCSI device error is detected while data from the initiator is still expected (the command PDU did not contain all the data and the target has not received a Data-Out PDU with the F bit set), the target must wait until it receives a Data-Out PDU with the F bit set in the last expected sequence before sending this response PDU.

The SCSI command response PDU contains several flags. In byte 1:

- o (**bidirectional overflow bit**) is set for bidirectional read residual overflow. In this case, the Bidirectional Read Residual Count indicates the number of bytes that were not transferred to the initiator because the initiator's expected bidirectional read data transfer length was not sufficient.

- u (**bidirectional underflow bit**) is set for bidirectional read residual underflow. In this case, the Bidirectional Read Residual Count indicates the number of bytes that were not transferred to the initiator out of the number of bytes expected to be transferred.

- O (**overflow bit**) is set for residual overflow. In this case, the Residual Count indicates the number of bytes that were not transferred because the initiator's expected data transfer length was not sufficient. For a bidirectional operation, the Residual Count contains the residual for the write operation.

- U (**underflow bit**) is set for residual underflow. In this case, the Residual Count indicates the number of bytes that were not transferred out of the number of bytes expected to be transferred. For a bidirectional operation, the Residual Count contains the residual for the write operation.

*Notes:*

- Bits O and U are mutually exclusive, as are bits o and u.

- Bits O, U, o, u must be 0 for a response other than "Command completed at target."

**Response** contains the iSCSI service response. The codes are

> 0x00—Command completed at target
>
> 0x01—Target failure
>
> 0x80–0xff—Vendor specific

All other response codes are reserved. A nonzero response field indicates a failure to execute the command, in which case the status and sense fields are undefined.

**Status** is used to report the SCSI status and is valid only if the response code is "Command completed at target." Some of the status codes defined for SCSI are

0x00—GOOD

0x02—CHECK CONDITION

0x08—BUSY

0x18—RESERVATION CONFLICT

0x28—TASK SET FULL

0x30—ACA ACTIVE

0x40—TASK ABORTED

A complete list and definitions of all status codes can be found in [SAM2].

**DataSegmentLength** is the length of the data segment, if any. If the value is zero, the response and status fields must also be zero. If it is nonzero, the data field holds the sense and/or response data, and the response and status fields have a nonzero value. The MaxRecvDataSegmentLength (negotiated value) limits the size of this data segment.

**ITT (initiator task tag)** is the unique value given to each task to identify the commands (as explained in Chapter 8, Command and Data Ordering and Flow).

**SNACK Tag** contains a copy of the SNACK Tag of the last **R-Data SNACK** accepted by the target on the same connection and for the command for which the response is issued. Otherwise it is reserved and should be set to 0.

After issuing an R-Data SNACK, the initiator must discard any SCSI status unless contained in an SCSI Response PDU carrying the same SNACK Tag as the last issued R-Data SNACK for the SCSI command on the current connection.

For a detailed discussion on R-Data SNACK, see SNACK Request.

**StatSN (status sequence number)** is a sequence number that the target iSCSI layer generates per connection and that in turn enables the initiator to acknowledge status reception. It is incremented by 1 for every response/status sent on a connection except for responses sent as a result of a retry or a SNACK. In case of responses sent because of a retransmission request, the StatSN must be the same as it was the first time the PDU was sent unless the connection was subsequently restarted.

**ExpCmdSN (expected command sequence number)** is the next expected CmdSN from the corresponding initiator. The target returns it to the initiator to acknowledge command reception. It is used to update a local register with the same name. An ExpCmdSN equal to MaxCmdSN+1 indicates that the target cannot accept new commands.

**MaxCmdSN (maximum CmdSN)** is the maximum command sequence number acceptable from the corresponding initiator. The target iSCSI returns it to the initiator. It is used to update a local register with the same name. If MaxCmdSN+1 equals ExpCmdSN, the initiator knows that the target cannot receive any additional commands.

In case MaxCmdSN changes at the target and the target has no pending PDUs to convey this information to the initiator, the target should generate a NOP-In to carry the new MaxCmdSN.

**ExpDataSN (expected data sequence number)** is the number of data-in (read) PDUs the target has sent for the command. This field is reserved if the response code is not "Command completed at target" (see Responses above). It is also reserved if the response is for a write operation.

**Bidirectional Read Residual Count** is valid only when either the u bit or the o bit is set. If neither bit is set, it should be zero.

If the o bit is set, the Bidirectional Read Residual Count indicates the number of bytes not transferred to the initiator because the initiator's expected bidirectional read transfer length was not sufficient. If the u bit is set, it indicates the number of bytes not transferred to the initiator out of the number of bytes expected.

**Residual Count** is valid only when either the U bit or the O bit is set. If neither bit is set, the field is supposed to be zero.

If the O bit is set, Residual Count indicates the number of bytes not transferred because the initiator's expected data transfer length was insufficient. If the U bit is set, it indicates the number of bytes not transferred out of the number of bytes expected.

**DataSegment (sense and response data)**—iSCSI targets have to support and enable a function called Autosense. Autosense requires the SCSI layer to retrieve the SCSI sense information automatically so that iSCSI can make it part of the command response whenever a SCSI CHECK CONDITION occurs. If the status is a CHECK CONDITION, the DataSegment contains sense data for the failed command. If the DataSegmentLength field is not zero, then the format of the DataSegment field is as shown in the figure.

| Byte | 0 | 1 | 2 | 3 |
|------|---|---|---|---|
| Bit | 0 1 2 3 4 5 6 7 | 0 1 2 3 4 5 6 7 | 0 1 2 3 4 5 6 7 | 0 1 2 3 4 5 6 7 |
| 0 to 3 | SenseLength | | | |
| 4 to *nn* | Sense Data | | | |
| *nn*+1 to *nn*+*xx* | Response Data | | | |

**SenseLength** is the length of the sense data.

**Sense Data** is the sense data returned as part of the status response and includes the sense key, additional sense codes, and a qualifier. It contains detailed information about a check condition; [SPC3] specifies its format and content.

**Response Data** for some iSCSI responses may contain vendor-specific response-related information (e.g., a vendor-specific detailed description of a target failure).

*Note:* Certain iSCSI conditions result in the command being terminated at the target as outlined in the following table.

The target reports the "Incorrect amount of data" condition if, during data output, the total data length is greater than FirstBurstLength and the initiator sent unsolicited nonimmediate data, but the total amount of unsolicited data is different from FirstBurstLength. The target reports the same error when the amount of data sent as a reply to an R2T does not match the amount requested.

| Reason | Sense key | Additional Sense Code (ASC) and Qualifier (ASCQ) |
|---|---|---|
| Unexpected unsolicited data | Aborted command—**0B** | ASC = hex **0c**, ASCQ = hex **0c** Write error |
| Incorrect amount of data | Aborted command—**0B** | ASC = hex **0c**, ASCQ = hex **0d** Write error |
| Protocol service CRC error | Aborted command—**0B** | ASC = hex **47**, ASCQ = hex **05** CRC error detected |
| SNACK rejected | Aborted command—**0B** | ASC = hex **11**, ASCQ = hex **13** Read error |

## SCSI Data-In PDU

The SCSI Data-In PDU for *read* operations has the following format.

| Byte | 0 | 1 | 2 | 3 |
|---|---|---|---|---|
| Bit | 0 1 2 3 4 5 6 7 | 0 1 2 3 4 5 6 7 | 0 1 2 3 4 5 6 7 | 0 1 2 3 4 5 6 7 |
| 0 to 3 | .\|.\|1 0 0 1 0 1 | F\|A\|0 0 0\|0\|U\|S | Reserved | Status or Reserved |
| 4 to 7 | 0 | DataSegmentLength | | |
| 8 to 15 | LUN or Reserved | | | |
| 16 to 19 | ITT | | | |
| 20 to 23 | TTT of Reserved (hex  FFFFFFFF) | | | |
| 24 to 27 | StatSN or Reserved | | | |
| 28 to 31 | ExpCmdSN | | | |
| 32 to 35 | MaxCmdSN | | | |
| 36 to 39 | DataSN | | | |
| 40 to 43 | Buffer Offset | | | |
| 44 to 47 | Residual Count | | | |
| 48 to 51 | Header Digest (if any) | | | |
| 52 (or 48) to *n* | DataSegment | | | |
| *n*+1 to *n*+4 | Data Digest (if any) | | | |

The SCSI Data-In PDU carries read data and may also contain status on the last Data-In PDU for a read command, as long as the command did not end with an exception (i.e., the status is GOOD, CONDITION MET, or INTER-

MEDIATE CONDITION MET). For bidirectional commands, the status is always sent in a SCSI Response PDU.

If the command is completed with an error, the response and sense data will be sent in a SCSI Response PDU, not in a SCSI data packet.

**F (final bit),** for incoming data, is 1 for the last input (read) data PDU of a sequence. Input can be split in several sequences, each one having its own F bit. This does not affect DataSN counting on Data-In PDUs.

The F bit may also be used as a "change direction" indication for bidirectional operations that need such a change. For bidirectional operations, the F bit is 1 for the end of the input sequences as well as for the end of the output sequences.

**A (acknowledge bit),** for sessions with an error recovery level of 1 or higher, is set to 1 to indicate that it requests a positive acknowledgment from the initiator for the data received.

The target should use the A bit moderately, setting it to **1** only once every MaxBurstLength bytes or on the last Data-In PDU that concludes the entire requested read data transfer for the task (from the target's perspective).

On receiving a Data-In PDU with the A bit set to 1, if there are no holes in the read data up to that PDU, the initiator must issue a SNACK of type DataACK.

The exception to this is when the initiator can acknowledge the status for the task immediately via ExpStatSN on other outbound PDUs. That assumes that the status for the task is also received.

When acknowledgment is accomplished through ExpStatSN, sending a SNACK of type DataACK in response to the A bit is not mandatory. However, if it is done, it must not be sent after the status acknowledgment through ExpStatSN.

If the initiator has detected holes in the read data before that Data-In PDU, it must postpone the DataACK SNACK until the holes are filled. Also, an initiator cannot acknowledge the status for the task before the holes are filled.

A status acknowledgment for a task that generated the Data-In PDUs is considered by the target an implicit acknowledgment of the Data-In PDUs with the A bit set.

O (**residual overflow bit**)—When set, the Residual Count indicates the number of bytes not transferred because the initiator's expected data transfer length was not sufficient.

This bit is only valid when the S bit is set to **1**.

U (**residual underflow bit**)—When set, the Residual Count indicates the number of bytes not transferred out of the number of bytes expected.

This bit is only valid when the S bit is set to **1**.

S (**status bit**) signals that status (or a residual count) accompanies this (the last) Data-In PDU for the corresponding command. If this bit is set, the F bit must also be set.

The S bit can only be set if the command did not end with an exception (i.e., the status must be GOOD, CONDITION MET, INTERMEDIATE, or INTERMEDIATE CONDITION MET).

The StatSN, status, and Residual Count fields have meaningful content only if the S bit is set to **1**.

Although targets may choose to send even nonexception status in separate responses, initiators must support nonexception status in Data-In PDUs.

**Status**—This PDU can return only status that does not generate sense (error conditions). Following are some of the acceptable status values:

Hex 00—Good

Hex 04—Condition met

Hex 10—Intermediate

Hex 14—Intermediate condition met

**DataSegmentLength** is the data payload length of a SCSI Data-In PDU. The sending of 0-length data segments should be avoided, although initiators must be able to receive them properly. The DataSegments of Data-In PDUs should be filled to an integer number of 4-byte words (real payload) unless the F (final) bit is set to 1. The DataSegmentLength must not exceed MaxRecvDataSegmentLength for the direction in which it is sent, and the total of all the DataSegmentLength of all PDUs in a sequence must not exceed MaxBurstLength.

**LUN (logical unit number)** is the number of the SCSI logical unit from which the data was taken. (See additional information under TTT, below.)

**ITT (initiator task tag)** is the unique value that the initiator gives to each task, used to identify the commands (as explained in Chapter 8, Command and Data Ordering and Flow) and returned with this PDU. In this case it is used as an identifier to enable the initiator to find the corresponding command that issued the request for the data, which arrives as part of this PDU.

**TTT (target transfer tag)**, on incoming data, must be provided by the target if the A bit is set to 1. The TTT and the LUN are copied by the initiator into the SNACK of type DataACK that it issues as a result of receiving a SCSI Data-In PDU with the A bit set to 1.

The TTT values are not specified by this protocol except that the value hex FFFFFFFF is reserved and means that the TTT is not supplied. If the TTT is provided, the LUN field must hold a valid value and be consistent with whatever was specified with the command; otherwise, the LUN field is reserved.

**StatSN (status sequence number)** is a sequence number that the target iSCSI layer generates per connection and which enables the initiator to acknowledge reception of status. It is set only when the S bit is set to 1.

**ExpCmdSN (expected CmdSN)** is a sequence number that the target iSCSI returns to the initiator to acknowledge command reception. It is used to update a local register with the same name. An ExpCmdSN equal to MaxCmdSN+1 indicates that the target cannot accept new commands.

**MaxCmdSN (maximum CmdSN)** is a sequence number that the target iSCSI returns to the initiator to indicate the maximum command the initiator can send. It is used to update a local register with the same name. If Max-CmdSN+1 is equal to ExpCmdSN, the initiator knows that the target cannot receive any additional commands.

**DataSN**, for input (read) or bidirectional Data-In PDUs, is the input data PDU number (starting with 0) in the data transfer for the command identified by the initiator task tag. R2T and Data-In PDUs used with bidirectional commands must share the numbering sequence (i.e., assign numbers from a common sequencer). The maximum number of input data PDUs in a sequence is $2^{32}$ (counting the first PDU, which is numbered 0).

**Buffer Offset** contains the offset of the PDU data payload within the complete data transfer. The sum of the buffer offset and the length should not exceed the expected transfer length for the command.

The order of data PDUs within a sequence is determined by Data-PDUInOrder (which when set to **Yes** means that PDUs have to be in increasing buffer offset order without overlays). DataSequenceInOrder determines the ordering between sequences. When set to **Yes**, it means that sequences have to be in increasing buffer offset order and overlays are forbidden. Additional descriptions of how buffer offset is used along with DataPDUInOrder and DataSequenceInOrder can be found in Chapter 8 (in the Data Ordering section).

**Residual Count** is valid only where either the U bit or the O bit is set. If neither bit is set, it should be zero.

If the O bit is set, this field indicates the number of bytes not transferred because the initiator's expected data transfer length was not sufficient. If the U bit is set, it indicates the number of bytes not transferred out of the number of bytes expected.

**DataSegment** contains the data sent from the target to the initiator with this PDU.

## SCSI Data-Out PDU

The SCSI Data-Out PDU for *write* operations has the format shown below.

| Byte | 0 | 1 | 2 | 3 |
|---|---|---|---|---|
| Bit | 0 1 2 3 4 5 6 7 | 0 1 2 3 4 5 6 7 | 0 1 2 3 4 5 6 7 | 0 1 2 3 4 5 6 7 |
| 0 to 3 | . \| . \|0 0 0 1 0 1 | F\| | Reserved | |
| 4 to 7 | 0 | DataSegmentLength | | |
| 8 to 15 | LUN or Reserved | | | |
| 16 to 19 | ITT | | | |
| 20 to 23 | TTT or hex  FFFFFFFF | | | |
| 24 to 27 | Reserved | | | |
| 28 to 31 | ExpStatSN | | | |
| 32 to 35 | Reserved | | | |
| 36 to 39 | DataSN | | | |
| 40 to 43 | Buffer Offset | | | |
| 44 to 47 | Reserved | | | |
| 48 to 51 | Header Digest (if any) | | | |
| 52 (or 48) to *n* | DataSegment | | | |
| *n*+1 to *n*+4 | Data Digest (if any) | | | |

**F (final bit)**, for outgoing data, is 1 for the last PDU of unsolicited data or for the last PDU of a sequence answering an R2T. For bidirectional operations, it is 1 for the end of the input sequences as well as for the end of the output sequences.

**DataSegmentLength** is the data payload length of a Data-Out PDU. The sending of 0-length data segments should be avoided, but targets must be able to receive them properly. The DataSegments of Data-Out PDUs should be filled to an integer number of 4-byte words (real payload) unless the F bit is set to 1.

The DataSegmentLength field must not exceed MaxRecvDataSegment-Length for the direction in which it is sent, and the total length of all DataSegments of all PDUs in a sequence must not exceed MaxBurst-Length (or FirstBurstLength for unsolicited data).

**LUN (logical unit number)** is the number of the SCSI logical unit to which the data applies. (For additional information, see TTT below.)

**ITT (initiator task tag)** is the unique value given to each task, used to identify the commands (as explained in Chapter 8, Command and Data Ordering and Flow). In this case it enables the target to find the corresponding command that requires the data carried in this PDU.

**TTT (target transfer tag)**, on outgoing data, is provided to the target if the transfer is honoring an R2T. In this case, it is a replica of the TTT provided with the R2T.

TTT values are not specified by this protocol. However, the value hex FFFFFFFF is reserved and means that the TTT is not supplied. If the TTT is provided, the LUN field must hold a valid value; otherwise, LUN is reserved.

**ExpStatSN (expected status sequence number)** acknowledges status responses that have been received on the connection (as explained in Chapter 7, Session Management).

**DataSN (data sequence number)**, for output (write) data PDUs, is the data PDU number (starting with 0) within the current output sequence. The current output sequence is identified by the ITT (for unsolicited data), or it is a data sequence generated for one R2T (for data solicited through R2T). The maximum number of output data PDUs in a sequence is $2^{32}$ (counting the first PDU, which is numbered as 0).

**Buffer Offset** contains the offset of this PDU data payload within the complete data transfer. The sum of the buffer offset and the length should not exceed the expected transfer length for the command.

The order of data PDUs within a sequence is determined by DataPDUIn-Order (when set to **Yes** it means that PDUs have to be in increasing buffer offset order without overlays). The order of sequences is determined by DataSequenceInOrder (when set to **Yes** it means that sequences have to be in increasing buffer offset order and overlays are forbidden). Additional descriptions of how buffer offset is used with DataPDUInOrder and Data-SequenceInOrder can be found in Chapter 8, the Data Ordering section.

**DataSegment** contains data sent from the initiator to the target with this PDU.

## SNACK Request PDU

SNACK (selective negative acknowledgment or serial number acknowledgment) is a request for retransmission of numbered responses (status, data, or R2T PDUs) from the target. Despite its name, SNACK has a positive acknowledgment function, which is useful during the input of a large amount of data.

| Byte | 0 | 1 | 2 | 3 |
|---|---|---|---|---|
| Bit | 0 1 2 3 4 5 6 7 | 0 1 2 3 4 5 6 7 | 0 1 2 3 4 5 6 7 | 0 1 2 3 4 5 6 7 |
| 0 to 3 | .\|.\|0 0 1 0 1 0 | 1\|Rsrvd\| Type | Reserved | |
| 4 to 7 | 0 | 0 | | |
| 8 to 15 | LUN or Reserved | | | |
| 16 to 19 | ITT or hex  FFFFFFFF | | | |
| 20 to 23 | TTT, SNACK Tag, or hex  FFFFFFFF | | | |
| 24 to 27 | Reserved | | | |
| 28 to 31 | ExpStatSN | | | |
| 32 to 39 | Reserved | | | |
| 40 to 43 | BegRun | | | |
| 44 to 47 | RunLength | | | |
| 48 to 51 | Header Digest (if any) | | | |

Support for all SNACK types is mandatory if the supported error recovery level of the implementation is greater than zero.

The SNACK request is used to request the retransmission of numbered responses, data, or R2T PDUs from the target. The SNACK request indicates the numbered responses or data "runs" whose retransmission is requested of the target, where the run starts with the first StatSN, DataSN, or R2TSN whose retransmission is requested and also indicates the number of Status, Data, or R2T PDUs requested, including the first. Zero has special meaning when used with Run fields. When used only in RunLength, it means all PDUs starting with the initial one indicated by BegRun. When used in both BegRun and RunLength, it means all unacknowledged PDUs.

It is suggested that the target support SNACK even if the error recovery level is zero—in case the initiator sends a SNACK when, for whatever reason, it wants to operate above its committed error recovery level.

**Type (byte 1, bits 4–7)** encodes the SNACK function as follows:

> 0—Data/R2T SNACK requests retransmission of a Data-In or R2T PDU.
>
> 1—Status SNACK requests retransmission of a numbered response.
>
> 2—DataACK positively acknowledges Data-In PDUs.
>
> 3—R-Data SNACK requests retransmission of Data-In PDUs with possible resegmentation and status tagging.
>
> All other values are reserved.

**LUN (logical unit number)** contains the LUN field from the Data-In PDU that had the A bit set. In all other cases this field is reserved.

**ITT (initiator task tag)** is the initiator-assigned identifier for the referenced command or hex FFFFFFFF. For status SNACK and DataACK, it is reserved with a value of hex FFFFFFFF. In all other cases, it must be set to the value of the ITT of the referenced command.

**TTT (target transfer tag) or SNACK Tag** must contain a value other than FFFFFFFF. When used as a SNACK Tag the initiator picks a unique non-zero ID for the task identified by the ITT. The value must be copied to the last or only SCSI Response PDU by the target into a field also known as SNACK Tag. For DataACK, this field must contain a copy of the TTT and LUN provided with the SCSI Data-In PDU with the A bit set to **1**.

In all other cases, the Target Transfer Tag field must be set to the reserved value of hex FFFFFFFF.

**ExpStatSN (expected status sequence number)** acknowledges status responses that have been received on the connection (as explained in Chapter 5, Session Management).

**BegRun** is the DataSN, R2TSN, or StatSN of the first PDU whose retransmission is requested (via Data/R2T and Status SNACK), or the next expected DataSN for a DataACK SNACK request.

It must be 0 for an R-Data SNACK.

**RunLength** is the number of PDUs whose retransmission is requested. A value of zero signals that all Data-In, R2T, or response PDUs carrying numbers equal to or greater than BegRun have to be resent.

The value must be set to 0 for a DataAck SNACK as well as for R-Data SNACK.

The first data SNACK issued after the initiator's MaxRecvDataSegmentLength decreases, for a command issued on the same connection before the change in MaxRecvDataSegmentLength, must use an R-Data SNACK and RunLength equal to 0.

The first data SNACK after a task management request of TASK REASSIGN (see the section Task Management Function Request PDU) for a command whose connection allegiance was just changed should be an R-Data SNACK with RunLength equal to 0.

## Resegmentation

If the initiator MaxRecvDataSegmentLength changes between the original transmission and the time the initiator requests retransmission, the initiator *must* issue an R-Data SNACK. With R-Data SNACK, the initiator indicates that it discards all the unacknowledged data and expects the target to resend it. It also expects resegmentation. In this case the retransmitted Data-In PDUs *may* be different from the ones originally sent, in order to reflect changes in MaxRecvDataSegmentLength. Their DataSN starts with the BegRun of the last DataACK received by the target (if any was received) or 0 otherwise, and is increased by 1 for each resent Data-In PDU.

A target that has received an R-Data SNACK *must* return a SCSI Response PDU that contains a copy of the R-Data SNACK "SNACK Tag." This SNACK Tag value must be placed in the SCSI Response SNACK Tag field as its last or only response. This means that if it has already sent a response containing another value in the SNACK Tag field or had the status included in the last Data-In PDU, it must send a new SCSI Response PDU. If a target sends more than one SCSI Response PDU due to this rule, all SCSI responses must carry the same StatSN. If an initiator attempts to recover a lost SCSI Response PDU (with a Status SNACK) when more than one response has been sent, the target will send the SCSI Response PDU with the latest content known to the target, including the last SNACK Tag for the command.

If a SCSI command is reassigned to another connection (Allegiance Reassignment), any SNACK Tag it holds for a final response from the original connection should be deleted and the default value of 0 should be used instead. If the new connection has a different MaxRecvDataSegmentLength than the old connection, the ExpDataSN (if greater than 0) that is sent on the Reassign Task Management Request may not be interpreted reliably by the iSCSI target. In such a case, the target must behave as if an R-Data SNACK were issued and retransmit all unacknowledged data. Also note that status-piggybacking is not to be used for delivering the response, even if it was used the first time for delivering the nonrecovery response on the original connection.

### Notes on the SNACK Request PDU

The numbered response(s) or R2T(s) requested by a SNACK have to be delivered as exact replicas of those transmitted originally—except for the ExpCmdSN, MaxCmdSN, and ExpDataSN fields, which must carry their current values. R2T(s) requested by SNACK must also carry the current value of StatSN.

The numbered Data-In PDUs requested by a Data SNACK (not R-Data SNACK), have to be delivered as exact replicas of those the initiator missed—except for the ExpCmdSN and MaxCmdSN fields, which must carry the current values.

Any SNACK requesting a numbered response, data, or an R2T that was not sent by the target must be rejected with a reason code of "Protocol error." A Data/R-Data/R2T/SNACK for a command must precede status acknowledgment for it. Specifically, the ExpStatSN must not be advanced until all Data-In or R2T PDUs have been received.

An iSCSI target that does not support recovery within a connection (because its error recovery level is 0) may reject status SNACK with a Reject PDU. This will probably cause the SCSI level to time-out and perform its own error recovery. It is therefore possible to build a very simple error recovery model in which iSCSI ignores these error types and lets the SCSI level retry the operation. The timeout will be fairly long, so hopefully this approach will not be used on "enterprise class" installations.

If the target supports an error recovery level equal to or greater than 1, it may still discard the SNACK, after which it must issue an asynchronous message PDU with an iSCSI event indicating a request logout. (However, this should be done only as a last resort.) If an initiator operates at error recovery level 1 or higher, it must issue a SNACK of type DataACK after receiving a Data-In PDU with the A bit set to **1**. However, if the initiator has detected holes in the input sequence, it must postpone the SNACK until the holes are filled. An initiator may ignore the A bit if it deems that the bit is being set aggressively by the target (i.e., before the MaxBurstLength limit is reached).

The DataACK is used to free resources at the target and not to request or imply data retransmission. This feature is useful when large amounts of data are being read, perhaps from tape, and the resources tied up by the operation in the target can be freed up incrementally, as the target can be sure that the data has arrived.

## Task Management Function Request PDU

Provides a way for the initiator to control task execution.

| Byte | 0 | 1 | 2 | 3 |
|---|---|---|---|---|
| Bit | 0 1 2 3 4 5 6 7 | 0 1 2 3 4 5 6 7 | 0 1 2 3 4 5 6 7 | 0 1 2 3 4 5 6 7 |
| 0 to 3 | .\|I\|0 0 0 0 1 0 | 1\|     Function | Reserved | |
| 4 to 7 | 0 | 0 | | |
| 8 to 15 | LUN or Reserved | | | |
| 16 to 19 | ITT | | | |
| 20 to 23 | Referenced Task Tag or hex  FFFFFFFF | | | |
| 24 to 27 | CmdSN | | | |
| 28 to 31 | ExpStatSN | | | |
| 32 to 35 | RefCmdSN or Reserved | | | |
| 36 to 39 | ExpDataSN or Reserved | | | |
| 40 to 47 | Reserved | | | |
| 48 to 51 | Header Digest (if any) | | | |

**I (immediate bit)** causes the request to be considered for immediate action.

**Function** holds the task management function codes that provide an initiator with a way to explicitly control the execution of one or more tasks (SCSI and iSCSI tasks). These functions are as follows. (For a more detailed description, see Chapter 10 and [SAM2].)

1. ABORT TASK—Aborts the task identified by the Referenced Task Tag field.

2. ABORT TASK SET—Aborts all tasks issued via this session on the logical unit.

3. CLEAR ACA—Clears the auto contingent allegiance condition.

4. CLEAR TASK SET—Aborts all tasks in the appropriate task set as defined by the TST field in the control mode page (see [SPC3]).

5. LOGICAL UNIT RESET—Performs a Clear Task Set for the LU and then resets various states within it.

6. TARGET WARM RESET—Performs a Logical Unit Reset for all LUs within the SCSI device (iSCSI target node).

7. TARGET COLD RESET—Performs a Target Warm Reset and then drops all connections.

8. TASK REASSIGN—Reassigns connection allegiance for the task identified by the ITT field on this connection, thus resuming the iSCSI exchanges for the task. It must be issued as an immediate command.

For all these functions, the task management function response PDU must be returned. The functions apply to the referenced tasks regardless of whether they are proper SCSI tasks or tagged iSCSI operations.

**LUN (logical unit number)** is required for functions addressing a specific LU (Abort Task, Clear Task Set, Abort Task Set, Clear ACA, Logical Unit Reset) and is reserved in all others.

**CmdSN (command sequence number)** enables in-order delivery of a given command to the target SCSI layer (as explained in Chapter 7, Session Management). Task management requests must act on all commands having a CmdSN lower than the task management CmdSN. If the task management request is marked for immediate delivery, it must be considered for execution immediately, but the operations involved (all or part of them) may be postponed to allow the target to receive all relevant tasks.

**ExpStatSN (expected status sequence number)** acknowledges commands that have been received on the connection (as explained in Chapter 7).

**ITT (initiator task tag)** is the unique value given to each task, used to identify the commands (as explained in Chapter 10, Task Management).

**Referenced task tag (RTT)** is the initiator task tag of the task to be aborted (Abort Task) or reassigned (Task Reassign). If the function is independent of any specific command to be aborted or reassigned, the value should be set to hex FFFFFFFF.

**RefCmdSN,** for the Abort Task function targeting non immediate commands, must always be set by the initiator to the CmdSN of the task identified by the RTT field, else, for immediate commands, must be set equal to this PDU's CmdSN. Targets must use this field when the task identified by the RTT is not with the target.

**ExpDataSN**—For recovery purposes the iSCSI target and initiator maintain a data acknowledgment reference number—the first input DataSN number unacknowledged by the initiator. When issuing a new command this number is set to 0. If the function is TASK REASSIGN, which establishes a new connection allegiance for a previously issued read or bidirectional command, ExpDataSN will contain either an updated data acknowledgment reference number or the value 0, the latter indicating that the data acknowledgment reference number is unchanged. The initiator *must* discard any data PDUs from the previous execution that it did not acknowledge, and the target *must* transmit all Data-In PDUs (if any) starting with the data acknowledgment reference number. The number of retransmitted PDUs may or may not be the same as the original transmission depending on whether there was a change in MaxRecvDataSegmentLength in the reassignment. The target *may* also send no more Data-In PDUs if all data has been acknowledged.

The value of ExpDataSN *must* be either 0 or higher than the DataSN of the last acknowledged Data-In PDU, but not larger than DataSN+1 of the last Data-In PDU sent by the target. The target *must* ignore any other value.

For other functions this field is reserved.

### Notes on the Task Management Function Request PDU

According to [SAM2], the iSCSI target must ensure that no tasks covered by the task management response (i.e., with a CmdSN less than the task management command CmdSN) have their responses delivered to the initiator SCSI layer after the task management response. However, the iSCSI initiator may deliver any responses received before the task management response. It is a matter of implementation if the SCSI responses—received before the task management response but after the task management request was issued—are delivered to the SCSI layer by the iSCSI layer in the initiator.

For Abort Task Set and Clear Task Set, the issuing initiator must continue to respond to all valid TTTs (received via R2T, Text Response, NOP-In, or SCSI Data-In PDUs) related to the affected task set, even after issuing the task management request. However, the issuing initiator should terminate these response sequences as quickly as possible (by setting the F bit to 1), preferably with no data. The target must wait for responses on all affected TTTs before acting on either of these two task management requests. A case in which all or part of the response sequence is not received for a valid TTT (because of digest errors) may be treated by the target as within-command error recovery (if it is supporting an error recovery level of 1 or higher). Alternatively the target may drop the connection to complete the requested task set function.

If the connection is still active (not undergoing an implicit or explicit logout), Abort Task must be issued on the same connection to which the task to be aborted is allegiant at the time the task management request is issued. If the connection is implicitly or explicitly logged out (i.e., no other request will be issued and no other response will be received on the failing connection), an Abort Task function request may be issued on another connection. This task management request will then establish a new allegiance for the command to be aborted, as well as abort it. The task aborted will not have to be retried or reassigned, and its status, if issued but not acknowledged, will be reissued followed by the task management response. (The initiator must be careful not to deliver the task management response to the SCSI layer until this missing status is reissued, received, and passed to the SCSI layer.)

The Target Reset function (Warm and Cold) is optional. Target Warm Reset may be subject to SCSI access controls for the requesting initiator. When authorization fails at the target, the appropriate response as described in the section Task Management Function Response PDU (following) must be returned by the target. The Target Cold Reset is not subject to SCSI access controls, but its execution privileges may be managed by iSCSI via Login Authentication.

For the Target Warm Reset and Target Cold Reset functions, the target cancels all pending operations on all LUs known to the initiator. Both functions are equivalent to the Target Reset function as specified by [SAM2]. They can affect many other initiators logged into the same servicing SCSI target port.

The use of Target Cold Reset may be limited by iSCSI access controls but not by SCSI access controls. It is handled as a power-on event so, when the Target Cold Reset function is complete, the target must terminate all of its TCP connections to all initiators (all sessions are terminated). Therefore, the service responses for this function may not be reliably delivered to the issuing initiator port.

For the Task Reassign function, the target should reassign allegiance to the connection on which this command is executed (and thus resume iSCSI exchanges for the task). The target must receive Task Reassign only after the connection on which the command was previously executing has been successfully logged out. The task management response must be issued before the reassignment becomes effective.

## Task Management Function Response PDU

| Byte | 0 | 1 | 2 | 3 |
|---|---|---|---|---|
| Bit | 0 1 2 3 4 5 6 7 | 0 1 2 3 4 5 6 7 | 0 1 2 3 4 5 6 7 | 0 1 2 3 4 5 6 7 |
| 0 to 3 | .\|.\|1 0 0 0 1 0 | 1\|    Reserved | Response | Reserved |
| 4 to 7 | 0 | 0 | | |
| 8 to 15 | Reserved | | | |
| 16 to 19 | ITT | | | |
| 20 to 23 | Reserved | | | |
| 24 to 27 | StatSN | | | |
| 28 to 31 | ExpCmdSN | | | |
| 32 to 35 | MaxCmdSN | | | |
| 36 to 47 | Reserved | | | |
| 48 to 51 | Header Digest (if any) | | | |

The target performs the requested task management function and sends the initiator a task management response Abort Task, Abort Task Set, Clear ACA, Clear Task Set, Logical Unit Reset, Target Warm Reset, Target Cold Reset, and Task Reassign. For Target Cold Reset and Target Warm Reset, the target cancels all pending operations across all logical units known to the issuing initiator. For Target Cold Reset, the target must then close all of its TCP connections to all initiators (i.e., terminate all sessions). As a result, the response may not be delivered to the initiator reliably. For Task Reassign, the new connection allegiance must only become effective at the target after the target issues the Task Management Function Response PDU.

**Response** is provided by the target, and it may take the values listed here. All other values are reserved.

0—Function complete

1—Task does not exist

2—LUN does not exist

3—Task still allegiant

4—Task allegiance reassignment not supported

5—Task management function not supported

6—Function authorization failed

255—Function rejected

The mapping of the response code onto an initiator SCSI service response code value, if needed, is outside the scope of this book. However, in symbolic terms, Response value 0 maps to the SCSI service response of FUNCTION COMPLETE. All other Response values map to the SCSI service response of FUNCTION REJECTED. If a Task Management Function Response PDU does not arrive before the session is terminated, the initiator SCSI service response is SERVICE DELIVERY OR TARGET FAILURE.

The response to Abort Task Set and Clear Task Set must be issued by the target only after

- All affected commands have been received by the target.

- The corresponding task management functions have been executed by the SCSI target.

- Delivery of all previous command responses has been confirmed (acknowledged through ExpStatSN) by the initiator on all connections of this session.

Responses to Abort Task are as follows:

- If the Referenced Task Tag identifies a valid task leading to a successful termination, the target must return the "Function complete" response.

- If the Referenced Task Tag does not identify an existing task, but if the CmdSN indicated by the RefCmdSN field in the task management function request is within the valid CmdSN window (between MaxCmdSN and ExpCmdSN), the target must consider the CmdSN received and return the "Function complete" response.

■ If the Referenced Task Tag does not identify an existing task, and if the CmdSN indicated by the RefCmdSN field in the task management function request is outside the valid CmdSN window, the target must return the "Task does not exist" response.

**ITT (initiator task tag)** is the unique value the initiator gives to each task, used to identify the commands (as explained in Chapter 10, Task Management) and returned on this response PDU.

**StatSN (status sequence number)** is a sequence number that the target iSCSI layer generates per connection and that in turn enables the initiator to acknowledge status reception. Task management PDUs are considered acknowledgeable events, which means that the StatSN local variable is incremented.

**ExpCmdSN (next expected CmdSN)** is a sequence number that the target iSCSI returns to the initiator to acknowledge command reception.

**MaxCmdSN (maximum CmdSN)** is a sequence number that the target iSCSI returns to the initiator to indicate the maximum CmdSN the initiator can send.

### Notes on the Task Management Function Response PDU

The execution of Abort Task Set and Clear Task Set consists of the following sequence of events on each of the entities:

■ The initiator:

1. Issues the Abort Task Set/Clear Task Set request.

2. Continues to respond to each valid TTT received (via R2T, Text Response, NOP-In, or SCSI Data-In PDUs) for the affected task set.

3. Receives any responses for the tasks in the affected task set (it may process them as usual since they are guaranteed to be valid).

4. Receives the task set management response, thus concluding all tasks in the affected task set.

■ The target:

1. Receives the Abort Task Set/Clear Task Set request.

2. Waits for all TTTs to be responded to and for all affected tasks in the task set to be received.

3. Propagates the command up to, and receives the response from, the target SCSI layer.

4. Takes note of the last-sent StatSN on each of the connections in the session and waits for acknowledgment of each StatSN (it may solicit acknowledgment by way of a NOP-In).

5. Sends the task set management response.

## Text Request PDU

The Text Request PDU allows the exchange of information and future extensions. It permits the initiator to inform a target of its capabilities or to request some special operations. (For a further explanation of this PDU, see Chapter 6, the section Text Requests and Responses.)

| Byte | 0 | 1 · | 2 | 3 |
|---|---|---|---|---|
| Bit | 0 1 2 3 4 5 6 7 | 0 1 2 3 4 5 6 7 | 0 1 2 3 4 5 6 7 | 0 1 2 3 4 5 6 7 |
| 0 to 3 | .\|I\|0 0 0 1 0 0 F\|C\| | | Reserved | |
| 4 to 7 | 0 | DataSegmentLength | | |
| 8 to 15 | LUN or Reserved | | | |
| 16 to 19 | ITT | | | |
| 20 to 23 | TTT or hex  FFFFFFFF | | | |
| 24 to 27 | CmdSN | | | |
| 28 to 31 | ExpStatSN | | | |
| 32 to 47 | Reserved | | | |
| 48 to 51 | Header Digest (if any) | | | |
| 52 (or 48) to *n* | DataSegment (Text) | | | |
| *n*+1 to *n*+4 | Data Digest (if any) | | | |

An initiator must have, at most, one outstanding text request on a connection at any time.

On a connection failure, an initiator must either explicitly abort any active allegiant text negotiation task or cause it to be implicitly terminated by the target.

**I** (**immediate bit**) ensures that the command is considered for handling without waiting. It must be the same for all requests in a sequence.

**F** (**final bit**), when set to **1**, indicates that this is the last or the only one in a sequence of text requests; otherwise, it indicates that more text requests will follow.

**C** (**continue bit**), when set to **1**, indicates that the text request (a set of key=value pairs) is not complete (it will be continued on a subsequent Text Request PDU); otherwise, it indicates that this Text Request PDU ends a set of key=value pairs. A Text Request PDU with the C bit set to 1 must have the F bit set to 0.

**DataSegmentLength** is the data payload length of the Text Request PDU. It should be filled with any number of text bytes, from one to $2^{24}-1$. However, its total size must be less than or equal to the variable known as MaxRecvDataSegmentLength (a per-connection and per-direction declared parameter).

**LUN** (**logical unit number**)—if the TTT is not hex FFFFFFFF, this field must be the LU sent by the target in the Text Response PDU.

**ITT** (**initiator task tag**) is the initiator-assigned identifier for this text request PDU. If the command is sent as part of a sequence of text requests and responses, the ITT must be the same for all the requests within the sequence.

**TTT** (**target transfer tag**) is set to the reserved value of hex FFFFFFFF when the initiator originates a Text Request PDU to the target. However, when the initiator answers a Text Response PDU from the target, this field must contain the value the initiator copies from that PDU.

The target sets the TTT in a Text Response PDU to a value other than the reserved value hex FFFFFFFF whenever it wants to indicate that it has more data to send or more operations to perform that are associated with the specified ITT. The target must do this whenever it sets the F bit to 0 in the response. By copying the TTT from the response into the next Text Request PDU it sends, the initiator tells the target to continue the operation for the specific ITT. The initiator must ignore the TTT in the Text Response PDU when the F bit is set to **1**.

When the initiator sets the TTT in this PDU to the reserved value hex FFFFFFFF, it tells the target that this is a new request and the target should reset any internal state associated with the ITT (resets the current negotiation state). This mechanism allows the initiator and target to transfer a large amount of textual data over a sequence of text command/text response exchanges, or to perform extended negotiation sequences. A target may reset its internal negotiation state if the initiator stalls an exchange for a long time or if it is running out of resources.

Long text responses are handled as in the following example:

```
I->T Text SendTargets=All (F=1,TTT=0xffffffff)

T->I Text <part 1> (F=0,TTT=0x12345678)

I->T Text <empty> (F=1, TTT=0x12345678)

T->I Text <part 2> (F=0, TTT=0x12345678)

I->T Text <empty> (F=1, TTT=0x12345678)

T->I Text <part n> (F=1, TTT=0xffffffff)
```

**CmdSN (command sequence number)** is unique across the session; it permits ordered delivery of this command for handling by the iSCSI layer.

**ExpStatSN (expected status sequence number)** acknowledges status responses that have been received on the connection (as explained in Chapter 7, Session Management).

**DataSegment (text field of this PDU)** contains key=value pairs, some of which can be used in Login Request/Response PDUs and some in Text Request/Response PDUs. (Appendix B contains a list of key=value pairs.) If not specified otherwise, the maximum length of an individual value (not its encoded representation) is 255 bytes, not including the delimiter (comma or null). The data length of a text request or response must not exceed MaxRecvDataSegmentLength (a per-connection, per-direction declared parameter).

A key=value pair can span text request or response boundaries (i.e., it can start in one PDU and continue in the next). In other words, the end of a PDU does not necessarily signal the end of a key=value pair.

The target sends its response back to the initiator. The response text format is similar to the request text format. That text response may refer to key=value pairs presented in an earlier text request, and the text in that request may refer to a still earlier response.

Text operations are usually meant for parameter setting/negotiations, but can also perform some long-lasting operations. Those that take a long time should be placed in their own Text Request PDU.

## Text Response PDU

The Text Response PDU contains the target's response to the initiator's text request. Its text field format matches that of the Text Request PDU.

| Byte | 0 | 1 | 2 | 3 |
|---|---|---|---|---|
| Bit | 0 1 2 3 4 5 6 7 | 0 1 2 3 4 5 6 7 | 0 1 2 3 4 5 6 7 | 0 1 2 3 4 5 6 7 |
| 0 to 3 | .\|.\|1 0 0 1 0 0 | F\|C\| | Reserved | |
| 4 to 7 | 0 | DataSegmentLength | | |
| 8 to 15 | LUN or Reserved | | | |
| 16 to 19 | ITT | | | |
| 20 to 23 | TTT or hex FFFFFFFF | | | |
| 24 to 27 | StatSN | | | |
| 28 to 31 | ExpCmdSN | | | |
| 32 to 35 | MaxCmdSN | | | |
| 36 to 47 | Reserved | | | |
| 48 to 51 | Header Digest (if any) | | | |
| 52 (or 48) to *n* | DataSegment (Text) | | | |
| *n*+1 to *n*+4 | Data Digest (if any) | | | |

**F (final bit)**—when set to **1** in response to a Text Request PDU that has its F
bit set to **1**, indicates that the target has finished the entire operation. An
F bit set to 0 in response to a Text Request PDU that has its F bit set to **1**
indicates that the target has more work to do (i.e., it invites a follow-on
text request). Other value settings are as follows:

- The F bit set to **1**, in response to a Text Request PDU with the F bit set
  to 0, is a protocol error.

- If the F bit is set to **1**, the PDU must not contain key=value pairs that
  require additional answers from the initiator.

- If the F bit is set to **1** the PDU must have its TTT field set to the reserved
  value of hex FFFFFFFF.

- If the F bit is set to 0, the PDU must have a TTT field set to a value
  different from the reserved hex FFFFFFFF.

**C (continue bit)**, when set to **1**, indicates that the text (a set of key=value
pairs) in this Text Response PDU is not complete (it will be continued on
a subsequent Text Response PDU). A C bit with a 0 value indicates that
the PDU ends a set of key=value pairs. A Text Response PDU with the C
bit set to **1** must have the F bit set to 0.

**DataSegmentLength** is the data payload length of the Text Response PDU.
The DataSegment (the text) should be filled with any number of text
bytes, from one to $2^{24}-1$. However, its total size must be less than or
equal to the variable known as MaxRecvDataSegmentLength.

**LUN (logical unit number)** may be set to a valid significant value if the TTT
is not hex FFFFFFFF; otherwise, it is reserved.

**ITT (initiator task tag)** matches the ITT in the initial Text Request PDU.

**TTT (target transfer tag)**—When a target has more text data than it can send
in a single Text Response PDU or it has to continue the negotiations (and
has enough resources to proceed), this field must be a valid value (not
the reserved value of hex FFFFFFFF); otherwise, it must be set to hex
FFFFFFFF.

If the TTT is not hex FFFFFFFF, the initiator must copy it and the LUN
field from this PDU into its next request to indicate that it wants the
rest of the data. Whenever the target receives a Text Request PDU with
the TTT set to the reserved value of hex FFFFFFFF, it resets its internal

information (resets state) associated with the given ITT. A target may reset its internal state—associated with an ITT (the current negotiation state) and expressed through the TTT—if the initiator fails to continue the exchange for some time. It may also reject subsequent text requests that have the TTT set to the same, now "stale," value.

When a target cannot finish the operation in single text response and does not have enough resources to continue, it should reject the Text Request PDU with a Reject PDU that contains the appropriate reason code (see Reject PDU).

**StatSN (status sequence number)** is a sequence number the target iSCSI layer generates per connection that enables the initiator to acknowledge reception of status. Text Request PDUs are considered acknowledgeable events, which means that the StatSN local variable is incremented and presented in this field.

**ExpCmdSN (next expected CmdSN)** is a sequence number that the target iSCSI returns to the initiator to acknowledge command reception. It is used to update a local register with the same name. An ExpCmdSN that is equal to MaxCmdSN+1 indicates that the target cannot accept new commands.

**MaxCmdSN (maximum CmdSN)** is a sequence number the target iSCSI returns to the initiator to indicate the maximum CmdSN the initiator can send. It is used to update a local register with the same name. If MaxCmdSN+1 is equal to ExpCmdSN, the initiator knows that the target cannot receive any additional commands.

**DataSegment (text field of this PDU)** contains responses in the same key=value format as in the text request, with the same length and coding constraints. A set of valid key=values and responses can be found in Appendix B.

A key=value pair can span Text Response PDU boundaries (i.e., a key=value pair can start in one PDU and continue in the next). In other words, the end of a PDU does not necessarily signal the end of a key=value pair. To get the missing part(s) of a key=value pair, an initiator may have to send an empty Text Request PDU. Text for text requests and responses can span several PDUs. If the length of a PDU does not allow it to hold the whole text request, the text response may refer to key=value pairs presented in an earlier text request.

Although the initiator is the requesting party and controls the request–response initiation and termination, the target can offer key=value pairs of its own as part of a sequence and not only in response to the initiator. The text response may refer to key=value pairs presented in an earlier text request, and the text in that request may refer to key=value pairs in still earlier responses.

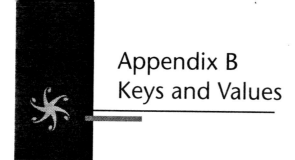

# Appendix B
# Keys and Values

In the following table, each keyword is described according to the following:

- When used (Use)

    IO—Only during connection login (initialize only).

    LO—Only during the leading (first connection) login (leading only).

    FFPO—Only during full-feature phase.

    All—During login or full-feature phase.

    S—Only during security negotiation phase.

    S&O—During security negotiation phase and operational negotiation phase.

    D—Declarative: can be combined with the above; can be used in security negotiation or operational phase. Nonsecurity and nondeclarative can be used only in the operational negotiation phase.

- Who uses it (Who)

    I—Initiator

    T—Target

    I&T—Both

- Scope of value (Scope)

    SW—Session-wide

    CO—Connection only

- Value or list used

- Default value

- Example use

- Comments

- The result function for

Minimum—The selected value cannot exceed the offered value.

Maximum—The selected value cannot be lower than the offered value.

AND—The result is the Boolean **AND** of the offered value and the responding value.

OR—The result is the Boolean **OR** of the offered value and the responding value.

| Key | Use/ Scope | Who | Value/List | Default |
|---|---|---|---|---|
| **AuthMethod** | IO, S /CO | I&T | **KRB**5, **SPKM**1, **SPKM**2, **SRP**, **CHAP, None** | **None** |
| | Example: **AuthMethod=SRP, CHAP, None** | | | |
| | Comment: Initiator offers, target selects. Note: private and public methods are also permitted, and use "Z–" and "Z#" see [iSCSI.] | | | |
| **AuthMethod** Keys | IO, S /CO | I&T | Method specific | Method specific |
| | Examples: | | | No default |
| CHAP_<key>, | CHAP_A=<A1, A2> | | | |
| KRB_<key>, | KRB_AP_REQ=<krb_ap_req> | | | |
| SPKM_<key>, | SPKM_REQ=<spkm-req> | | | |
| SRP_<key> | SRP_U=<userid> | | | |
| | Comment: The authentication-specific key syntax is authentication method (**CHAP**), then _, then the method's key (**CHAP_A=<A1, A2>**). | | | |

| Key | Use/ Scope | Who | Value/List | Default |
|---|---|---|---|---|
| Authentication SRP Unique Key: **TargetAuth** | IO, S /CO | I&T | **Yes** or **No** | No default |
| | Example: **SRP-U=xyzid TargetAuth=yes** | | | |
| | Comment: Used only with **SRP_U=<userid>**. | | | |
| **DataDigest** | IO /CO | I&T | **CRC-32C, None** | **None** |
| | Example: **DataDigest=CRC-32C, None** | | | |
| | Comment: The initiator or target offers; the responder chooses. Note: private and public methods are also permitted using "Y–" and "Y#" see [iSCSI]. | | | |
| **DataPDUInOrder** | LO /SW | I&T | **Yes** or **No** | **Yes** |
| | Example: **DataPDUInOrder=No** | | | |
| | Comment: **No** indicates that the data PDUs within a sequence can be in any order. **Yes** indicates that the data PDUs within a sequence have to be at continuously increasing addresses and that overlays are forbidden. The result function is **OR**. | | | |
| **DataSequence InOrder** | LO /SW | I&T | **Yes** or **No** | **Yes** |
| | Example:   **DataSequenceInOrder=No** | | | |
| | Comment: If set to **No**, the data PDU sequence may be transferred in any order. If set to **Yes**, the sequence must be transferred using continuously increasing offsets except for error recovery. The result function is **OR**. | | | |
| **DefaultTime2Retain** | LO /SW | I&T | **0–3600** | **20** |
| | Example: **DefaultTime2Retain=100** | | | |
| | Comment: **Max** seconds that connection and task allegiance reinstatement is still possible following a connection termination or reset and the **Time2Wait** interval. The results function is **Min**. Zero means no reinstatement is possible. Also known as **Time2Retain**. | | | |
| **DefaultTime2Wait** | LO /SW | I&T | **0–3600** | **2** |
| | Example: **DefaultTime2Wait=300**                                        *(continued)* | | | |

| Key | Use/ Scope | Who | Value/List | Default |
|---|---|---|---|---|
| | Comment: **Min** seconds to wait before attempting connection and task allegiance reinstatement after a connection termination or a connection reset. The results function is **Max**. A value of zero means that task reassignment can be done immediately. Also known as **Time2Wait**. | | | |
| **ErrorRecoveryLevel** | LO /SW | I&T | **0–2** | **0** |
| | Example: **ErrorRecoveryLevel=1** | | | |
| | Comment: Recovery levels represent a combination of recovery capabilities. Each level includes all the capabilities of the lower recovery level. The result function is **Min**. | | | |
| **FirstBurstLength** | LO /SW | I&T | **512** to $(2^{24})-1$ | 64K bytes |
| | Example: **FirstBurstLength=2048** | | | |
| | Comment: Maximum SCSI payload, in bytes, of unsolicited data an initiator may send to the target. Includes immediate data and a sequence of unsolicited Data-Out PDUs. Zero (don't care) can be used. Must be **<= MaxBurstLength**. The result function is **Min**. | | | |
| **HeaderDigest** | IO /CO | I&T | **CRC-32C, None** | **None** |
| | Example: **HeaderDigest=CRC-32C,None** | | | |
| | Comment: The initiator or target offers the value list; the other chooses. Note: private and public methods are also permitted using "Y–" and "Y#" see [iSCSI]. | | | |
| **IFMarker** | IO /CO | I&T | **Yes** or **No** | **No** |
| | Example: **IFMarker=Yes** | | | |
| | Comment: Turns on or off the target-to-initiator markers. The result function is **AND**. | | | |
| **IFMarkInt** | IO /CO | I&T | **1–65535[~ 1–65535]** or **Reject** | **2048** |
| | Example: **IFMarkInt=1024~ 8192** | | | |

| Key | Use/ Scope | Who | Value/List | Default |
|---|---|---|---|---|
| | Comment: Interval value (in 4-byte words) for target-to-initiator markers. The interval is measured from the end of one marker to the beginning of the next one. The offer can have only a range; the response can have only a single value (picked from the offered range) or **Reject**. | | | |
| **ImmediateData** | LO /SW | I&T | **Yes** or **No** | **Yes** |
| | Example: **ImmediateData=No** | | | |
| | Comment: Either the initiator or target can turn off **ImmediateData**. (See table that follows). The result function is **AND**. | | | |
| **InitialR2T** | LO /SW | I&T | **Yes** or **No** | **Yes** |
| | Example: **InitialR2T=No** | | | |
| | Comment: Turns off the default use of R2T; allows an initiator to start sending data to a target as if it had received an initial R2T. The result function is **OR**. | | | |
| **InitiatorAlias** | All, D, S&O /SW | I | **<iSCSI-local-name-value>** | No default |
| | Example: **InitiatorAlias=Mother_System** | | | |
| | Comment: Sent to the target in the login PDU. | | | |
| **InitiatorName** | IO, D, S&O /SW | I | **<iSCSI-name-value>** | No default |
| | Example: **InitiatorName=iqn.2002-01.com.jump:ee** | | | |
| | Comment: Must be sent on first login request per connection. | | | |
| **MaxBurstLength** | LO /SW | I&T | **512** to $(2^{24})-1$ | 256K bytes |
| | Example: **MaxBurstLength=4096** | | | |
| | Comment: Maximum SCSI data payload in bytes for data-in or for a solicited data-out sequence. Zero (don't care) can be used. The responder's number is used. The result function is **Min**. | | | |
| | | | | *(continued)* |

| Key | Use/Scope | Who | Value/List | Default |
|---|---|---|---|---|
| **MaxConnections** | LO /SW | I&T | **1–65535** | **1** |
| | Example:    **MaxConnections=25** | | | |
| | Comment: The initiator and target negotiate the maximum number of connections that can be requested or are acceptable. The result function is **Min**. | | | |
| **MaxOutstandingR2T** | LO /SW | I&T | **1–65535** | **1** |
| | Example: **MaxOutstandingR2T=500** | | | |
| | Comment: The maximum number of outstanding R2Ts. The responder's value is used. The result function is **Min**. | | | |
| **MaxRecvData-SegmentLength** | All, D /CO | I&T | **512** to $(2^{24})-1$ | **8192** |
| | Example: **MaxRecvDataSegmentLength=1024** | | | |
| | Comment: The maximum amount of data that either the initiator or the target can receive in any iSCSI PDU. Zero (don't care) can be used. I&T can specify (declare) the **Max** they can receive. This is a connection- and direction-specific parameter. The actual value used for targets will be **Min (This value, MaxBurstLength**) for data-in and solicited data-out data. **Min (This value, FirstBurstLength**) for unsolicited data. | | | |
| **OFMarker** | IO /CO | I&T | **Yes** or **No** | **No** |
| | Example: **OFMarker=Yes** | | | |
| | Comment: Turns on or off the initiator-to-target markers. The result function is **AND** | | | |
| **OFMarkInt** | IO /CO | I&T | **1–65535** [~ **1–65535**] or **Reject** | **2048** |
| | Example: **OFMarkInt=2048~8192** | | | |
| | Comment: The interval value (in 4-byte words) for initiator-to-target markers, measured from the end of one marker to the beginning of the next. The offer can have only a range; | | | |

| Key | Use/ Scope | Who | Value/List | Default |
|---|---|---|---|---|
| | the response can have only a single value (picked from the offered range) or **Reject**. | | | |
| **SendTargets** | FFPO /SO | I | **ALL, <iSCSI Target name>, <nothing>** | **<Current session's Target Name>** |
| | Example: **SendTargets=ALL** | | | |
| | Comment: See Chapter 5, the section Discovery Session | | | |
| **SessionType** | LO, D, S&O /SW | I | **Discovery** or **Normal** | **Normal** |
| | Example: **SessionType=Discovery** | | | |
| | Comment: The initiator indicates the type of session needed and the target can accept or reject it. **Discovery** indicates that the only purpose of the session is discovery. | | | |
| **TargetAddress** | All, D, S&O /SW | T | **Domain-name [:port] [,portal-group-tag]** | No default |
| | Example: **TargetAddress=10.0.0.1:5003,65** | | | |
| | Comment: Returned in the **SendTargets** response. | | | |
| **TargetAlias** | All, D, S&O /SW | T | **<iSCSI-local-name-value>** | No default |
| | Example: **TargetAlias=Database_volumes** | | | |
| | Comment: Sent to the initiator in a login response PDU. | | | |
| **TargetName** | IO, S&O, → All ⟶ D /SW | I T | **<iSCSI-name-value>** | No default |
| | Example: **TargetName=iqn.2001-02.com.wonder.zz** | | | |
| | Comment: Must be sent by the initiator on the first login request per connection. Not sent by the initiator on discovery session. Sent by the target in response to a **SendTargets** command. *(continued)* | | | |

| Key | Use/ Scope | Who | Value/List | Default |
|---|---|---|---|---|
| **TargetPortal-GroupTag** | IO, D, S&O /SW | T | **<16 bit Binary-Value 0- to 65535>** | No default |
| | Example: **TargetPortalGroupTag=1** | | | |
| | Comment: Value is the 16-bit TPGT of the connection. It is returned to the initiator in the first login response PDU of the session. | | | |
| **X-<Vendor-SpecificKey>** | All | I&T | **<Vendor Specific Values>** | No default |
| | Example: **X-com.ibm.DoTheRightThing=ofcourse** | | | |
| | Comment: The vendor's reverse DNS name should follow the **X-** and precede the function name. | | | |
| **X#<IANA-registered-string>** | All | I&T | **<IANA-Registered values>** | No default |
| | Example: **x#my_stuff=5** | | | |
| | Comment: The key and the values must be registered by IANA. | | | |

The following table is a summary of unsolicited data options.

| InitialR2T | ImmediateData | Result (up to FirstBurstLength) |
|---|---|---|
| No | No | Unsolicited data in data PDUs only |
| No | Yes | Immediate and separate unsolicited data |
| Yes | No | All types of unsolicited data disallowed |
| Yes | Yes | Immediate unsolicited data only |

# Appendix C
# SCSI Architecture Model

The following information is from [iSCSI]. It describes the relationship between the SCSI architecture model and SCSI devices and ports, the I-T nexus, and iSCSI. This relationship implies implementation requirements in order to conform to the [SAM2] model and other SCSI operational functions. These requirements are detailed in the section Consequences of the Model.

## SCSI–iSCSI Mappings

The following paragraphs outline mappings of SCSI architectural elements to iSCSI.

**SCSI device**—According to [SAM2], an entity that contains other SCSI entities. For example, a SCSI initiator device contains one or more SCSI initiator ports and zero or more application clients. A SCSI target device contains one or more SCSI target ports and one or more logical units. For iSCSI, the SCSI device is the component within an iSCSI node that provides SCSI functionality. As such, there can be only one SCSI device within a given iSCSI node. Access to the SCSI device can only be achieved in an iSCSI normal, operational session. The SCSI device name is the iSCSI node name, and its use is mandatory in the iSCSI protocol.

**SCSI port**—According to [SAM2], an entity in a SCSI device that provides SCSI functionality to interface with a service delivery subsystem or transport. For iSCSI, the definition of a SCSI initiator port and that of a SCSI target port are different.

■ The *SCSI initiator port*—Maps to the endpoint of an iSCSI normal operational session, which is negotiated through the login process between an iSCSI initiator node and an iSCSI target node. At successful completion of this process, a SCSI initiator port is created within the SCSI initiator device. Its name and SCSI identifier make up the iSCSI initiator name, together with a label that identifies it as an initiator port name/identifier and the ISID portion of the session identifier.

■ The *SCSI target port*—Maps to an iSCSI target portal group. The SCSI target port name and the SCSI target port identifier are both defined to be the iSCSI target name, together with a label that identifies it as a target port name/identifier and the target portal group tag.

■ The *SCSI port name*—Mandatory in iSCSI, when used in SCSI parameter data. SCSI port names have a maximum length of 255 bytes. It should be formatted as follows, in the order given:

  ➤ The iSCSI name in UTF-8 format

  ➤ A comma separator (1 byte)

  ➤ The ASCII character **i** (for SCSI initiator port) or the ASCII character **t** (for SCSI target port)

  ➤ A comma separator (1 byte)

  ➤ The hexadecimal representation of the 6-byte value of the ISID (for the SCSI initiator port) or the TPGT (for the SCSI target port), including the **0X** and the terminating null.

  ➤ Zero to three null pad bytes so that the complete format is a multiple of four bytes long.

**I-T nexus**—A relationship between a SCSI initiator port and a SCSI target port. For iSCSI, this relationship is a session, defined as a relationship between an iSCSI initiator's end of the session (the initiator port) and the iSCSI target's portal group. The I-T nexus can be identified by the conjunction of the SCSI port names or the SSID. Specifically, its identifier is the tuple (`iSCSI initiator name + i + ISID`, `iSCSI target name + t + target portal group tag`). Note that the I-T nexus identifier is not the same as the session identifier (SSID).

## Consequences of the Model

Between an iSCSI (SCSI) initiator port and an iSCSI (SCSI) target port, at any given time only one I-T nexus (session) can exist. Said another way, no more than one nexus relationship is allowed (no parallel nexus).

These assumptions lead to the conclusions and requirements in the following paragraphs.

**ISID rule**—Between an iSCSI initiator and an iSCSI target portal group (SCSI target port), there can be only one session with a given ISID that identifies the SCSI initiator port. The ISID contains a naming authority component that facilitates compliance with this rule.

The iSCSI initiator node is expected to manage the assignment of ISIDs prior to session initiation. The ISID rule does not preclude the use of the same ISID from the same iSCSI initiator with different target portal groups on the same iSCSI target or on other iSCSI targets. Allowing this is analogous to a single SCSI initiator port having relationships (nexus) with multiple SCSI target ports on the same SCSI target device or the same SCSI target ports on other SCSI target devices. It is also possible to have multiple sessions with different ISIDs to the same target portal group. Each such session is considered to be with a different initiator even when the sessions originate from the same initiator device. A different iSCSI initiator may use the same ISID because it is the iSCSI name together with the ISID that identifies the SCSI initiator port.

A consequence of the ISID rule and the specification for the I-T nexus identifier is that two nexus with the same identifier should not exist at the same time.

**TSIH rule**—The iSCSI target selects a nonzero value for the TSIH at session creation (when an initiator presents a zero value at login). After being selected the same TSIH value must be used whenever the initiator or the target refers to the given session and a TSIH is required.

## I-T Nexus State

Certain nexus relationships contain an explicit state (e.g., initiator-specific mode pages) that may need to be preserved by the target (or, more correctly, the device server in a logical unit) through changes or failures in the iSCSI layer (e.g., session failures). For that state to be restored, the iSCSI initiator should reestablish its session (relogin) to the same target portal group using the previous ISID. In other words, it should perform session recovery (as described in Chapter 11) because the SCSI initiator port identifier and the SCSI target port identifier form the datum that the SCSI logical unit device server uses to identify the I-T nexus.

**SCSI Mode Pages**

If the SCSI logical unit device server does not maintain initiator-specific mode pages, and if an initiator makes changes to port-specific mode pages, the changes may affect all other initiators logged in to that iSCSI target through the same target portal group.

Changes via mode pages to the behavior of a portal group via one iSCSI target node should not affect the behavior of this portal group with respect to other iSCSI target nodes, even if the underlying implementation of a portal group serves multiple iSCSI target nodes in the same network entity.

# Appendix D
# Numbers, Characters,
# and Bit Encodings

The sections that follow describe iSCSI numbers, characters, and bit encodings.

## Text Format

The initiator and target send a set of key=value pairs encoded in UTF-8 Unicode. All the text keys and text values in this book are case sensitive and should be used in the case in which they appear.

(a-z, A-Z) letters
(0-9) digits
" " (0x20) space
"." (0x2e) dot
"-" (0x2d) minus
"+" (0x2b) plus
"@" (0x40) commercial "at"
"_" (0x5f) underscore

"=" (0x3d) equal
":" (0x3a) colon
"/" (0x2f) solidus (also known as slash)
"[" (0x5b) left bracket
"]" (0x5d) right bracket
null (0x00) null separator
"," (0x2c) comma
"~" (0x7e) tilde

A key name is whatever precedes the first = in the key=value pair.

The term "key" is used frequently in this book with the meaning of "key-name." A value is whatever follows the = up to a 0-byte delimiter that separates one key=value pair from the next one or marks the end of the data (for the last key=value pair if the PDU C bit is set to 0).

The following definitions apply to key=value pairs:

**Standard-label:** a string of one or more characters consisting of letters, digits, dot (.), minus (–), plus (+), commercial at (@), and underscore (_). A key-name must begin with a capital letter and must not exceed 63 characters.

**Key-name:** a standard label.

**Text-value:** a string of 0 or more characters consisting of letters, digits, dot (.), minus (–), plus (+), commercial at (@), underscore (_), slash (/), left bracket ([), right bracket (]), and colon (:).

**iSCSI-name-value:** a string of one to 223 characters consisting of minus (–), dot (.), colon (:), and any character allowed by the output of the iSCSI **string-prep** template as specified in [STPREP-iSCSI].

**iSCSI-local-name-value:** a UTF-8 string with no null characters allowed. This encoding is to be used for localized (internationalized) aliases.

**Boolean-value:** the string **Yes** or **No**.

**Hex-constant:** a hexadecimal constant encoded as a string starting with **0x** or **0X**, followed by 1 or more digits or the letters **a, b, c, d, e, f, A, B, C, D, E,** and **F.** Hex constants are used to encode numerical values or binary strings. With numerical values the excessive use of leading 0 digits is discouraged and the string following **0X** (or **0x**) represents a base16 number starting with the most significant base16 digit followed by all other digits in order of decreasing significance and ending with the least significant base16 digit. With binary strings, hex-constants have an implicit byte length made up of 4 bits for every hexadecimal digit of the constant, including leading zeroes (i.e., a hex-constant of $n$ hexadecimal digits has a byte length of (the integer part of) $(n+1)/2$).

**Decimal-constant:** an unsigned decimal number—zero or a string of 1 or more digits starting with a nonzero digit. Decimal-constants are used to encode numerical values or binary strings. Decimal-constants can be used to encode binary strings only if the string length is explicitly specified. There is no implicit length for decimal strings. Decimal-constants must not be used for parameter values if those values are allowed to be equal to or greater than $2^{64}$ (numerical) or for binary strings that are allowed to be longer than 64 bits.

**Base64-constant:** a string starting with **0b** or **0B** followed by 1 or more digits or letters, or plus (+), slash (/), or equal (=). The encoding is according to [RFC2045], and each character, except equal, represents a base64 digit or a 6-bit binary string. Base64-constant encodes numerical values or binary strings. With numerical values the excessive use of leading 0 digits (encoded as **A**) is discouraged. The string following **0B** (or **0b**) represents a base64 number starting with the most significant base64 digit followed by all other digits in order of decreasing significance and ending with the least significant base64 digit. Pad digits (encoded as equal) not considered part of the number may optionally follow the least significant base64 digit. With binary strings, base64-constant has an implicit byte length that includes 6 bits for every character of the constant excluding trailing equals. That is, a base64-constant of *n* base64 characters excluding the trailing has a byte length of ((the integer part of) ((*n*+3)\*3/4)). Correctly encoded base64 strings cannot have *n* values 1, 5, . . . K\*4 + 1.

**Numerical-value:** an unsigned integer less than $2^{64}$ encoded as a decimal-constant or a hex-constant. Unsigned integer arithmetic applies to numeric-value.

**Large numerical-value:** an unsigned integer that can be larger than or equal to $2^{64}$ encoded as a hex-constant or base64-constant. Unsigned integer arithmetic applies to large numeric-values.

**Numeric-range:** two numerical-values separated by a tilde (~) where the value to the right of the tilde must not be lower than the value to the left.

**Regular-binary-value:** a binary string of not longer than 64 bits encoded as a decimal-constant, a hex-constant, or a base64-constant. The length of the string is either specified by the key definition or is the implicit byte length of the encoded string.

**Large-binary-value:** a binary string longer than 64 bits encoded as a hex-constant or a base64-constant. The length of the string is specified by the key definition or is the implicit byte length of the encoded string.

**Binary-value:** a regular-binary-value or a large-binary-value. Operations on binary values are key specific.

**Simple-value:** text-value, iSCSI-name-value, Boolean-value, numeric-value, numeric-range, or binary-value.

**List-of-values:** a sequence of text-values separated by commas.

If not otherwise specified, the maximum length of a simple-value (not its encoded representation) is 255 bytes, not including the delimiter (comma or zero byte).

Any iSCSI target or initiator must be able to receive at least 8,192 bytes of key=value data in a negotiation sequence. When proposing or accepting authentication methods that require support for very long authentication items (such as public key certificates), the initiator and target must be able to receive 64 kilobytes of key=value data.

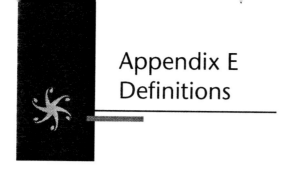

# Appendix E
# Definitions

What follows is a quick index of various iSCSI-related terms. Much, but not all, of it is from the [iSCSI].

**Alias** Allows an organization to associate a user-friendly string with the iSCSI name, but is not a substitute for that name. An alias string can also be associated with an iSCSI node.

**CID (connection ID)** A unique ID for a connection within the session. It is generated by the initiator and presented to the target during login and logout request.

**Connection** TCP/IP Connection. It is the medium of communication between the initiator and the target. Connections carry control messages, SCSI commands, parameters, and data within iSCSI protocol data units (iPDUs).

**iSCSI device** A SCSI device using an iSCSI service delivery subsystem. Service delivery subsystem is defined by [SAM2] as a transport mechanism for SCSI commands and responses.

**iSCSI initiator name** The iSCSI worldwide unique name of the initiator.

**iSCSI initiator node** Also known simply as the initiator, an iSCSI node within the iSCSI client network entity.

**iSCSI (SCSI) initiator port** See SCSI initiator port.

**iSCSI (SCSI) target port** See SCSI target port.

**iSCSI layer** Builds/receives iSCSI PDUs and relays/receives them to/from one or more TCP connections that form an initiator–target "session."

**iSCSI name**    The name of an iSCSI initiator or target.

**iSCSI node**    Represents a single iSCSI initiator or target. There are one or more iSCSI Nodes within a network entity, accessible via one or more network portals. The separation of the iSCSI node name from the addresses used by and for the node allows multiple iSCSI nodes to use the same addresses and the same iSCSI node to use multiple addresses.

**iSCSI client network entity**    An iSCSI network entity on the initiator side.

**iSCSI server network entity**    An iSCSI network entity on the target side.

**iSCSI target name**    The worldwide unique iSCSI name of the target.

**iSCSI target node**    Also known simply as the target, an iSCSI node within the iSCSI server network entity.

**iSCSI task**    An iSCSI request for which a response is expected.

**iSCSI transfer direction**    Defined with regard to the initiator; thus, outbound transfers are from the initiator to the target, whereas inbound transfers are from the target to the initiator.

**ISID (initiator session ID)**    The unique identifier an initiator assigns to its session endpoint, which when combined with the iSCSI initiator name provides a unique name in the world for the SCSI initiator port.

**I-T nexus**    According to [SAM2], a relationship between a SCSI initiator port and a SCSI target port. For iSCSI, this relationship is a session, defined as a relationship between an iSCSI initiator's end (SCSI initiator port) and an iSCSI target's portal group. The I-T nexus can be identified by the conjunction of the SCSI port names; that is, the I-T nexus identifier is the tuple (iSCSI initiator name + ",i," + ISID, iSCSI target name + ",t," + portal group tag).

**Network entity**    Represents a device or gateway accessible from the IP network. A network entity must have one or more network portals, each of which can be used to gain access to the IP network by some iSCSI nodes contained in that network entity.

**Network portal**    A component of a network entity that has a TCP/IP network address and may be used by an iSCSI node within that entity for the connection(s) within one of its iSCSI sessions. A network portal in an initiator is identified by its IP address. Its IP address and its listening TCP port identify a network portal in a target.

**Originator**    In a negotiation or exchange, the party that initiates the negotiation or exchange.

**PDU (protocol data unit)**    The boundary units into which initiators and targets place their messages. Also known as iSCSI PDU.

**Portal Groups**    Defines a set of Network portals within an iSCSI node that supports the coordination of a session with connections spanning these portals. Not all network portals within a portal group participate in every session connected through that group. One or more portal groups may provide access to an iSCSI node. Each network portal as utilized by a given iSCSI node belongs to exactly one portal group within that node.

**Portal Group Tag**    A 16-bit bitstring that identifies the portal group within an iSCSI node. All network portals with the same portal group tag in a given iSCSI node are in the same portal group.

**Recovery R2T**    An R2T generated by a target upon detecting the loss of one or more Data-Out PDUs through one of the following means: a digest error, a sequence error, or a sequence timeout. A recovery R2T carries the next unused R2TSN, but requests part of or the entire data burst that an earlier R2T (with a lower R2TSN) had already requested.

**Responder**    In a negotiation or exchange, the party that responds to the originator of the negotiation or exchange.

**SCSI Device**    According to [SAM2], an entity that contains one or more SCSI ports that are connected to a service delivery subsystem and supports a SCSI application protocol. For example, a SCSI initiator device contains one or more SCSI initiator ports and zero or more application clients; a SCSI target device contains one or more SCSI target ports and one or more device servers and associated logical units. The SCSI device is the component within an iSCSI node that provides SCSI functionality. There can be at most one such device within a node. Access to the SCSI device can only be in an iSCSI normal operational session. The SCSI device name is the iSCSI name of the node.

**SCSI layer**    Builds/receives SCSI CDBs (command descriptor blocks) and relays/receives them with other command-execute parameters to/from the iSCSI layer (see [SAM2]).

**Session**    The group of TCP connections that link an initiator with a target and thus form a session (loosely equivalent to a SCSI I-T nexus). TCP connections can be added and removed from a session. Across all connections within a session, an initiator sees one and the same target.

**SSID (session ID)**   Identifies a session between an iSCSI initiator and an iSCSI target. A session ID is a tuple composed of an initiator part (ISID) and a target part (target portal group tag). The initiator, at session establishment, explicitly specifies the ISID. The target portal group tag is implied by the initiator through the selection of the TCP endpoint at that time. The target portal group tag key may also be returned by the target as a confirmation during session establishment.

**SCSI initiator port**   Maps to the endpoint of an iSCSI normal operational session. An iSCSI normal operational session is negotiated through the login process between an iSCSI initiator node and a iSCSI target node. At successful completion of this process, a SCSI initiator port is created within the SCSI initiator device. The SCSI initiator port name and initiator port identifier are both defined to be the iSCSI initiator name together with (a) a label that identifies it as an initiator port name/identifier and (b) the ISID portion of the session identifier.

**SCSI port**   According to [SAM2], an entity in a SCSI device that provides the functionality to interface with a service delivery subsystem. For iSCSI, the definition of the SCSI initiator port and target port are different.

**SCSI port name**   Made up of UTF-8 characters; includes the iSCSI name + ",i," or ",t," + ISID or portal group tag.

**SCSI target port**   Maps to an iSCSI target portal group.

**SCSI target port name and SCSI target port identifier**   Both defined to be the iSCSI target name together with (a) a label that identifies it as a target port name/identifier and (b) the portal group tag.

**TPGT (Target Portal Group Tag)**   a numerical (16 bit) identifier for an iSCSI target portal group.

**TSIH (Target Session Identifying Handle)**   A target-assigned tag for a session with a specific named initiator. The target generates the TSIH during session establishment, and its internal format and content are not defined by this protocol except for the value 0 that is reserved and used by the initiator to indicate a new session. The TSIH is given to the target during additional connection establishment for the same session.

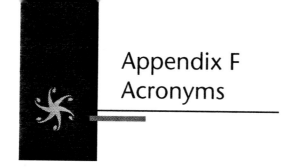

# Appendix F
# Acronyms

The following acronyms were extracted from this book, the [iSCSI], and related publications.

| | |
|---|---|
| 3DES | Triple Data Encryption Standard |
| ACA | auto contingent allegiance |
| ACK | Acknowledgment |
| ACL | access control list |
| AEN | asynchronous event notification |
| AES | Advanced Encryption Standard |
| AH | additional header |
| AH | authentication header (with IPsec) |
| AHS | additional header segment |
| API | application programming interface |
| ASC | additional sense code |
| ASCII | American Standard Code for Information Interchange |
| ASCQ | additional sense code qualifier |
| ATA | advanced technology attachment |
| BHS | basic header segment |
| BIOS | Basic Input Output Service |
| BIS | Boot Integrity Service |
| BOF | birds of a feather |
| CAT.5 | category 5 (for Ethernet cable) |
| CBC | cipher block chaining |
| CD | compact disc |
| CDB | command descriptor block |
| CHAP | Challenge Handshake Authentication Protocol |
| CID | connection ID |

| CIFS | Common Internet File System |
| CO | connection only |
| CPU | Central Processing Unit |
| CRC | cyclic redundancy check |
| CRC-32c | cyclic redundancy check, version with 32 bits |
| CRL | certificate revocation list |
| CSG | current stage |
| CSM | connection state machine |
| DA | directory agent (with SLP) |
| DD | discovery domain |
| DDP | direct data placement |
| DES | Data Encryption Standard |
| DHCP | Dynamic Host Configuration Protocol |
| DMA | direct memory access |
| DNS | Domain Name Server |
| DOI | Domain of Interpretation |
| DVD | digital versatile disc |
| EKAD | keys, authentication methods, and digests |
| ESP | encapsulating security payload |
| EUI | extended unique identifier (for EUI-64) |
| eui | enterprise unique identifier (for iSCSI names) |
| FC | Fibre Channel |
| FCIP | Fibre Channel over Internet Protocol |
| FFP | full-feature phase |
| FFPO | full-feature phase only |
| FIM | fix interval marker |
| FQDN | fully qualified domain name |
| Gbps | Gigabits per second |
| HBA | host bus adapter |
| HDD | hard disk drive |
| HMAC | hashed message authentication code |
| HW | hardware |
| IANA | Internet Assigned Numbers Authority |
| ICV | integrity check value (with IPsec) |
| ID | identifier |
| IDN | internationalized domain name |
| IEEE | Institute of Electrical & Electronics Engineers |
| IETF | Internet Engineering Task Force |
| iFCP | Internet Fibre Channel Protocol |

| IKE | internet key exchange |
| I/O | input/output |
| IO | initialize only |
| IP | Internet Protocol |
| IPR | intellectual property rights |
| ips | IP storage |
| IPsec/IPSec | Internet Protocol Security |
| IPv4 | Internet Protocol version 4 |
| IPv6 | Internet Protocol version 6 |
| iqn | iSCSI qualified name |
| iSAN | iSCSI-based storage area network |
| iSER | iSCSI Extension for RDMA |
| iSCSI | SCSI over IP |
| iSNS | Internet Storage Name Service |
| ISID | initiator session ID |
| I_T | Initiator_Target |
| I_T_L | Initiator_Target_LUN |
| ITN | iSCSI target node or iSCSI target name |
| ITT | initiator task tag |
| JBOD | just a bunch of disks |
| KRB5 | Kerberos version 5 |
| LFL | lower functional layer |
| LAN | local area network |
| LTDS | logical-text-data-segment |
| LO | leading only |
| LONP | login operational negotiation phase |
| LU | logical unit |
| LUN | logical unit number |
| MAC | message authentication codes |
| MAN | metropolitan area network |
| MC/S | multiple connections per session |
| MIB | management information base |
| MD-5 | Message Digest version 5 (algorithm used with IPsec) |
| NA | not applicable |
| NAS | network attached storage |
| NFS | network file system |
| NIC | network interface card |
| NOP | no operation |
| NSG | next stage |

| OC | optical connection |
| OS | operating system |
| OUI | organization unique identifier |
| PDU | protocol data unit |
| PKI | public key infrastructure |
| PXE | pre-execution environment |
| R2T | ready to transfer |
| R2TSN | ready to transfer sequence number |
| RAM | random access memory |
| RAID | Redundant Array of Independent Disks |
| RAS | reliability, availability, and serviceability |
| RDMA | remote direct memory access |
| RFC | Request for Comments |
| SA | Security Association (with IPsec) |
| SA | Service Agent (with SLP) |
| SAM | SCSI Architectural Model |
| SAM2 | SCSI Architectural Model 2 |
| SAN | storage area network |
| S-ATA | Serial ATA |
| SCSI | Small Computer Systems Interface |
| SHA1 | Secure Hashed Algorithm version 1 |
| SHA2 | Secure Hashed Algorithm version 2 |
| SLP | Service Location Protocol |
| SN | sequence number |
| SNP | security negotiation phase |
| SNACK | sequence number acknowledgment or selective negative acknowledgment |
| SNMP | Simple Network Management Protocol |
| SoHo | small office/home office |
| SNIA | Storage Networking Industry Association |
| SPKM-1 | Simple Public Key Mechanism version 1 |
| SPKM-2 | Simple Public Key Mechanism version 2 |
| SRP | secure remote password |
| SSID | session ID |
| SW | session-wide software |
| TCB | task control block |
| TCO | total cost of ownership |
| TCP | Transmission Control Protocol |
| TOE | TCP/IP Offload Engine |

| | |
|---|---|
| TPGT | target portal group tag |
| TSIH | target session identifying handle |
| TUF | TCP Upper-Level-Protocol Framing |
| TTT | target transfer tag |
| UA | user agent (with SLP) |
| UDP | User Datagram Protocol |
| UFL | upper functional layer |
| ULP | upper level protocol or upper layer protocol |
| URL | uniform resource locator |
| URN | uniform resource name |
| UTF | Universal Transformation Format |
| VPN | virtual private network |
| WAN | wide area network |
| WG | working group |
| XCBC | extended cipher block chaining |
| XOR | exclusive OR |

# Appendix G
# References and Web Pointers

The references are divided into four groupings:

- References that have a direct impact on iSCSI (other than SCSI and security)

- References that are related to the SCSI specifications

- References that are related to security features of iSCSI and IPsec/IKE

- References that are indirectly associated with the iSCSI specification

## Basic References for iSCSI

[BOOT] P. Sarkar et al., "iSCSI Boot," *http://www.ietf.org/rfc/rfc4173.txt.*

[Castagnioli] G. Castagnoli, S. Braeuer, and M. Herrman, "Optimization of Cyclic Redundancy-Check Codes with 24 and 32 Parity Bits," *IEEE Transact. on Communications,* 41(6), June 1993.

[CRC] ISO 3309, *High-Level Data Link Control.*

[DHCP iSNS] J. Tseng, "DHCP Options for Internet Storage Name Service," *http://www.ietf.org/rfc/rfc4174.txt.*

[EUI] "Guidelines for 64-bit Global Identifier," *http://standards.ieee.org/regauth/oui/tutorials/EUI64.html.*

[iSCSI] J. Satran, "iSCSI," *http://www.ietf.org/rfc/rfc3720.txt.*

[iSCSI-REQ] M. Krueger, R. Haagens, "Small Computers Interface Protocol over the Internet," *http://www.ietf.org/rfc/rfc3347.txt.*

[iSCSI-SLP] M. Bakke, "Finding iSCSI Targets and Name Servers Using SLP," *http://www.ietf.org/rfc/rfc4018.txt.*

[iSNS] J. Tseng, "Internet Storage Name Service (iSNS)," *http://www.ietf.org/rfc/rfc4171.txt.*

[MIB] M. Bakke, "Definitions of Managed Objects for iSCSI," Internet draft, *http://www.ietf.org/internet-drafts/draft-ietf-ips-iscsi-mib-11.txt.*

[MIB-AUTH] M. Bakke, "Definitions of Managed Objects for User Identity Authentication," *http://www.ietf.org/internet-drafts/draft-ietf-ips-auth-mib-07.txt.*

[MIB-iSNS] K. Gibbons, "Definitions of Managed Objects for iSNS," *http://www.ietf.org/internet-drafts/draft-ietf-ips-isns-mib-07.txt.*

[NDT] M. Bakke et al., "Naming and Discovery," *http://www.ietf.org/rfc/rfc3721.txt.*

[OUI] "IEEE OUI and Company_ID Assignments," *http://standards.ieee.org/regauth/oui/index.shtml.*

[Performance] J. Menon and C. Fuentes, "iSCSI Performance and Architecture and Comparison to Other Network Protocols," IBM Hursley, Feb 21, 2000.

[RFC1737] K. Sollins, "Functional Requirements for Uniform Resource Names," *http://www.ietf.org/rfc/rfc1737.txt.*

[RFC1982] R. Elz and R. Bush, "Serial Number Arithmetic," *http://www.ietf.org/rfc/rfc1982.txt.*

[RFC2044] F. Yergeau, "UTF-8, a Transformation Format of Unicode and ISO 10646," *http://www.ietf.org/rfc/rfc2044.txt.*

[RFC2045] N. Borenstein and N. Freed, "MIME (Multipurpose Internet Mail Extensions) Part One: Mechanisms for Specifying and Describing the Format of Internet Message Bodies," *http://www.ietf.org/rfc/rfc2045.txt.*

[RFC2131] Droms, R., "Dynamic Host Configuration Protocol," *http://www.ietf.org/rfc/rfc2131.txt.*

[RFC2373] R. Hinden and S. Deering, "IP Version 6: Addressing Architecture," *http://www.ietf.org/rfc/rfc2373.txt.*

[RFC2396] T. Berners-Lee, R. Fielding, and L. Masinter "Uniform Resource Identifiers," *http://www.ietf.org/rfc/rfc2396.txt.*

[RFC2732] R. Hinden, B. Carpenter, and L. Masinter, "Format for Literal IPv6 Addresses in URL's," *http://www.ietf.org/rfc/rfc2732.txt.*

[STPREP-iSCSI] M. Bakke, "String Profile for iSCSI Names," *http://www.ietf.org/rfc/rfc3722.txt.*

[StringPrep] P. Hoffman and M. Blanchet, "Preparation of Internationalized Strings," *http://www.ietf.org/rfc/rfc3454.txt.*

[UNICODE] Unicode Standard Annex #15, "Unicode Normalization Forms," *http://www.unicode.org/unicode/reports/tr15.*

## References for SCSI-Related Items

[SAM] "SCSI-3 Architecture Model (SAM)," ANSI X3T10-994D, *ftp://ftp.t10.org/t10/drafts/sam/sam-r18.pdf.*

[SAM2] "SCSI Architecture Model (SAM-2)," T10/1157D, *ftp://ftp.t10.org/t10/drafts/sam2/sam2r23.pdf.*

[SBC] "T10-996D SCSI-3 Block Commands (SBC)," NCITS.306-1998, *ftp://ftp.t10.org/t10/drafts/sbc/sbc-r08c.pdf.*

[SBC-2] "SCSI Block Commands–2 (SBC-2)," T10/1417-D, *ftp://ftp.t10.org/t10/drafts/sbc2/sbc2r06.pdf.*

[SPC-2] "SCSI Primary Commands (SPC-2)," T10/1236-D, *ftp://ftp.t10.org/t10/drafts/sam2/sam2r23.pdf.*

[SPC-3] "SCSI-3 Primary Commands (SPC-3)," T10/1416-D, *ftp://ftp.t10.org/t10/drafts/spc3/spc3r07.pdf.*

## References for iSCSI Security and IPsec/IKE

[AESCBC] S. Frankel, S. Kelly, and R. Glenn, "The AES Cipher Algorithm and Its Use with IPsec," *http://www.ietf.org/rfc/rfc3602.txt.*

[AESCTR] R. Housley, "Using AES Counter Mode With IPSec ESP," *http://www.ietf.org/rfc/rfc3686.txt.*

[CHAP] See [RFC1994].

[Kerberos] "The Kerberos Version 5 GSS-API Mechanism," RFC1964, *http://www.ietf.org/rfc/rfc1964.txt.*

[RFC1510] J. Kohl, C. Neuman, "The Kerberos Network Authentication Service (V5)," *http://www.ietf.org/rfc/rfc1510.txt.*

[RFC1964] J. Linn, "The Kerberos Version 5 GSS-API Mechanism," June 1996, *http://www.ietf.org/rfc/rfc1964.txt.*

[RFC1994] W. Simpson, "PPP Challenge Handshake Authentication Protocol—(CHAP)," *http://www.ietf.org/rfc/rfc1994.txt.*

[RFC2025] C. Adams, "The Simple Public-Key GSS-API Mechanism (SPKM)," *http://www.ietf.org/rfc/rfc2025.txt.*

[RFC2246] T. Dierks, C. Allen, "The TLS Protocol Version 1.0, *http://www.ietf.org/rfc/rfc2246.txt.*

[RFC2401] S. Kent, R. Atkinson, "Security Architecture for the Internet Protocol," *http://www.ietf.org/rfc/rfc2401.txt.*

[RFC2402] S. Kent, "IP Authentication Header (AH)," *http://www.ietf.org/rfc/rfc2402.txt.*

[RFC2404] C. Madson and R. Glenn, "The Use of HMAC-SHA-1-96 within ESP and AH," *http://www.ietf.org/rfc/rfc2404.txt*.

[RFC2406] S. Kent and R. Atkinson, "IP Encapsulating Security Payload (ESP)," *http://www.ietf.org/rfc/rfc2406.txt*.

[RFC2409] D. Harkins and D. Carrel, "The Internet Key Exchange (IKE)," *http://www.ietf.org/rfc/rfc2409.txt*.

[RFC2451] R. Pereira and R. Adams, "The ESP CBC-Mode Cipher Algorithms," *http://www.ietf.org/rfc/rfc2451.txt*.

[RFC2945] T. Wu, "The SRP Authentication and Key Exchange System," *http://www.ietf.org/rfc/rfc2945.txt*.

[SEC-IPS] B. Aboba et al., "Securing Block Storage Protocols over IP," Internet draft, *http://www.ietf.org/rfc/rfc3723.txt*.

[SEQ-EXT] S. Kent, "IP Encapsulating Security Payload (ESP)," Internet draft, *http://www.ietf.org/internet-drafts/draft-ietf-ipsec-esp-v3-10.txt* (in progress).

[SRP] See [RFC2945].

## References That Indirectly Affect iSCSI

[AC] J. Hafner, "A Detailed Proposal for Access Control," *ftp://ftp.t10.org/t10/document.99/99-245r9.pdf*.

[CAM] "Common Access Method-3," ANSI X3.232-199X.

[RFC790] J. Postel, "Assigned Numbers," *http://www.ietf.org/rfc/rfc790.txt*.

[RFC791] Internet Protocol, DARPA Internet Program Protocol Specification, *http://www.ietf.org/rfc/rfc791.txt*.

[RFC793] Transmission Control Protocol, DARPA Internet Program Protocol Specification, *http://www.ietf.org/rfc/rfc793.txt*.

[RFC1035] P. Mockapetris, Domain Names—Implementation and Specification, *http://www.ietf.org/rfc/rfc1035.txt*.

[RFC1122] R. Braden (ed.), "Requirements for Internet Hosts—Communication Layer," *http://www.ietf.org/rfc/rfc1122.txt*.

[RFC1766] H. Alvestrand, "Tags for the Identification of Languages," *http://www.ietf.org/rfc/rfc1766.txt*.

[RFC2026] S. Bradner, "The Internet Standards Process—Revision 3," *http://www.ietf.org/rfc/rfc2026.txt*.

[RFC2119] S. Bradner, "Key Words for Use in RFCs to Indicate Requirement Levels," *http://www.ietf.org/rfc/rfc2119.txt*.

[RFC2234] D. Crocker and P. Overell, "Augmented BNF for Syntax Specifications: ABNF," *http://www.ietf.org/rfc/rfc2234.txt*.

[RFC2407] D. Piper, "The Internet IP Security Domain of Interpretation of ISAKMP," *http://www.ietf.org/rfc/rfc2407.txt.*

[RFC2434] T. Narten and H. Avestrand, "Guidelines for Writing an IANA Considerations Section in RFCs," *http://www.ietf.org/rfc/rfc2434.txt.*

# Index